India's Military Power

A General Reflects

Attention Authors

'We Convert Fighters into Writers'. That has been the motto of Manas Publications, since more than four decades. Our message to the world is that India can win the battle, not only by the bullet but also by the pen. There is no dearth of intellectuals in our country, but their knowledge is confined to them only. No sincere effort has been made by any other publisher to channelise their knowledge in national interest. That is why the talent of a large number of intellectuals, remains latent. An author transforms his knowledge, into a manuscript, and it is our job to spread his/her knowledge by converting it into a beautiful book.

For over four decades, Manas has been motivating the intellectuals by publishing their manuscripts and would like to publish your manuscript too. If you or your colleagues have any manuscript, ready for publication or are working on it, kindly contact us with detailed synopsis and the list of contents. We would transform your work, into a valuable publication. If you wish, we can also suggest you, the suitable subjects for writing books, related to your area of expertise. Manas is known for its publishing quality and commitments. We take utmost care in production and give wide publicity to the book, as well as its author, through our national and international distribution network.

India's Military Power

A General Reflects

Lt Gen HC Dutta
PVSM (Retd)

Manas Publications
(We Convert Fighters into Writers)
New Delhi-110002 (INDIA)

MANAS PUBLICATIONS

(We convert Fighters into Writers)

(Publishers, Distributors, Importers & Exporters)
4402/5-A, Ansari Road (Opp. HDFC Bank)
Darya Ganj, New Delhi-110 002 (India)
Off. 23260783, 23265523, Res. 23842660
Fax: 011-23272766
E-mail: manaspublications@gmail.com
manaspublications@yahoo.com
Website: www.manaspublications.in

ISBN 978-81-7049-517-8

₹ 795/-

Designed at Innovative Processors
Printed in India at
R.K. Print Services, Delhi and
Published by Mrs Suman Lata for
Manas Publications, 4402/5-A, Ansari Road (Opp. HDFC Bank),
Darya Ganj, New Delhi-110 002 (INDIA)

To

my dear wife Shobha,
who has been my constant source of inspiration
and my son, the late Rajiv and my daughter Sweetie,
who live on in our fond memories.

Contents

Foreword 9

Preface 13

1. How I Came to Join the Indian Army 17
2. My Initial Years in the Army 38
3. Counter Insurgency Operations and Sino-Indian War of 1962 63
4. Indo-Pak War 1965 77
5. Taking Command of 114 Infantry Brigade, in Ladakh 96
6. Commander, Senior Command Course 116
7. Commandant Army College of Combat, Mhow 135
8. Deputy Chief of the Army Staff, Delhi 150
9. Command of 1 Corps, Mathura 169
10. Problems Confronting the Army 189
11. The Indian Security Edifice 213
12. The Need for Formulating National Security Doctrine 228

Index 259

Foreword

This book is an interesting account of the life and times of the author who had a very successful career in the Army. I am reminded of a biography of Chengiz Khan written by Charles Lamb many years ago. He wrote how Mongol soldiers talking at their home round a burning fire describing strange people, strange lands and their campaigning experiences in a fireside talk at their home and others with mouths wide open listening to their amazing stories. In modern times, successful Generals have kept that tradition by writing their memoirs. General Dutta's autobiography falls in that category shedding much light on his Army career. This can be a source of both learning and inspiration for the younger generation of military officers. Non-military readers of this book will get acquainted with matters military.

The author joined the Indian Army in 1947. Although he is from the second batch of post Second World War Officers, his batch was the first one of officers commissioned after Independence. His batch was exceptional in terms of having a very large number of officers who attained a General's rank in our highly pyramidical rank structured Army. Quite a few reached the penultimate rank of Army Commander. Lt Gen Dutta has been a brilliant officer who reached that high rank, with varied experience who served as our Central Army Commander. I have had the privilege of knowing him for over six decades.

General Dutta begins this book with his lineage going back a few centuries. In keeping with his family's high family traditions of service to the country, he chose to join the Army. I was very impressed going through the contents of this book because I found that it reminded me of my own career as I had preceded him in various appointments. I was amused to find that as Instructor at Defence Services Staff College at Wellington, he had lived in the same house, called *Crinken* in which I had lived a few years earlier and also revived my reminisces of places and appointments where I had preceded him. We were also colleagues as Principal Staff Officers at Army Headquarters in late Seventies, he as Deputy Chief of Army Staff and I as Adjutant General. He made a significant contribution in all appointments that he held in his Army career. He has also made useful suggestions in the fast changing world of future warfare including Space and Cyberspace warfare. He has been a role model that the new generation of Army Officers can emulate.

Towards the end of his book, as a thinking General, the author has given his analytical views concerning organisation and functioning of our Higher Defence Command. He has brought out the major shortcomings therein which led to the debacle of 1962. Marginalising the Army in the process of decision making on military matters was one of the main reasons for this. Derailing the Kargil Committee Report with meaningless cosmetic changes have skirted the fundamental issue. It is a pity that this grave shortcoming has not yet been rectified in our functioning at the highest level.

In 1947 the Indian Army overnight got transformed from a colonial to a national army. Instead of being viewed as an instrument of oppression it now became the most popular institution of the Government among the people of India. This metamorphosis took place because of the Army's role in defending the Nation against foreign aggression, assistance in maintaining law and order when required and providing succour to people in distress during natural disasters. The

Army played a significant but silent role in bringing about the Independence of the country, forcing the British to quit. It has also been the only apolitical Army of the developing world. Yet the fear among the political leaders of the man on horseback and the insatiable ambition of the civilian bureaucracy to have stifling control over the Army have led to the present unhappy situation. The emoluments and protocol status of officers and soldiers of the Army have been persistently lowered in comparison with their civilian counterparts. The Army though an integral part of the Military Power of India, is the most Neglected service of the Nation.

I commend this book to all those interested in national security matters and particularly to our new generation of Officers in the military.

New Delhi

Lt Gen (Retd) S.K. Sinha, PVSM
Former Vice Chief of Army Staff
Former Ambassador to Nepal
Former Governor of Assam and J&K

Preface

This book is a tribute to the Indian soldier; ever uncomplaining and steadfast, he has always been true to his salt and to a code of personal honour, whether as part of Mughal forces or British Indian Army. So, from the hills of Haldi Ghati and the hot plains of Basra-Baghdad, to the icy slopes of Monte Cassino, history has been witness to the battle cries of *"Har Har Mahadev"*, *"Durga Mata Ki Jai"*, and *"Jo Bole So Nihal"*, and the like. The legendary Gorkhas, with whom I had the honour to serve, went charging into battle with flashing khukris and the proud battle cry of *"Ayo Gorkhali"* (The Gorkhas have come).

This book is also a tribute to the Indian officer who has always led from the front and earned the trust of his soldiers by his gallantry and professional ability. He has also been a fast learner. When Independence came in 1947, there were only a handful of Indian officers who had the experience of commanding battalions, leave alone commanding brigades and divisions. Yet, when rushed into battle in Jammu & Kashimir within a few weeks of gaining Independence, they took to higher command with aplomb, learning quickly as they fought. Owing to their superb performance, the fledgling army of Independent India was transformed into a veteran force, almost overnight.

Thereafter, in 1965, the Indian Army led by our gallant officers went into successful battle campaigns against Pakistan with massed tank and infantry formations. The war of 1971 was won even more convincingly. Next, in Kargil in 1999, the Army turned a sticky situation into victory against fearful odds. However, it faltered against China in 1962 and was caught on the wrong foot in Sri Lanka in 1987, for various reasons. The nation owes a debt of gratitude to these brave leaders and soldiers of the Indian Army.

Regrettably, the picture is not so sanguine for the future. The army has been neglected with regard to its modernization. The entire strategic scenario is askew owing to a number of anomalies and imbalance in the national power structure. Relations between the armed services and the Ministry of Defence (MoD) are strained apart from rivalries within the armed services, resulting in doctrinal dissonance, and lack of operational integration between them. The higher defence control organization is awry, resulting in knee-jerk responses at the strategic level. There is need to devise a National Security Doctrine and National Security Strategy relevant to the core interests and goals of the country, and to institute an organization for central planning and execution under a Chief of Defence Staff (CDS). The CDS system is also critical for prioritizing acquisition of weapons and equipment in contrast to the prevailing practice of ad-hoc purchases. However, these much needed reforms though accepted at the highest level, seem to be stuck owing to turf wars and bureaucratic opposition or inertia.

India needs to carry out a thorough analysis and research into the likely shape of future wars under the nuclear overhang. Probably the pattern will be that of a series of intense, short and swift land battles with the Army playing a central role together with dedicated close air support including helicopter support for attack and transport. Indeed, there is need for total integration between the armed services with a structure of integrated command, and integrated entities all the way down to battle teams, supplanting the present regime of corps, divisions, brigades and regiments. A possible architecture of inter-service integration is given in a later chapter of the book which could form the basis of discussion. Under all circumstances, the Army must have assured and integral support of the Air Force. Should such far-reaching restructuring of the forces prove unacceptable for any reason, the only viable alternative would be that the requisite elements of air assets (close support aircraft and helicopters) should be made integral to the Army. Likewise, intimate support of the Indian Navy to the overall battle is also of paramount importance.

For various reasons as enumerated in the body of this book, the profession of arms has lost its sheen and has become less attractive as evident from the shortages in the officer cadre, especially that of the Army. Worse, the shortages are most pronounced in the junior ranks which does not augur well for future wars. The country also got embroiled in an ugly row between the ex-servicemen and the government regarding pensions, known as "One Rank One Pension" (OROP) which was not handled in the proper manner in the early stages creating a feeling of rancor and mistrust amongst the pensioners. Fortunately, the present government has acted with wisdom and fairness and a degree of settlement seems to have been reached. However, the incident has highlighted the need for understanding the problems of the ex-servicemen.

This book has been written as a personal narrative. I have done so in all humility without any intention of blowing my own trumpet or by way of justifying my shortcomings. I hold that in the final reckoning, an officer's work should speak for itself. However, I am persuaded that there is some merit in sharing my views on various aspects concerning the armed forces and in particular, the Indian Army which has borne the brunt of all the wars and struggles since Independence. Unfortunately it has been sadly neglected for prestige and modernization, though it remains integral to India's Military Power.

In the course of writing this book, I have thoroughly enjoyed recalling many happy memories of my years in the Army and remembering so many good friends. Nevertheless, I must confess that I have been pushed into doing this by my family, my high spirited younger son Aditya, my very able and caring daughter-in law Sumita and my highly talented grandchildren, Sarina and Arjun. Above all, my support group was headed by my cheerful dear wife Shobha. She has been a tower of strength to me at all times in all ventures in the past sixty three years.

Reminiscing the story of my life, my thoughts often went to the memory of my two children who are no more. My daughter Sweetie (Jyoti) died on 18 August 1979 and my son Rajiv passed away on 31 January 2011. They were both an integral part of my life. Specially after my retirement, Rajiv was my constant companion, friend and a loving son.

Both of them would have been so happy to see this book, had they been alive.

Lt Gen (Retd) HC Dutta, PVSM

1

How I Came to Join the Indian Army

My family hails from the area of the Salt Range and the Potohar Plateau which is now a part of Pakistan. My ancestors migrated and settled down in this region centuries ago. This is a stretch of country lying between the Indus and Jhelum rivers after their emergence from the mountains. Rising abruptly from the Punjab plains west of the River Jhelum and ending equally precipitously on the Indus, one hundred and eighty kilometres to the west, the Salt Range is a mass of sheer escarpments, jagged peaks, rolling hills and desolate ravines gouged out by rivers that have long since ceased to flow except in rare deluges. Nestling in-between, are fairly wide and fertile valleys irrigated by spring fed streams with prosperous small villages. In the past, the area was further cut up by salt marshes dominated by salt bearing hills of Khewra which gave its name to the rock salt mines extant even today. This turbulent, twisted and broken landscape bred hardy and doughty hill fighters who were fiercely independent. The population consisted of Rajput tribes of *Janjuas*, *Gakkhars* and others plus a few tribes of warrior Brahmins. The region saw intense fighting till Babur managed to conquer the region. He had the marshes drained out and granted *mansabs* to the *Janjuas* and *Gakkhars* and other tribes including some of the *Kshatryias* and Brahmin tribes after converting them to Islam. My tribe of warrior Brahmins called *Mohyals*, among a small number of tribes, refused to convert. This region is known for people who live by a certain code of honour which endures to this day. As a matter of fact, this ethos of loyalty and sense of honour runs through my community too. They constitute ideal material to "do or die for the king and country" (read established authority and the nation). Consequently, members of my community have readily taken to service in the armed forces, police and administrative services in large numbers, earning a lot of praise.

Interestingly, the area of Potohar Plateau is still considered a prime area for recruitment of soldiers for the Pakistan Army and the *Janjuas* and *Gakkhars* are considered prime soldier material. Indeed, *Janjuas* and *Gakkhars* feature prominently in the upper echelons of Pakistani armed forces and the government.

My Ancestors

My tribe, the Mohyal Brahmins, was one of the few that held out against conversion to Islam and stayed put till the Partition forced them to flee to India. The origin of the Dutts (also spelt as Duttas, Datts and Dattas) as also a few allied subtribes of like-minded persuasion (the whole group going by the name of Mohyal Brahmins) — is lost in the mists of time. Some claim that the group belonged to a sect of Saraswat Brahmins, who took to arms and tilling of land, renouncing the traditional priestly functions, even prior to the Mahabharata times.

Going by the folklore and stories recounted by countless generations of elders, the Dutt clan has a colourful history. We hear of a Dutt clan that had migrated to Arabia, participating in the battle of Karbala in 687 AD. A chieftain named Rahib Sidh Dutt fought in an internecine war after the death of Hazarat Mohammed. He sided with Hazarat Imam Hussain (one of the relatives claiming to be the true successor to the Caliph). Rahib Sidh Dutt fought in the bloody battle against a vastly superior force sacrificing seven of his sons. Later in 728 AD, Rahib Sidh Dutt had to leave Arabia, migrating to Afghanistan as the enemies of the Imam let loose a vendetta against his followers.

The historical documentation of the above legend may be lost in antiquity but the Mohyal community cherish the legend that has been handed down through generations. Interestingly, there are authentic accounts of Mohyal Brahmins celebrating Muharram alongside Shia Muslims in different parts of India such as Allahabad, Pune, etc., to this day. The Duttas take out *Tazias* bedecked with flowers and mourn the death of Imam Hussain in Allahabad and they are known as Hussaini Brahmins: www.FirstPost.com/living/meet the hussaini brahamins-hindus-who observe-muharram-alongside-muslims-1788623.html.

Next, the name of Rahib Dutt surfaces through a British historian named Sir A Cunningham who mentions that there is strong evidence of a dynasty of Dutts ruling in Afghanistan for a period of 120 years, 830 AD–950 AD, with its capital at a place called Ohind on the River Indus near Taxila. For the next five centuries or so, the power of the Dutt tribe seems to have waned as their habitat often tended to be in the path of various invading armies. About the year of 1527 AD, we hear of Dewan Rai Pun Dutt, a descendent of one Shiv Dutt, capturing a large swath of territory around Pathankot and establishing his capital at Paniad (between Gurdaspur and Dinanagar). The town of Paniad features poignantly in the psyche of Dutts as that is where they fought and perished to the last man against superior Mughal forces. It is said that on directions from Babur, a large force under governor of Lahore, attacked the Dutt stronghold of Paniad. The attack was repulsed with heavy losses three times. Finally, through the treachery of a cook, the defenders were caught unawares. In the ensuing battle, each and every Dutt of the entire region was massacred with the usual ferocity of the Mughals. Thus, the Dutt tribe was annihilated except for two boys who had gone visiting their maternal grandfather in Samba, near Jammu.

The carnage took place on a Thursday; so it is an inauspicious day for the Dutts, proscribing start of any venture or journey. Besides, they don't even drink water or stay overnight in Pạniad. Later, when Babur's son, Humayun lay mortally ill, the Ulemas proclaimed that he was under a curse of the Dutts. So, the two surviving boys of Dutt clan, Shah Sarup and Dholan were brought to Delhi and implored to pray for his life. By way of making amends, Shah Sarup was bestowed 13 villages in the district of Gurdaspur and Dholan was given a similar number of villages in Sialkot district. In due course of time, both Zaffarwal and Kanjrur became strongholds of the Dutts.

At some point of time later, my immediate ancestors moved from Zaffarwal to Jhelum district and settled at Bhaun, on the fringes of the Potohar Plateau. Our oldest known ancestor was Mehta Balak Ram Dutta. He was my father's great grandfather. Not much is known about him except that he was a legal advisor in the court of the Mughal governor at Lahore. His son, Mehta Anokh Rai Dutta rose to be a Commissioned Officer in the British Police Cavalry. He is known to have served with distinction in the Mutiny of 1857. So, our lands in Chak SB in village Phularwan, district Sargodha, were probably built on a grant from the British which was expanded by the acumen of his son (my grandfather). Apparently a distinguished officer, Anokh Rai had earned a reputation for competence and dedication to duty. He was commended by the Commissioner of Jalandhar who while writing a recommendation for his son, my grandfather, (Mehta Ganda Mal Dutta) wrote, "He is the son of a most deserving father (Anokh Rai). If he resembles his father, he will do well". His wife, (my father's grandmother) was a pious lady of the "Krishna" sect. She had lost her eyesight in an accident at a young age but since she had been betrothed to Anokh Rai even before her birth, common practice of the times, he married her just the same. As a child, I heard stories of her graciousness. Once she accidently fell in a shallow well. A rescue party roped down to her. She received them with great courtesy as if receiving guests in her *haveli.* She was quite uncomplaining but when the men tried to pick her up, she casually mentioned that her left arm had fractured. Being an only child, she inherited a lot of property around Bhaun, probably this influenced the relocation of my family to the Bhaun area. She is said to have wielded great influence on her son, consequently my grandfather, is the only known vegetarian in my family.

My grandfather, Mehta Ganda Mall Dutta had a commanding personality and enormous capacity for hard work. I had the good fortune to meet him on a number of occasions. An aware, alert person and "no nonsense" man, he was anxious to keep abreast of the times. I was a student of high school when my father took me along to our lands in Bikaner. My grandfather once asked me, "Harish, what is this movement called 'Fascism'?" In spite of being well informed smartee, I was a bit taken aback. I must have waffled something. A shrewd man, he saw through me in a few minutes but not to embarrass me, he just nodded and changed the subject. It seems that his father (Anokh Rai) had passed away early, so my grandfather had to work his way up in life by sheer grit and dint of hard work. Starting up the ladder of revenue officials from a *Kanungo*, and so on, he became a *Naib Tehsildar* in Gurdaspur where he seems to have made his mark. For his outstanding work in that appointment, he was awarded a gold watch with an inscription by the Governor of Punjab. He rose to the position of a *Tehsildar*, where he made a name as a specialist in matters of land settlement. He was deputed to Mandi State in Himachal Pradesh as Assistant Settlement Officer, with the task of building up a record of landholdings and setting up a system of levying taxes. Gradually, he seems to have made himself almost indispensable in the state administration. He is known to have attended the Delhi Durbar of 1911 and was entrusted with the task of presenting the Raja of Mandi (then a babe-in-arms) to King George V. He distinguished himself during World War I by obtaining recruits and collecting war loans for the British.

In his yearly report to the Viceroy, the officiating Superintendent of the state (larger states used to have agents but smaller states were assigned superintendents), Mr H.W. Emerson, ICS, in his capacity as officiating superintendent, wrote, "From what I have seen of his work in matter of appeals and in other ways, I have no hesitation in endorsing the very high opinion of M. Ganda Mal, penned earlier by Mr Gordon Walker, ICS, Superintendent of Mandi State". My mother, Ram Rakhi, had very fond memories of her days in Mandi while staying with my grandfather (her father-in-law).

My grandfather was a visionary and a builder. In fact, he laid the foundations of our family fortunes. He consolidated the lands obtained by his father in Sargodha District, which he expanded to a holding of a full *Chak* of 25 squares (of 25 acres each), comprising more than 600 acres of land. We lost all the Sargodha lands in the Partition. Much later, by way of partial compensation, we were allotted a much smaller piece of land measuring 600 *bighas* (approximately 110 acres) in Ambala district.

Earlier, my grandfather happened to attend the coronation of Maharaja Ganga Singh of Bikaner in 1925, to which a number of prosperous landlords from canal colonies of Punjab had been invited. The Maharaja spoke to him of his desire to open up the sandy wastes of his lands to cotton farming by constructing a grid of irrigation canals as had been done in Punjab. To realise his dream he said, he was keen to invite landlords from the Punjab with their experienced farm hands. He offered to sell land at concessional prices, payable in instalments if so desired. Never the one to look a gift horse in the mouth, my grandfather bought a lot of sandy lands in Gajsinghpur at throw away prices and built up a holding of one whole *Chak* of 25 Squares of land. On the Maharaja's instruction, he also laid out the grain market (*mandi)* as also the new town of Gajsinghpur. He built a large house for his family close to the railway station. It is said that he worked day and night on setting up the farm in the inhospitable land in ferocious climate. My father suggested that he should expand the established and fertile farmlands in Sargodha instead of working so hard on the raw land in Bikaner. My grandfather is reported to have replied that the Sargodha lands could be lost someday, but the assets built in the Hindu state of Bikaner would be safe for generations. This was in the year 1925, which shows remarkable prescience on his part. He got his first grandson, Romesh, my eldest brother, admitted in the newly established Agricultural College at Lyallpur, saying that we should learn the modern methods and progressive technologies of farming. Once, somebody suggested that he should get his sons to come and help him on the farms. He replied that he did not want his grandchildren to grow up as country yokels, they should get educated in convents and mission schools in the cities. They would become landlords and not just tillers of soil.

My Parents

My father, Mehta Dinanath Dutta, was born in Bhaun near the *tehsil* town of Chakwal in Jehlum district on 26 October 1891, as the first son, besides three sisters and a younger brother. The younger brother, Iqbal Nath, unfortunately died young, while studying in the Medical College at Lahore which devastated my grandfather as he had expected great things of the younger son. My father had grandiose visions of going to England for further studies but my grandfather put paid to his plans by getting him married to my mother, Ram Rakhi, daughter of Sardar Sher Singh Bali, who had retired as *Risaldar* from "Guides Cavalry". He had joined under the Siladari System wherein the volunteers came with their own mount. He had fought in the Anglo-Sikh wars, losing his younger brother in battle. He retired as a *Risaldar*, on a princely pension of Rs 2/- per month, such being the value of money in those times.

My mother was the only sister of four brothers and hence a spoilt young girl. All her life, she only wore silk and never ventured into the kitchen. I remember her as a strikingly beautiful and kind lady. She raised a happy family of five strapping (and perpetually warring) sons which turned her into a virtual saint. The rowdy sons apart, she also had to cope with an imperious husband. A fine figure of a gentleman, my father was a tall, well built person and a picture of self-assurance. He was a wizard at all sports. In the large compound of our house in Kangra, Himachal Pradesh, he laid out a cricket field. Our "eleven" comprised of my father as the captain, all five brothers of varying age and height, some retainers and my father's peon as his team. We would play most afternoons and on all Sundays. But it was an unequal match. Once my father got the strike, we were in for a whole afternoon of fielding, with him hitting the ball all round. Ultimately, we got him to agree to restrict his time at the crease. He had joined the excise department as a sub inspector, graduating to an inspector and then senior inspector. But he always seemed to have time for games and fun time with us. He was a prominent member of various sports clubs specially those for cricket and tennis. (He said he was so good that he finished his work superfast). To his bad luck the Partition robbed his chances of further promotion to an excise officer. He said the Partition was the British perfidy to do him down as he had to retire at fifty.

My father Mehta Dinanath Dutta and mother Ram Rakhi.

My father was a natty dresser and had trunks full of fine clothes, which had to be aired at the beginning and end of the winter season. He sported a riding horse which was housed in a cottage at the edge of the compound. The horse caretaker (called *cyce* in Urdu) and his wife, an old Muslim family, lived there. Once, out of curiosity, I stole into their cottage when they were out on an errand. I took one pull at his *hookah* and ran back out coughing violently. That was my first brush with smoking. Thereafter, I have smoked cigarettes, cigars and a pipe, but never ventured near a *hookah* or a hubble-bubble as it used to be called by the British.

Two of my maternal uncles were Sikhs and two were non-Sikhs as per the prevailing custom. Their children followed similar pattern of half-and-half, for their children, with the result that even today I have a number of turbaned cousins and their extended families. The system worked fine till some fissures developed between the Sikhs and Hindus, although even now, mixed marriages between them are quite common. The remarkable part is that, though born of the same parents, the sons brought up as Sikhs, ended up imbibing the aggressive and the warrior culture associated with Sikhs. Indeed as per the custom of yore, the stronger son used to be brought up as a Sikh. It is understandable because the Sikh sect originally evolved to fight against the Mughal oppression.

My Educational Career

Like most service children, my schooling followed the pattern of my father's postings. I did my middle level schooling at Mission School, Rawalpindi, and passed my matriculation examination from the Government Intermediate College, Campbellpur near Nowshera. Thereafter, I came to Gordon College, Rawalpindi for the intermediate level, finally graduating from the Forman Christian College, Lahore. I was not quite the top boy in my class but nearly there most of the time. I was very good in most subjects but mathematics was my nemesis. I was a favourite of my teachers in English, Economics and Political Science who would all be waiting anxiously outside the examination hall to meet me coming out of the mathematics examination. However, I scraped through with a second division. I once talked to General Manekshaw about my travails with mathematics; he laughed and said that he had passed his matriculation level in third division. Interestingly, he sent the certificate in original for display in the Field Martial Manekshaw Museum at our Regimental Centre at Shillong.

I enjoyed my stay at the FC College. Lahore was a very happening town and a great place for a young man. I learnt good things and bad, common to the young at this stage of life. My roommate was a boy called Jaspal Singh Bedi who like me, had arrived from Gordon College Rawalpindi. Bedis are revered as descendants of the Sikh gurus, but I picked up smoking and drinking from him. He was a spoilt son of a rich family but like all such spoilt brats, he was good fun to be with. I found myself frequenting cinemas and restaurants of Lahore. So, one fine morning I was facing the terrible Mr Sinclair, the unforgiving Dean of the College, in his office. He had me up for bunking a lot of classes. After an unpleasant interview, I escaped with a warning and admonition to work up my attendances. However, I was too far gone on attendances for the optional subject of Urdu, which was the forte of one very irascible master who used to mark our answer sheets of assigned essays in a manner so strict that getting five marks out of a total of fifty placed one at the top of the class. Anyhow, the net result was that although I made up on attendances for other subjects before the finals, I failed to make up enough in the optional of Urdu. So, I had to forego the examination for the subject of English Honours much to my regret and surprise of a very nice teacher, Professor Painter, who used to hold classes in his house in a very convivial atmosphere. I also recall

I was friendly with another student, Joginder Singh, a village lad from Punjab but a very fine boy of studious nature. We were both avid readers of George Bernard Shaw. We must have read though all his plays and more so, his scintillating prefaces to the plays. One day, in a fit of enthusiasm, we sat down and wrote a letter to him saying as how we were such avid readers of his writings and so on. We posted the letter as a lark without expecting a reply. But lo and behold, we got a reply after three or four weeks! He had written a long letter in his hand, filling a British "penny post card" to the brim. He was very kind and all that, but what I remember most is his advice to a would-be author. He said that as long as he remembered, he would never go to sleep at night until he had written at least 3000 words. So, he said, the key to becoming an author was perseverance. I let Joginder keep the letter. He was so keen on it. I hope he has preserved it as it would be worth a lot of money to-day.

I Join the Indian Army

World War II was drawing towards an end in 1945. My course of studies was coincidentally also in the final year of graduation at F.C. College, Lahore. I was thinking about a likely career. Fortunately, the Army, Navy and Air Force recruiting teams were still actively combing colleges for officer material. I remember one such team, headed by a British Brigadier, resplendent with a chest full of medals, extolling the attractions of a military career, as a glorious life full of adventure, games and mouth-watering outdoorsy fun like hunting, fishing and camping. And, he said "No studies, no exams and such like pests"! For me, that hit the proverbial nail on the head, though, later in service I was to discover that such utopias seldom exist. However, that incident left a seed of attraction for a career in the army in my mind.

After graduation, I was loafing around Bombay and Pune, burning up my brother's money. One day, he brought me a form to fill, casually mentioning that it was for joining the army (no commitment mind you, just show of interest!) and it will give me a free ticket, first class, to Bangalore—something like "money for jam". Forever ready for a lark, I signed on the penciled crosses marked very helpfully by my brother. The rest as they say is history. However, I must admit that I never regretted joining the army. I took to it as a duck taking to water, and would do it happily if I were to re-live my life.

My sojourn in Bangalore was pleasant enough, though not quite what I had planned. The selection board processes have evolved over the years, so have a logic of their own and the rush of events leaves little time to relax or reflect. For one, it is expected that everyone arriving is wound up tight to succeed and will kill to pass. It was certainly not my frame of mind. The organisers would have thrown a fit, if I had told them that I was only mildly interested and that I had really come for a swan round the town. But as an opinionated cocky young man amidst a bunch of about 20 odd hopefuls, I was swept along the current and before I knew it, I found myself in the thick of it, wanting to succeed. They keep you on the run and pack in a lot of activity, a clever mix of the physical and the mental. There was a group discussion, leaderless on purpose. I did not know if it was like that, so, without a second thought, I ploughed right in and took charge, which turned out to be the correct approach. There was a cleverly laid out obstacle course with marks assigned for each obstacle. The aim was to tote up the maximum score in a given time. It was before the time of Nintendo and Mario computer games but I took it with the same gaming mindset.

On the morning of the fourth day, there was one final meeting with the top man. He just spoke in general terms saying that I seem to have done well. So, it came as a surprise when three of us (Rebello, Elijah and myself) were trooped to a sort of medical centre. Somebody whispered that we had passed. That was that. In retrospect, I honestly think that there were quite a few others who were better than me. The only difference was that they were trying too hard. Later, when I was senior enough to advice, I suggested that the first essential of the selection system should be to put candidates at ease and in a relaxed frame of mind so that they could perform at their true best.

Soon we got busy in the logistics of returning to our homes. The army arrangements were flawless as usual. The news of my success at Bangalore had preceded me and on arrival at home, I got a happy reception. However, there were a few smirks and unkind remarks that my goose was cooked and that hereafter, instead of being a demanding snob round the house, I would be chased round by drill sergeants! It was also a bit deflating to discover that the whole thing had been planned between my father and my elder brother. There was a reason behind that; my rather grandiose notions of studying in England (it seems to run in the family). And of all things, I had decided on a six year stint to become a chartered accountant. In view of my prowess in mathematics, it would have been an unmitigated disaster but the young will always have dreams.

A Gentleman Cadet at the Indian Military Academy

We arrived at Dehradun on 8 August 1946. It was a hot and sultry afternoon, which became more uncomfortable as we arrived all "dressed up" in coat and tie with outsized boxes and kitted up with lists sent to our homes. First, we were told to lug our boxes to our assigned rooms and settle down. We were the Second Regular Course instituted post World War II, so there were seniors from the First Course to help us, which basically amounted to them ordering us around. But we were special in that we were going to be the First Course of Independent India. The training commenced in right earnest after two days of "rest" but which in actual fact turned out to be ragging, though it was clean fun and mainly lots of runs and marches at night.

We were expecting the course to be tough and hard going. It proved to be just that. However, in retrospect, our course at the Indian Military Academy proved truly remarkable, and indeed, transformational. We had arrived from colleges and homes, not quite aware of what lay ahead, except with the optimism of youth and a sense of self-importance of being the chosen ones. In general, the rigorous regime of training was targeted at our physical, mental and psychological grooming. We came in as a bunch of spirited boys but went out as focused and competent young leaders of free India. We now moved and carried ourselves better, we learnt to speak and write clearly and authoritatively. We learnt to dress as gentlemen without being gaudy or showy. We imbibed a sense of purpose and dedication.

The welcome speech was by Company Sergeant Major (CSM) Gahan. Soon after our arrival, we were stood in three lines and the CSM said, "Gentlemen, you are indeed lucky, for you have been selected to join the Army. Hereafter, we will feed you, clothe you, house you and train you to be officers. If you fall ill we will treat you. When you get married, we will look after your wife and children, AND when you die we will give you a decent burial", all in all, an excellent example of the worldview of a British Sergeant.

As a matter of fact, I am of the view that some such regimen of grooming as we got at the IMA should also be devised for youngsters taking up other professions. The emphasis will perforce be different but the general direction could be the same, i.e., overall grooming of mind, body and spirit with equal emphasis on self-organisation. As it is, one often hears the lament that the majority of young men and women being churned out in droves by our universities are found largely unemployable. When I was the Deputy Chief of the Army at Army Headquarters, I once suggested to the then Prime Minister Indira Gandhi whilst escorting her to the Army Commanders' meeting, that some attachment to the Armed

At the IMA, Dehradun, 1946

Services or a "Boot Camp" on leadership, organisational skills and dedication to duty should be mandated for all Class One Officers. She seemed to see merit in the suggestion but thought it would not pass muster with the *burra babus*.

Expectedly, the first target of our training was deportment which in practical terms meant proper turn-out or dress and holding ourselves erect, and to walk correctly, with head high and shoulders square. This was achieved through endless hours of drill movements on the Drill Square. Indeed, we were not considered fit to go out of the boundary of the IMA to visit the town, till we had passed the 'Drill Square'. Till then we also had to polish our leather boots and belts, and do up our beds. Mercifully, these chores were assigned to our bearers again after we had passed the Drill Square.

Tremendous importance was accorded to drill and drill movements. The Drill Square was hallowed ground and never to be used for loitering or making short cuts. Considerable time and effort was devoted to teach us drill movements and battle formations which was considered the bedrock of military tactics. Indeed, the ability to adopt and hold various battle formations was considered a battle winning factor. This was so from the earliest time through history of warfare through the era of the Greek Phalanx and later the Roman Legions. The ability of the armies to wheel and deploy in proper battle formations in the din and bedlam of war with practiced ease often proved decisive. In fact, seeing the superiority of the British and French forces, various Indian Rajahs, notably Ranjit Singh of Punjab and Tipu Sultan of Hyderabad hired European instructors after the Napoleonic Wars. The alchemy of drill was also seen to be a major tool for instilling discipline and obedience. Again, it was a confidence building measure as troops attacking in formation in battle took heart from their comrades to the right and left. As a battalion commander, I always found the ceremonial drill parade to be an excellent instrument to achieve cohesion and discipline in the unit.

Apart from pre-eminence accorded to drill, especially in the early stages, our training syllabus followed several broad modules, namely, military craft, toughening regime including doing the obstacle course, academics, art and science of leadership, moral imperatives, apolitical nature of army and the soldier's credo and lastly, the elusive but all important, matter of style. The importance accorded to deportment, dress, carriage, and personality continued throughout. In between, various military subjects were interwoven, such as handling of weapons, use of obstacles and the ubiquitous "crawling" (to get close to the enemy unseen). We were to learn all these subjects later taught in detail at army schools. On an average each officer gets to attend upwards of 10-12 such specialist courses during the length of his service. So, unlike in the civil services, the in-service training in the armed forces is a continuous process.

Toughening exercises get high importance because warfare is an exceptionally physical and gory business which demands high degree of physical fitness and endurance. Further, physical fitness is linked to mental toughness and ability to face danger. This requirement puts the armed forces in a special class by themselves, because, unlike civil services, men of the army, navy and air force must be prepared to operate in an environment of danger on a continuous basis for long periods. We did long marches through days and nights, with heavy backpacks. It goes on for the rest of our service. I often tell people that during my service of 37 years in the infantry, I must have walked for lakhs of miles. It has also continued even after retirement as a force of habit.

The obstacle course vied with the drill square in importance. It continues for years and an obstacle course is a regular fixture in all cantonments and unit lines, containing all manner of obstacles to hone fitness of limb and mind. It took time to get used to. I remember my old friend, Joe Rebello from Bangalore. He could never bring himself to vault over the nine-foot ditch because he would be unnerved by the bundles of barbed wire piled at the bottom. Again, some boys felt claustrophobic panic while crawling through a concrete pipe.

Discipline and obedience were accorded due importance. This was the exclusive domain of the British sergeants. We were designated as Gentlemen Cadets. The sergeants addressed us as "Sir" while we addressed them as "staff". There the pretence ended; the sergeant was the boss both on and off the parade ground.

The British sergeant is in a class by himself. Patterned after the Roman centurion and cohort, he is highly regarded and judged to be the back-bone of the British army. But they can be quite autocratic and overbearing. "Sir, you are a bloody fool, Sir". A slight exaggeration but close. But as a smart and truculent graduate from Lahore, I was not going to be pushed around by a semi-educated cockney. Hence, I was frequently on the wrong side of (their) law, and being marched up to my Company Commanders' office every so often and punished for disobedience and answering back. Once loafing around with my beret in hand, I espied the dreaded Sergeant bearing down on me. I quickly donned my cap but I must have done it the wrong way (badge on the right eye against the regulation left eye). I hotly contested the Sergeant's admonishment. I was marched up to the Company Commander. I denied the allegation by saying that I had told the Sergeant that I was wearing the cap on the *right* eye (meaning the correct eye); the Company Commander dismissed the charge with a knowing smile. When just the two of us were in his office, my Company Commander, a young major, but wise beyond his years, sat me down and gave me a lecture which I have not forgotten till today. Basically, he said "all organisations are built upon hierarchy, chain of command or pecking order and there are rules to be obeyed". He explained that command/obedience, authority/responsibility, power/restraint, are two sides of the same coin. Therefore, he said, as I went up the ladder, I will be giving orders to subordinates but also receiving orders from above. In the army, there is a place for honest difference of opinion but no place for a rebel. You cannot buck the system. You must conform and play by the rules and be a *"part of a team."* He then went and had a placard made out, that said:

"If you want to command, you must first learn to obey"

He asked me to put it up in my room. Thence, Major Atikur Rehman (called Turk by his peers) became my mentor and guide. In time, he also appointed me an Under Officer. Much later, when he came on a visit to India, he was pleased to meet me and know that I had gone up to be an Army Commander.

The course was strewn with academic lessons in various subjects with special emphasis on history and study of warfare. We were required to deliver short lectures, on a subject of our choice to teach us and to get us used to hearing the sound of our own voice. Colonel Gould, Head of Academics, advised us to devote time and effort on voice modulation and spoken and written language as a necessary part of interpersonal skills. I learnt the value of his advice as in the Service one is frequently making "presentations" or writing papers on various issues, when skills of written and spoken language became important.

On arrival, our English teacher, Major Wright, divided the course into three classes depending on our proficiency in the language. My room-mate, Janjua, much to his discomfiture, got dumped in class three, which he just could never wriggle out of despite all his efforts and kow-towing to Major Wright. Later, Brig Amir Gulistan Janjua rose to be a Governor in Pakistan and an Ambassador. Once, I met him passing through Delhi. By then, he was Pakistani Ambassador to Nepal. He was still unhappy about the "class three" ignominy. However, later, when I mentioned about my friend Janjua, to the Pakistani High Commissioner in Delhi, he told me as how Janjua's diplomatic dispatches from Nepal often caused a lot of mirth in their foreign service. So, Major Wright had a point after all!

Leadership took a prime position in our training. Indeed, throughout the course, it was dinned into our head that the primary function of an officer was to lead troops into battle even at the cost of his life. Hence, the officer must be a paragon of all virtues such as, honour, courage and initiative. He must train his troops and make sure that his command was fully prepared for battle. He should have the moral courage to speak up to his superior if the tasks assigned or the decisions/plans made at higher echelon were wrong or beyond the capacity of his troops. It was his responsibility to create and maintain the requisite team spirit and cohesion of his command. At all times, his was the responsibility to ensure success. He carries the life of his troops in his hands. The troops will follow him to hell and beyond, if they believe in him and trusted his professional ability.

Much later, in a seminar, I was once asked about the "fear factor" for a commander in war. My answer was that in war, for the commander himself, surrounded by his troops and the array of weapons all round him as he is, there is little fear in the personal sense. But the element of fear for him is the fear of failing his men and endangering their lives because in an attack there is often a hair breadth of difference between success and failure. That is the meaning of moral courage and that is the meaning of leading troops into battle. To achieve this bond of mutual trust takes a lifetime of reputation of flawless character, unimpeachable integrity and professional ability.

There is a story that during a lull in the Battle of Gallipoli, a senior officer going the rounds asked a British NCO where his officers were, he is said to have replied, " they must be somewhere around sir, but when it comes time to die, they will be with us".

That kind of mutual trust and confidence between the officers and men is the Gold Standard of officership. Ours was to be a life of hardships and high ideals and we had to be a model of probity and honesty regardless of laxity of morals elsewhere. We were a group of young men from all regions and all religions, so we learnt about national integration at an early stage of life. We were fired by the national zeal for Independent India. We also learnt about the soldier's credo to be apolitical. The British laid great stress on the need for the army to be above politics. So, besides a legacy of leadership, we also inherited from them the valuable principle of an "*apolitical army*". It is a matter of pride that the Indian Army of free India has lived up to this ideal.

Passing out Parade at the IMA

It was eleven o'clock of the morning of December 21st in the year 1947. Some friends such as Bhupinder, Amrit Verma, Amar Cheema and I, and a few others, had gathered in the officers' mess. The long awaited "Passing Out Parade" was over, marking the end of our Course at the Indian Military Academy, Dehradun, and what was more significant, we were now Commissioned Officers in the Indian Army in the rank of 2nd Lieutenant from that day (21 December1947). This was the all-important day for which we had slogged and slaved for over 17 months. The magic hour had arrived, and as previously planned, a bunch of us cronies had gathered together to celebrate the occasion with champagne. We were not quite jumping with joy but there was a feeling of palpable relief and a sense of "thank God it is over". There was a sense of deep satisfaction but there was also an air of a sort of anticlimax and emptiness. As it is said, it is better to travel hopefully than to arrive. Besides, our minds were already turning towards the thrills and challenges awaiting us as officers and leaders of troops. More significantly, we were acutely conscious of the fact that, we were the first batch of officers being commissioned in independent India, and that we were officers of the Indian Army and not the British Indian Army.

Indeed, the special significance of this occasion was amply highlighted in the Parade. For the first time in the history of the Indian Military Academy (IMA), the Indian Tricolour was unfurled instead of the British Union Jack, and the salute was taken by no less a person than Sardar Baldev Singh as the first Defence Minister of free India. He gave a long inspiring speech on the occasion, creating a ripple of excitement in our hearts. We stood taller and stuck our chests out that much more.

2

My Initial Years in the Army

I was commissioned as Second Lieutenant on 21 December 1947 in the 4th Battalion of the 2nd King Edward VII's Own Gurkha Rifles, which was later re-designated as 5th Battalion of the 8 Gorkha Rifles.

In early March 1948, as I prepared to take a train to Calcutta to join my Battalion I was excited and perhaps a bit nervous. Events were unfolding swiftly at the national level. It was a historically momentous period in the history of the subcontinent. But as a Second Lieutenant fresh out of the IMA, I was perhaps too young to grasp the full significance of it at that time.

The Independence and Partition of India into two dominions of India and Pakistan brought about sweeping changes across the entire board affecting different parts of the erstwhile British Indian Army. The major changes involved were:

a. Accretion of Gorkha Battalions to India.
b. Trans-posting of officers between India and Pakistan.
c. Restructuring of one class regiments.
d. Restructuring of all class regiments.
e. Division of assets, i.e., Stores, Depots, Cantonments.

Impact of Partition on the Army

Division of Gorkha Regiments

As per "The Tripartite Agreement, between Britain-India-Nepal 1947", the 10 Gurkha regiments of the erstwhile British Indian Army were to be divided: 6 regiments coming to the Indian Army, and 4 regiments to be taken away by Britain as the British Gurkhas. Further, the regiments going to the British were to take only two battalions each, leaving the rest to India. A referendum was carried out and most gurkha troops opted to stay in the Indian Army. India had to raise new battalions for our six regiments plus a new Regiment 11GR for gurkhas who had chosen to stay. Hence, in effect India became the beneficiary of upwards of 50 battalions of these legendary soldiers which have since been a valuable asset to the country. In addition, as hitherto all Gurkha regiments had been exclusively officered by the British, India had now to find the requisite number of Indian officers to take their place. The privilege of providing officers in a large single block fell on our course; so about fifteen of us newly commissioned officers were posted to Gorkha regiments, the remaining shortfall being made up by officers relieved by the Muslim regiments going to Pakistan, as the rest of the Indian Army was also being divided on the 2/3rd, 1/3rd basis. The Indian Army (Military Secretary's

Branch) had to shuffle a large number of officers in the chaos of partitioning. In the atmosphere of hurry and scurry, it is doubtful if the larger significance of assimilation of Gorkhas into the Indian Army or special selection of officers for them was properly realized.

Trans-postings of Officers

On Partition, officers of the majority community in their country had to stay with their country's army. While officers of the minority community in either country had the option of joining either the Indian or the Pakistani army. So, there was total chaos because the Muslim regiments going to Pakistan had to shed non-Muslim officers and pick up Muslim officers from regiments staying in India. On top of it all, India had to find more than a few hundred officers for the newly acquired (and newly Indianized) Gurkha battalions (now rechristened as Gorkhas) In the confusion, many square pegs got sent to round holes and *vice versa*. For instance, when I joined my unit in Alipore Camp, Calcutta, I found ex-officers from as many as seven different regiments. The 2nd in command, a colourful character called Major Ajit Ohara Sen had mostly served in the ENSA groups (equivalent of Indian Army "Dikush Sabha" groups for the entertainment of Indian trops in war). His forte was to come singing British songs aloud to the mess. Obviously, he had done little soldiering with troops. Mass movement to and fro was hard enough but considering that movement of officers also entailed movement of their baggage and wives and children, one can imagine the magnitude of the logistic problem.

Division of One Class and All Class Regiments

The British Indian Army had undergone restructuring at various points in history. Till the Mutiny of 1857, most of the regiments were of one class type depending upon the state from which they were recruited, the bulk consisting of Muslim sepoys from Central India. After the mutiny, the British mixed the soldiers by religion and region, i.e., each regiment having Muslims and non-Muslim soldiers, on the basis of "half-and-half", to guard against conspiracies and possible rebellion. After Indian Independence, the mix had to be unraveled all over again. In other words, all Muslim components had to go to Pakistan and non-Muslim elements transferred from Pakistan to India. It was bad enough for the regiments of infantry and armour, but regiments of other arms like artillery, signals and a whole host of service units had a mix of all religions and regions; so in their case, cross-postings of masses of individual soldiers had to be resorted to.

Division of Fixed Assets

Fixed assets, such as ordnance and other stores were mostly scattered in the interior of India, whereas, the army cantonments were concentrated in North West (only threat was perceived from Russia). For the stores in depots, the formula of 2/3rd and 1/3rd was used but the cantonments stayed *in situ*. For Army Headquarters, India's portion remained in Delhi whereas Pakistan had to establish a new Army Headquarters out of the erstwhile Northern Command located at Rawalpindi.

The division of numerous other common assets was a herculean task. It was generally agreed to be divided on the basis of 80:20, but working out the assets in detail was well-nigh impossible. Hence, it was decided that a sum of Rs 75 crore would be paid by India to Pakistan. A sum of 20 crore was actually paid but then Pakistan invaded Kashmir (tantamount to invading India since Kashmir had acceded to India). Consequently, the balance 55 crore rupees was withheld on the argument that, if paid, it would only augment the war-making capacity of Pakistan. On this point, Mahatma Gandhi went on a fast, which was deemed to be unfair coercion by many Hindu nationalists. Later, this was mentioned as one of the main provocations for the assassination of Gandhiji by Nathuram Godse.

Siano Leftain (Little Lieutenant)

Award of PVSM by the President, N. Sanjeeva Reddy

I found myself in a train bound for Calcutta in early March 1948 to join my battalion. Immediately on commissioning on 21 December 1947, our entire batch was sent to attend short courses in weapons at Saugor and tactics at Mhow before joining our units. In the units, following the end of the Second World War, almost every officer was at least a captain; hence a 2nd Lieutenant was a rarity. As a duty-officer of the week, going through the unit family lines, the Gorkha women would come rushing out to take a peek at the *Siano Leftain* (little lieutenant). I was appointed a Platoon Commander. So, as taught at the IMA, I set about to know my men by name and the village and district they came from. It was hard to distinguish between them. They all looked alike with round faces with Chinky eyes. So, after memorizing their names, I would stand them in a line and then ask them to step up turn by turn as I shouted out the name and village of the soldier. In the beginning, I made many mistakes identifying the soldiers which caused some confusion and laughter, but this proved useful in breaking the ice and making friends. There was a youngster, Harka Bahadur from Lamjhung district of Nepal which I often mispronounced as *"lahmjhunge"*. The class would break out into peals of laughter till my Subedar told me one day that *"lahmjhunge"* in Nepali language meant "long moustache". I think that's the nickname they had given me. I also learnt something about the Gorkhas. I found that despite their reputation as fearless fighters, they were the most friendly and gentle human beings.

Internal Security Duties

I had come full of grandiose visions of being a dashing leader of men but the reality was deflating, since my first assignment turned out to be moving sections around on internal security duty. Hindu-Muslim riots had broken out since independence had been declared. Calcutta was on fire. At one time, five or six battalions of Gorkhas were deployed in penny packets all over the lanes and by-lanes of the vast city to maintain order. I was on the move day and night, checking on posts and frequently running after miscreants. On one occasion, we found a group of very excited Bengalis, mostly lumpen elements, chasing after some Muslims urchins who were armed with burning torches. The Bengalis were chasing them with long *thows* (kind of long daggers) shouting that the Muslims were trying to set fire to their homes. We pacified the agitated Bengalis and I sent a batch of my Gorkhas to catch the Muslim miscreants but they disappeared into a maze of narrow lanes. The troops were advised to avoid getting lost in the back lanes. The rule book solution is to have a magistrate handy and to get him to permit opening of fire or even entering miscreant's homes. However, there were only a few magistrates available, so the orders were: no opening of fire and avoid entering into private houses. The army is taught to use only minimum force and to avoid getting into trouble. In point of fact the army finds the internal security duty (IS Duties) very distasteful. You are damned for what you do and damned for what you do not do.

The unit was woefully understaffed, so I moved up fast from handy man to platoon commander to adjutant to company commander. The Commanding Officer, Colonel

N.K. Chatterji and Adjutant Captain Chakrabarti were both ex-Baluch Regiment, bachelors, and very good officers. I got along well with them and learnt a lot. The CO seemed to like me and gave me an extremely good "end of the year" report but in one line, he said that this young officer tends to be a bit "garrulous". I thought it was a word of praise but on checking the dictionary, I was sobered to know that the word meant "talkative". The rest of the officers were a mixed bag of good and indifferent. On the very first evening, the Adjutant told the Mess Sergeant that I should not be served a drink unless I asked for it in Gorkhali (Gorkha language). I mastered the words within an hour! The Subedar Major (originally called "native commandant") was one Sardar Bahadur Balesore Rana, OBI. He was an imposing Gorkha with a chest full of medals. As per the custom he selected a batman (soldier helper) for me who was to be my guide in the matter of drinking and spending money.

Partition – The Monumental Blunder

India gained independence on 15 August 1947 but it came wrapped in untold misery for millions of people. Partition of the country into India and Pakistan caused savage rioting through the length and breadth of the country. Men behaved like wild animals. There was wholesale migration of populations. Hundreds of thousands of men, women, children, young and old, were on the march to and fro; multitudes of Hindus and Sikhs from Pakistan to India and a vast number of Muslims from India to Pakistan leaving their homes and hearths with whatever belongings they could carry on their person. There was total upheaval and mass killings. In fact, the Partition of India will go down in history as the greatest blunder and unparalleled crime on the part of the British rulers. An endeavour of such vast magnitude was undertaken without adequate preparation resulting in horrendous loss of life and property, sowing seeds of acrimony and discord between India and Pakistan that may continue for generations. Figures are mind boggling — between one to two million perished and 7-10 million people were displaced. And, all this happened when India had possibly a galaxy of luminaries and able leaders headed by no less a person than Mahatma Gandhi.

It is hard not to believe that Indians were somehow hustled into the Partition by the uncanny British whose overweening desire seemed to be to concede Pakistan to the Muslims. So, the Indian leaders tried hard to prevent it but the implacable Jinnah had his way. Though the Indian leaders had languished in jails for years in the struggle for independence, Jinnah or his partymen had not been in prison even for a single day, but he got his way. Characteristically, Jinnah refused to support the Quit India Movement launched by Mahatma Gandhi on 9 August 1942; as a matter of fact, the Muslim League volunteers helped the authorities to round up Congress leaders during the Movement. The Quit India Movement was crushed within two months by severe repressive measures by deploying a force of more than 50 battalions. However, it became clear to the British that nothing short of total independence would be acceptable to Indian leaders. England was in dire straits herself. The Empire had been bled white in the two World Wars. Apart from crippling losses in manpower, her economy was in recession. Nevertheless, the British reacted very aggressively to Gandhi's "Quit India" movement as World War II was poised at a critical point and the Allies could not allow any let-up in India's war effort. Alarmed at the Quit India Movement, President Truman sent a personal emissary to India to discuss measures to ensure continued Indian cooperation for the war effort.

Mountbatten came to India with plenipotentiary powers to negotiate Indian independence with Indian leaders. In the context of implacable attitude of Jinnah, Mountbatten seemed to have conceded the notion of two nations at an early stage, unless we presume that he came with this preconceived notion or worse, that this was his secret mandate from the powers in UK. Be that as it may, the thrust of negotiations got centered on coercing the Indian leaders to accept the Partition. How and when this shift in the British perception came about, is lost in the fog of discussions, arguments and counter arguments. The Indian position was firm against the breakup of the country till 1945, when Wavell had to call an abrupt end to the Simla Conference in June 1945. But within a few months of the arrival of Mountbatten, the British attitude seemed to have hardened and tilted finally in favour of Jinnah. Various reasons are adduced — one theory was that since the British could not hold the whole of India any longer, they conspired to carve out a smaller and more pliable slice of the country (Pakistan); the Muslims were the current favourites, and conceivably, there may also have been a Saudi Arabia angle (Truman factor). Theories and conjectures abound. The only thing which seemed beyond doubt was the British resolve to create Pakistan. Then, Mountbatten advanced the date of independence from June 1948 to 15 August 1947. There is a story that the British were alarmed at the failing health of Jinnah and it was evident that should Jinnah die, the chances for Pakistan will die with him. This story has been controverted but it will just not go away (He died 13 months after Partition). In any case, no reason, plausible or otherwise, was given. Perhaps, the British just got tired of the obduracy of Jinnah, or got simply fed up with the argumentative Hindus. Perhaps they just wanted to get out as quickly as possible.

Whatever the motivation, it should have been obvious to the British and more so to the Indian leaders that it would be impossible to organize an orderly migration of masses at such a short time. The Indians knew nothing about administration — all they had learned was politics of agitation and arousing communal passions. But the British lapse in this regard is highly condemnable. If they could marshal the enormous state power to crush the countrywide Quit India Movement within a matter of two months, there is no excuse as to why it could not be done for management of Partition. It shows an attitude of total disregard for public safety, amounting to willful dereliction of duty, indeed genocide. The Indian leaders are equally culpable for not insisting on a longer timeline.

We invited Lord Louis Mountbatten to be India's first Governor General, which has been criticized in most quarters. It is felt that it was the duty of the new government to organise a functional cabinet. There was so much to be done. We should have organised a proper defence committee of the cabinet to coordinate functioning of railways, appointment of armed guards of military or police to ensure safety of passengers. We should have organised protection of marching columns, and administrative arrangements for staging camps, diverting of masses to refugee camps, and so on. It is said that an effort was made by the British to organise some arrangements by way of armed guards for refugee trains and organisation of refugee camps and control of their flow but sheer numbers were overpowering and there were not enough troops. So, the suffering and bloodshed was horrendous. At the top level, we did not seem to understand that formation of a government entails much more than just nomination of ministers. Again, unlike Pakistan, India had inherited a functioning secretariat and by now, Sardar Patel was supposed to have organised the administrative services and the police. It is very reprehensible that instead of taking on our legitimate responsibility, we allowed the British to continue to handle the matters of higher policy of the government even after independence. The same applied to intelligence matters. Hence, the British were privy to all classified information, as they still held all key appointments including, C-in-Cs of both dominions. Hence, the monumental blunder of partition of the country came about not as a result of proper deliberations by the Indian leaders but through British manipulation and a state of helpless drift on our part.

The whole truth will never be known even though a lot of books have been written on the subject. Was it an honest miscalculation on the part of British through an intention to grant independence without delay and give some sort of concessions to the minorities (read grant of Pakistan)? Or was it diabolic malevolence of the rulers to leave India as a fractured mess of numerous states in eternal conflict with each other. We came pretty close to it, but for the personality and sagacity of Sardar Patel who managed to persuade all the 565 states to accede to India barring Hyderabad, Junagarh and still festering Kashmir. Annexation of Hyderabad was also largely the work of Patel. Same is said about Junagarh.

Anyhow, whichever way one may look at it, the Partition failed to achieve its chief objective, namely 'to provide a homeland for Muslims' as more Muslims got left behind in India than those moving to the newly created Pakistan. In the event the large and burgeoning Muslim minority in India is creating its own problem and a potential threat to India in the long run.

I was a cadet at the IMA when all this was happening. My family as well the family of my wife to be, were going through great hardship getting out of Pakistan and finding refuge in India. Each family has its tale of woe and scars of this unforgettable tragedy. We lost all our lands in Sargodha and became "landlords without land" overnight as it were. Otherwise, my father and family were a little more fortunate. They got away in good time in army transport arranged by my older brother who as a serving captain and happened to be stationed in Rawalpindi. However, our entire household goods were "safely stored" in the cantonment, never to be seen again. We lost a flourishing farm of more than 600 acres in Sargodha, West Punjab. Later, we got only one tenth of the acreage in India by way of compensation.

My future wife's family had a rougher time. My father-in-law, a Garrison Engineer in Army MES service was stationed in Jhelum. Since his properties and lands lay in Rawalpindi and village Khurd near Jhelum, he initially opted to stay on in Pakistan (many Hindus did so) but soon one of his Muslim friends came to tell him that the local branch of the Muslim League had his name on top of the list for extermination. So, he scrambled to prepare to leave. He stored his belongings including his car with some Muslim friends who also helped him to withdraw bulk of his money from the bank (Pakistan had put an embargo on it for the departing Hindus) and managed to move in some military trucks to the town of Mirpur in just the clothes they were wearing. From there, along with a few other families, he managed to hire a bus (bribing the driver with petrol from the black market) and persuaded him to take them to Jammu. The bus broke down just short of Akhnoor, so all including women and children walked in the dark to the small town, in constant fear of an attack by miscreants.

After a fearful night with a Hindu family in Akhnoor, they managed to hire a boat next morning to take them to Jammu by the Akhnoor-Jammu canal. Totally exhausted and wet, they tottered up to the house of my wife's uncles in Jammu late next day. By now the father had fallen ill due to the strain of the journey and anxiety for saving his family. Somehow the family managed to get one seat and sent him to Delhi by a returning military plane. The family stayed back for a few more days, getting new clothes stitched, before joining the father in Delhi by another harrowing journey by bus, truck, and finally by train from Amritsar to Delhi. This was the typical experience of most Hindus fleeing out of Pakistan. Many were not so fortunate, falling prey to depredations and abductions by Muslim mobs roaming the countryside. The Muslim families would have had similar experiences.

Indo-Pak War 1947-48

Soon after, a desperate Pakistan took a suicidal step! It launched a tribal invasion on Kashmir on 27 October 1947, barely 9 weeks after Partition, a thinly disguised military offensive with a view to annex the State of Jammu and Kashmir to achieve a *fait accompli.* However, the gamble backfired as the dithering Maharaja Hari Singh panicked and signed the Instrument of Accession to India, making it possible to fly in Indian troops to secure Srinagar in the nick of time. These events triggered the longest insurgency in history though Kashmir remains in Indian possession (less a larger chunk of the territory in Pakistani hands referred to as POK and Gilgit and Baltistan) even after 68 years. This was also the beginning of first of the four wars between the two neighbours. The Indian army steadily pushed the Pakistani invaders, by now reinforced by its regulars, out of a part of Kashmir when India declared a unilateral ceasefire and took the matter to the UN. Since then, a number of elections have been held and the accession has been ratified by the State Constituent Assembly. Yet Pakistan has fomented and is stoking a virulent insurgency, forever trying to infiltrate *jihadists* into the Valley, forcing a state of perpetual mobilization on us. It is wasteful in manpower and resources though excellent training experience for the Indian Army. There is a 740 km long LOC (Line Of Control) manned and patrolled, day and night, by both the Pakistan and Indian armies, with frequent exchange of fire.

Accession of Kashmir to India

The high drama of signing of the accession document by the Maharaja of Jammu and Kashmir has been recounted in many documents, the chief being the narrative told by the then Prime Minister of the State, Justice Mehar Chand Mahajan. Mahajan was sent to Nehru by the Maharaja for emergent help of the Indian Army to save Srinagar, on October 26, 1947. The letter of accession with a similar appeal had been sent earlier on October 24 with Deputy Prime Minister Batra. Nehru who disliked the Maharaja, tended to prevaricate but yielded on the intervention of Sheikh Abdullah and Sardar Patel. Later, Nehru, under the unfortunate influence of Lord Mountbatten, added the *suo moto* caveat about ascertaining the wishes of the people of the State on return of normalcy *after the withdrawal of Pakistani forces.* This contentious clause got inserted into the Indian brief to the UN. Ever since then, this reference to "wishes of the people", which morphed into a promise of Plebiscite, has created endless trouble for India, albeit it was contingent upon the withdrawal of Pakistani forces, which has not happened till date. There is controversy about Nehru's referring of the issue to the UN (again on advice from Mountbatten, it is believed) before we could clear the entire state of Pakistani tribals and Pakistani forces, which seemed feasible at that stage of operations. K. Natwar Singh, who served later in the PMO under Indira Gandhi, calls it a "monumental blunder" to have referred the matter to the Security Council. Further, Natwar Singh has stated that we made the mistake of approaching the UN under Chapter VI of the UN Charter, which addresses "disputes" and advocates negotiations, whereas it should have been more appropriate to make a reference to Chapter VII, which deals with "aggression" and "breach of peace".

Adventure in Gulmarg

My unit 5/8 Gorkha Rifles, having done its tour of IS duties in crowded Calcutta, got orders to move to the Tithwal Sector in north Jammu and Kashmir. It turned out to be a very different experience and closer to real soldiering. Tithwal had been an area of high endeavour in the 1947-48 Indo-Pak War. Indian 19 Division under the dynamic leadership of General Thimayya, had stopped the intrusion of Pakistani tribals, (now fully reinforced by their regular army), and launched a counteroffensive with 161 Brigade under Brigadier L.P. Sen on the direct Jhelum–Muzzafarabad axis and 163 Brigade under the intrepid Brigadier Harbakhsh Singh to carry out a daring outflanking move over the 3000 meter plus high Nastachun Pass to Kishen Ganga River and then to Tithwal. Harbakhsh succeeded brilliantly, capturing a huge swath of territory from Handwara to Tithwal. On arrival, that is where my Battalion was deployed in pickets on the high ridges guarding the approaches to Tithwal. Fresh vegetables were always in short supply, so after a while one of our platoon pickets once discovered a tempting spinach like growth near a small stream (*khola* in gorkhali) which they avidly cooked and ate for supper. Next day the platoon commander found the men groggy and floundering. The local Kashmiris told us later that they never touched the stuff as it was highly toxic and sleep inducing. We warned all troops to avoid this spinach!

The Ski School in Gulmarg

General Thimayya, forward looking as ever, dreamed up a Ski School in the high meadows of Gulmarg, for the army to gain expertise in operating in snow and extreme cold conditions since almost his entire operational area used to be snow bound in winter. Hence, a call up went out for volunteers for attending this course of training. I did not need much coaxing for this promising venture. So, 4 to 5 of us from Tithwal Brigade did a day long trudge of 16-18 miles of snow trails over the Nastachun Pass in December 1948 as the Pass used to be closed to vehicular traffic for the six months of winter. We 3 reached Chowkibal, a staging post on the other side, which was used for summer stocking. There the Captain-in-Charge, surprised at the bedraggled party of youngsters, proved most hospitable providing us hot tea and basins full of hot water to help thaw our frozen feet. I got a scare as due to a leak in the sole of one of my boots, the hot soak turned the skin black. Next day we went to Tangmarg at the foot of the Gulmarg massif by truck and did another slog up to the meadow at the top reaching late in the evening. Worried about the blackened foot, I took care to keep wearing thick woolen socks during the medical inspection next morning, which mercifully escaped the notice of the harried doctor. Later, the offending skin peeled off leaving me none the worse for my lapse.

We were the first course at the Ski School. Two officers of the Swiss Army, Major Gahluser and Lieutenant Zurbrigan arrived to take us in hand. We were issued long wooden skis with boots fastened with steel bindings and ski poles. The initial lessons were mainly to make us comfortable with the new-fangled contraptions starting with learning to stand without falling. We learned fast and got used to the sensation of gliding over snow. Our instructors were good and concentrated on toughening exercises and coordination training. At the end of the six week's course, two of us were retained as instructors; so through four such courses we built up a cadre of eight instructors, with which we managed the next year.

I worked at the school for three winters, from 1948 through 1950. We used to do serious soldiering with our units in summer and gathered back at the school with the first snowfall. It was pure joy and possibly the happiest time of my life. Skiing is a popular sport in the western countries, so it was a wonder that we did it as part of duty. Over time, we ran basic courses and advanced courses. Starting with officers' courses only, we branched out to courses for other ranks and introduced many innovations, like climbing and skiing down with weapons and military gear, stopping en route to fire. It was hilarious to watch plainsmen from Rajasthan and Haryana who had never seen snow in their life, zipping down the slopes. We organised slalom, downhill and cross-country ski races.

One year, I paired up with a good friend, Major Nandu Jayal of Garhwal Rifles. We got red polka dotted shirts stitched in Srinagar, for the occasion. I remember it because that year we won both slalom and downhill races. As a special treat, a bunch of us instructors used to go out exploring new trails in the short breaks in between the courses (six weeks for basic courses and eight weeks for advance courses). We once did a cross country skiing trip to Baramula, covering some 18-19 miles, much to the amazement and admiration of the divisional staff. We were having the time of our lives but the people in Srinagar looked upon us as heroes. Many of us later graduated to mountain climbing which is a mix of pleasure, hard work and sometimes, tragedy. Nandu Jayal died on Cho Oyu (in Tibet) in 1952. Later, in 1965, John D. Dias died climbing with a US Army team in Alaska. I felt particularly bad because I knew John and his wife Joan rather well and I had climbed with him on Panchachule, a mountain in Kumaon Himalayas.

We must have done good groundwork at Gulmarg as the School subsequently blossomed into a full-fledged Mountain Warfare School ranking as one of the best in the world. Furthermore, apart from operations in snow and extreme cold, the Indian Army now also specializes in operating at high altitudes and also trains in ice and rock work. Gulmarg has also grown into a major ski resort. For me personally, I developed an abiding love for the mountains. Thereafter, I organized adventure courses for young officers wherever I happened to be serving and encouraged adventure sports. I tell people that we are lucky to have unlimited opportunities and special equipment for such activities in the army in the course of duty, whereas these kind of facilities are only available to our civilian counterparts at great expense and with difficulty.

Recently in 2012, I had an opportunity to visit my Battalion in Palampur, Yol with the back drop of the majestic Dhauladhar mountain range. My family and I had the great opportunity to get an audience with his Holiness, the Dalai Lama in Dharamsala which was an uplifting experience. I also found that many more facilities for sport have come up there like Paragliding, mountain hiking, and even serious mountaineering beyond Dharamsala. I suggested that the Unit should encourage and organize hikes, motorbike excursions and the like. Much can be done also together with their young wives. In the past, officers were not allowed to spend annual leave in station. They had to go out and see the country and meet people, often touring their recruiting areas.

Several years ago, a friend in the academic line asked me to write a paper on the subject of "what is wrong with the youth of our time". The burden of my paper was that the fault lies with parents of our time and that we do not invest enough time and effort in quality parenting. We are too busy striving to get ahead or making a living. We forget that main job of parents is to be a role model and that the best way to teach is by setting a personal example. In the same manner, the commanding officers of today get so engrossed in the minutiae of soldiering that they are not able to devote time and effort to develop the requisite qualities in the young officers.

Summer and Winter Life in J&K

Besides our shenanigans for three to four winter months in Gulmarg, my real vocation of soldiering in the unit continued apace. Summer months were actually a busy period. We repaired our bunkers, maintained the tracks and intensified patrolling between posts. There was a lot of administrative work too, for the posts had to be restocked for the following winter. The region of J&K lacks the resources to sustain a large military, so every bit of food and other necessities like petrol, oil, etc., had to be brought from supply depots from plains of India. Stocking of posts over mule paths, required an army of ponies and porters. Besides, dry rations, the units were issued onions, potatoes and condiments for 6 months of winter. For fresh vegetables, 3-4 month worth of hard wearing vegetables such as *Knol-khol* (*Kohlrabi*) were supplied. Meat was another problem for canned meat was unknown then. Instead, the unit would be issued a lot of goat carcasses (male goats only for Gorkhas) which we would bury in snow-lined pits as soon as winter came. It would last a few months for the rest, so we went vegan for the rest of winter. After subsisting on *Kohlrabi* for three winters, this is one vegetable that I cannot stand to this day.

One can imagine the enormous effort needed on administration, a perennial bugbear of commanders down the ages. It was a good lesson to learn for the budding leaders for history of warfare, which abounds in examples of entire campaigns floundering for want of adequate administration and poor logistical support. This problem further intensifies when logistics depend upon mules and porters. Fortunately, Kashmir has a surfeit of ponies and porters. Be that as it may, the army's requirement generated vast wealth for the locals and a lucrative avenue of employment, often quoted as cause of their vested interest in continuing the insurgency.

The unit was headquartered at a place called Chamkot on the unpaved road en route from Tangdhar to Tithwal. The Brigade HQ was at Tangdhar. The Brigade Commander, Brigadier Bikram Singh, a fire-eating, foul-mouthed Sikh, whose idea of active command was to ring up and ball-out the unit colonels once or twice a day. Our Commanding Officer (CO) was a conscientious and hardworking Parsi gentleman who simply loathed the shouting tyrant. As an Adjutant, I tried my best to shield my CO, keeping him away from the telephone on one pretext or another, and taking the flak myself. At some point before the arrival of our unit, the Brigadier had been gifted a tiny bear cub, its mother having been killed. The little bear had the free run of all the cook houses and soon grew to be a formidable size, but still quite playful. It is said that one day he playfully grabbed the unsuspecting Brigadier from behind, giving him the scare of his life. Thereafter, the poor fellow was ordered to be securely chained whenever the Brigadier Sahib was around.

National Defence Academy, Khadakvasla

After service in the unit including the Gulmarg interlude, I was posted to my alma mater, IMA Dehradun as an instructor, which is always welcome news to a young officer. On arrival, I was assigned to the Joint Services Wing of the IMA. It was to move to its new home, at Khadakvasla outside Pune, where a new National Defence Academy was set up, an ambitious and farsighted Tri Service University to train young cadets for the army, navy, and air force, prior to them going to their respective service academies. Specially selected young boys would be studying for a university degree together with service training. The aim would be to feed full-fledged graduates in arts, science or technology to the respective services. Accordingly, officers of the rank of captain and equivalent were posted as Instructors from all the three Services along with a large complement of civil professors. The Academy was situated in a beautiful new campus spread over 7000 acres against the backdrop of mountains dominated by Shivaji's Fort Simhagad. My first task was to be a part of the Pilot Committee (naval equivalent of "Advance Party") along with Lieutenant Nayar of the Indian Navy, and a Flight Lieutenant of the Indian Air Force, to receive special trains with men and stores arriving from Dehradun and to help settle them in the new location.

Working at a tri-service institution was very good exposure for me at an early stage of service. Thereafter it is a happy experience to meet my contemporaries from the navy and air force as also the professors and lecturers. The first passing out parade was unique as it amalgamated features from the three Services such as a quarter deck (Navy) and an aerial fly past (Air Force). At the academy, there were extensive facilities for hobbies like horse riding, sailing in the adjoining lake, and glider training. We used tri-service terminology such as battalions, squadrons (for companies) and troops (for platoons). We got a large number of visitors to this show piece such as Nehru escorting Chou En-lai along with a clutch of grizzled Chinese Marshals. We also hosted Marshal Zukhov of Russia and the Shah of Iran with his beautiful queen.

My Marriage and Life Thereafter

As a landmark in my personal life, I got married while at Khadakvasla, which again came about through the machination of my brother, a Major now. He found a very attractive sister to the wife of a fellow Major. They cooked it up well and quick, getting my father's approval. So, one fine morning, I got a telegram that said; "Congratulations, you are engaged". It has been a standing joke in the family ever since that both my wife and I were "fixed" without even having seen each other. In the event, like many other such lucky breaks in my life, the marriage proved extremely fortuitous and through no effort on my part, I was blessed with a lovely young wife who has since been a tower of strength and an anchor to my life. Marriage followed engagement, and I was soon standing to attention in the Commandant, General Habibulah's office requesting permission to marry as per the old custom. He gave me permission and one weeks' leave of absence. I got back with my brand new wife and we were wined and dined by our young friends, many also newly married, day after day. Such is the beauty of service camaraderie that we did not to get to start our kitchen in our newly built house for a good 10-12 days.

As a bachelor, I had had a rather chaotic life style, so my young wife Shobha, was appalled to see a pile of unpaid bills. From then onwards, she learnt not to trust my sense of financial management. Like most young officers, we led a grand life somehow financially keeping our head above water. But lucky for me, my wife proved to be a solid home manager, besides being a great companion. Later in life, through years of teaching and counseling of young officers, I always stressed the virtues of stability in personal life — financial, domestic and emotional stability, as essential attributes of a good officer. I have seen many a promising career ruined for lack of such balance in life.

We worked hard and played hard and made many lifelong friendships. We went on many outings and excursions on our motorbikes — only a few boasted cars. We were not rich by any standard but we were happy and contented with a sense of fulfillment in our professional and personal life. Soon, we were blessed with our first child, a lovely doll of a baby girl. The firstborn is truly a life-altering experience, and a thing of wonder and sheer magic.

It was a very good year for me and I soon got another lucky break. It came in the form of a messianic wellwisher, Captain K.K. Kaul of Deccan Horse, fresh from a triumph at the competitive exam for the Staff College and winning a nomination for a course in the UK. He was aghast at my cavalier approach to the profession and promptly took me in hand. The Army has exams, written as well as oral at every rung on the promotion ladder. The *creme de la creme* is the exam for entry into the Staff College which separates men from the boys. He put me in the run for both Part D (written exam for promotion to Major) and the Staff College exam. Next started a grueling pace of studies and written answer sheets. He would give me sample question papers every day, demanding I should read up the relevant books and training pamphlets and produce full essay type answers within two days. On the next visit he would discuss my answers in merciless detail, giving back my answer sheets full of corrections in red ink. Hard work apart, it was a bit deflating for a self-assured person like me; so I was pricked to get down to serious work for a change. In truth, I had never worked so hard in my life. This professional boot camp went on nonstop for a full three months. I was quite peeved with the whole business though my wife found it quite amusing.

Canadian Army Staff College

I may have chucked it but then, my friend Kaul seemed to prove his point in that I passed the written Part D exam in all subjects in one shot. In fact I surprised myself. So hereafter, I was his willing acolyte. To cut a long story short, he chaperoned me through studies for the Staff College exam so well that I passed with flying colours. What is more, I was selected to attend a course at the Canadian Army Staff College. As per the Officer Exchange Programme, we used to send an officer each to UK, Canada and Australia every year. I was going to be the man for Canada. The only fly in the ointment was that my wife was not allowed to accompany me as India was passing through a dollar crunch.

Soon, on 15 November 1957, I was boarding a luxurious P&O Liner, Chusan in Bombay docks for London, en route to Canada. Our *babus* in the finance who had perhaps not heard of air travel, decreed that I should travel by ship, without realizing that first class single cabin ship fare cost more (plus daily allowance as icing on the cake). Anyhow, that gave me a leisurely sea voyage plus a two week sojourn in London with a regimental friend, Jerry Nagle "between ships". The London-Canada leg was on even a more luxurious ship. The Atlantic in winter tends to be quite choppy. I discovered that I was a good sailor, so I got exclusive treatment in the dining hall as more than half the passengers were nursing their seasickness in their cabins. I landed at Halifax on the Eastern seaboard of Canada, sailing past Newfoundland, famed for the earliest Viking settlement. Then on to Ottawa after a daylong train journey, where I was received by a Canadian captain who very kindly took me to his home for X-mas dinner. The next day I took a train to Kingston, where I was received by an Instructor of the college at the railway station which was more like a simple siding. The tradition of grand monument-like railway stations is absent in practical Canada. Canadians are a very friendly and hospitable people and I received great kindness throughout my stay there. Only three students stayed in the mess, a German, a Turk and I. It was bitterly cold. Even a short walk to the classrooms took ones' breath away, so I had to ask my friend in London to ship out a heavy woollen overcoat on priority.

The course of training was interesting and it was not too unlike our courses in content and style as the Canadian Army was largely patterned on the British Army like ours. I settled down quickly and was taking part in the proceedings, matching up with the Canadians. Apart from the hosts, nearly one-third of the students were foreigners. There were officers from NATO and Commonwealth countries besides large contingents from the USA and the UK. Not surprisingly, the foreigner group was a clear notch above the local contingent, since like me they had obviously gone through a rigorous selection process. Interestingly, the Pakistani student, Major Azhar Sadik, originally my course mate in IMA Dehradun, was handsomely installed in a rented house with a princely allowance of 12 dollars per day as against the measly 3 dollars per day sanctioned by the Indian ministry for me. Anyhow, it was a great opportunity and a mind broadening experience to be exposed to the norms and views of officers from other countries and well worth the expense to our exchequer. I suggested in my end of course report that we should send another 3 or 4 officers from the Indian Army, at our own expense if need be, in addition to the one allowed under the exchange protocol.

During the course a large number of foreign dignitaries visited us. I had the unique experience of meeting the legendary FM Lord Montgomery. He was a diminutive person with bird-beak of a nose, but with tremendous presence and aura. I was presented as Captain Dutta from India. He graciously shook my hand and asked, "How is the Indian Army?" I was taken aback for a moment but I heard myself say, "Indian Army is doing very well, Sir". I do not know what he thought of it but he moved on with a polite nod. I must have recounted the story a thousand times thereafter to whoever would listen!

One of the highlights of the course was a grand tour of Canadian military establishments and places of interest. Notably, we were taken to their military "Post" at Fort Hudson Bay close to the Arctic Circle, a fairly large establishment, all covered and heated. It was a virtual enclosed and covered town containing all appurtenances of a small-sized cantonment. Of special interest to me was to meet the Eskimo instructors who took us out for a night camp in the wilderness. We were also given a tour of the Niagara Falls and the towns of Montreal and Quebec. It was interesting to see the famous Quebec Heights which was captured by the English under the legendary, 26 year old, General Wolfe. Our commandant at the college was Brigadier Roger Rowley DSO, MC. The instructors were all Colonels and equal ranks of the navy and air force. I think I got on with them very well and made a good impression. I earned a good course report, which had a good impact on my career. So, I did well for myself besides having a great time.

3

Counter Insurgency Operations and Sino-Indian War of 1962

Rejoining 5/8 GR at Yol

On return from Canada in the end of February 1959, I rejoined my unit, 5/8 GR, located at Yol near Dharamsala in Himachal Pradesh. Against the backdrop of a beautiful valley in the foothills of the Himalayas, the Yol Cantonment was located on a broad hill slope about 10 kms from the old military station of Dharamsala. For training, the units would go down to the plains. In fact, within a day of my arrival, I was called to join my unit on training near Kangra. So, I just put my family in the house allotted to me and putting together some uniforms and military gear, I left by the vehicle sent to fetch me. I was away on training for a good two months before returning to meet my family. Communications between the training area and base camp in Yol were quite primitive. There was nothing like cell phones in those days, so my wife was quite worried about my well-being. She told me later that she seriously thought of alerting the police but then was horrified to learn that there was no police station within 50 km! When I returned to Yol, my wife and young daughter Sweetie were aghast to see me tanned and burned black by the sun.

In Yol Cantonment, the unit offices and sheds for the troops were located way down the slope, while the wooden cottages/bungalows for officers were located a good bit higher on the slope. So, we had to go down and climb back up at least thrice a day, involving a trudge of 4-5 km, and a round trip of 2 hours. The day started with going down at six in the morning for an hour of Physical Training (PT), after which we would climb back up for a shower and breakfast, and again we would go down for the day's work. We climbed back for a quick lunch and then went down again to play games with the men, returning around seven in the evening — a very hectic schedule which kept us all fit (and tired). It so happened that two of our Majors and an elderly Captain were childless. This gave rise to some ribald humour in the station as to how all the climbing up and down tired out the officers of 5/8 GR so much that at the end of the day, all they could do was to flop down and sleep. Obviously, it did not affect the younger crowd because my wife and I were blessed with a baby boy on 6 May 1960 whom we joyfully named Rajiv. By then, I was officiating as the Brigade Major of the Brigade and was actually out on an exercise in the plains when I got the happy tidings.

Around this time, I got into a bit of a misunderstanding with my Commanding Officer (CO), Colonel Manmohan Bakshi. The Brigade Major (BM) of our Brigade was posted out. The Brigade Commander, Brigadier Hardial Singh Randhawa was very fond of me, so he wrote to the authorities asking that he wanted me to be posted as his BM. I was eminently qualified and due for a posting of this type anyway, so he took it for granted that his request will be granted and had me move over to start functioning as BM. This was all the more needed as the Brigade was preparing for a Corps Exercise. Meanwhile the unit had received orders for a move to Nagaland and quite understandably, the CO wanted me to go with the unit. So, he dashed off a letter to General Manekshaw (he was the Colonel of the Regiment) stating as how he wanted me to go with the unit. He did not show me his letter (he did not have to), but I

Inspecting the Guard of Honour of 5/8 GR

could not help worrying that the incident would show me in a bad light. Anyhow, my CO had his way and that was that.

Counter Insurgency Duties in Nagaland

The unit moved to Nagaland in Northeast India, on Counter Insurgency (COIN) duties. Entraining at Pathankot on 14 October 1960, we crossed the length and breadth of India to reach Dimapur, en route crossing the Brahmaputra River on a steamer at Mokama Ghat, to Assam and entraining again to arrive at our destination. Since then a bridge has been constructed over the mighty river so the trains pass through without the passengers having to cross the river on a steamer. Dimapur was the railhead for the landlocked state of Nagaland which was in the throes of a raging insurgency. The Nagas, a fierce warrior people had risen in armed revolt against India, demanding an independent status. In truth, these fierce head hunters living in the mountainous border of India and Burma had never been fully subjected to foreign rule. Before Indian Independence, the British had exercised a rather "flexible control" over these tribals, somewhat similar to their arrangements with Pakhtun tribes on the northwestern boundary of India. The two million Nagas, belonging to 27 groups called tribes followed a primitive lifestyle and lived free, untouched by modern civilization. They had their own customs and rituals, which they considered superior to the plains people of Assam, whom they regularly raided for plunder and women.

Historically, the Nagas had been fighting against the British incessantly from 1833 to 1879. Finally, on about 27 March, 1880 an accord was reached between the two, solemnized by a quaint Naga ritual. It is said that a circle was drawn on the ground with representatives of both sides getting into it. Then a cat was brought in, whose head was held by the Naga representative, and the body was held by the British representative. Then the cat was sliced at the neck. This was to signify that there was to be no more fighting between the parties and that the defaulting party would meet the same fate.

The British were verbally allowed to establish military bases as "friends and guests". Later, the British carved out a part of the highland Naga territory and established a Naga Hill District as settled British territory. It is reported that the Nagas were bemused to see, what they thought to be, a meaningless ceremony of unfurling of the Union Jack. There had been no formal treaty. Hence, soon after India gained independence, according to their simplistic logic, the Nagas took it to mean independence for them also. The government of India thought otherwise. Perhaps our officials on the ground or the local leaders could not fathom the nuanced relationship which had existed between the British and the Nagas. Anyhow, this was the beginning of the Naga insurgency which erupted in 1958 and sputtered on for more than a decade (it has recently resurfaced).

The Nagas continued to harass and raid other tribes. They also continued the practice of extracting money from the traders and the trucks carrying stores from Dimapur to destinations inland. In fact by the time our unit was inducted into the area they seemed to have perfected the system of collecting the blood money. As per the marketplace rumour mill, their system was better enforced than the taxation system of the government. In any case, the pragmatic *banias* who were plying their trade were quite comfortable with the system and considered the money paid as cost of production. They just hiked their prices accordingly and the villagers paid.

The situation defined the role of the army. The battalions were stationed at important points to keep the peace and to ensure safe passage of civilian trucks. My battalion was tasked to control and ensure peace in a large swath of territory from Dimapur to Kohima which was the district headquarters as also the location of our Divisional Headquarters. So, we set up company posts at places en route and escorted convoys up and down. As a Company Commander, I took out patrols to sanitize my assigned area, and laid ambushes on likely trails and organized cordon and search operations in the hamlets and villages in the sparsely populated area. For a while I also escorted civilian convoys. We would marshal all the trucks at Dimapur in the morning and allot army detachments throughout the column. To the amusement of the civilians and army jawans, the word got out that a Canada-returned Major had come to escort convoys of civilian trucks. I doubt if the ragamuffin drivers were much impressed, but it was satisfying that there were no ambushes or raids during my watch. In fact it was a tribute to the operating procedures adopted by my unit because the Nagas used to carefully observe newly inducted units to gauge their vigilance and operational drills. They would pounce hard on any laxity, often inflicting casualties and heavy losses.

The Hunt for Mau Angami

A few months after our arrival in the area, I learnt an object lesson about counter-insurgency operations. The Brigade HQ got an important piece of intelligence about a dreaded

Angami leader known as Mau Angami. Apparently, he had established a major camp miles away from the road and in a dense bamboo forest. Intelligence agencies further reported that it is his main camp, well-established and being used for training new recruits. To make matters more interesting, a young fearless Indian officer (Captain Judge of the Parachute Regiment) currently employed with the Divisional Intelligence Company, managed to capture a Naga hostile, who admitted to have been recently trained in that camp. He said he knew the location of the camp and could show us the route to it. It all sounded a bit too good to be true. However, the Brigade Commander Brigadier N.K. Chatterji (my old CO from Calcutta days) told my CO to rig up a strong force under me for the task.

So, I assembled a decent sized force, a company plus (about 150 men) with a troop of artillery (25 pounder guns) in support, Captain Judge duly delivered the captured Naga and after a few sessions with the captive Naga, we set off in the second week of November 1960. To ensure secrecy and surprise, we covered the 40 km distance mostly by night marches. As we reached within the last two-three km of the anticipated site of the camp, I sent out "stops" (small squads to prevent escape on the flanks on likely escape routes. A bamboo forest is a very rough and noisy going, so I thought it very likely that the enemy would have got some warning about our presence. My artillery captain (Sharma) was keen to fire some shots for ranging but I disallowed that. The Naga prisoner was no help; all he could say was that it was a huge fortified camp when he was there. Just then, one of our stops on a dry *nala* (small stream) reported the capture of three fleeing hostiles from the direction of the campsite. There was no holding back Captain Sharma then; I allowed him to fire two or three ranging shells, which was a mistake because it alerted the Nagas and further hastened their exodus. Simultaneously, I rushed up with advance elements of our force, only to glimpse the last of the fleeing hostiles, shooting down two of them.

We coursed through the whole camp which was spread over a large area. There were many bamboo shacks for living and sleeping, cooking places and a fair number of pots and pans (a few still had warm food in them). However, there were no signs of any fortifications. It was obvious that the much feared Mau Angami had no plans to make a stand and resist an attack. It was mainly a camp for training and rest. We destroyed the makeshift structures without any difficulty, collected the two wounded hostiles, one of them grievously injured, and retuned. Meanwhile, our ambush party deployed to block the escape routes on the flanks, joined up with the main force with three Nagas whom they had captured from their ambush. We made camp for the night and reached back to our unit after 2-3 days march. I made the able-bodied captives carry the two wounded men and had them admitted to our military hospital. The Nagas are a very hardy people. So, when I visited the hospital a few days later even the most severely wounded prisoner had survived and was out of danger.

In retrospect, my expedition had been only partially successful. We had misjudged the Naga strategy. Theirs was not to fight and resist an attack but to follow a strategy of "hit and run" and they did not resort to building strong defences at their camps, no matter how large. The object lesson to be learnt is that counter-insurgency operations demand actions by small parties and not by large forces. Further, there should be clarity of mission: whether the aim is to destroy a major camp, capture an individual or wreak maximum attrition.

I Learn about Armour Tactics

Around this time (February 1961), I was posted as GSO 2 (General Staff Officer Grade 2) in our one and only Armoured Division located at Jhansi in Madhya Pradesh. I owed this opportunity to the initiative and farsightedness of its then General Officer Commanding (GOC), General Badhwar, who asked for an infantry officer to be posted on the division's operational team since the armoured division was composed of an armoured brigade and a brigade of infantry (then) on ordinary troop carrying vehicles as against the present armoured personnel carrier vehicles (APCs). Besides being a leg-up in my career, it was a wonderful opportunity for me to understand how the armour fights. Hence, whenever the tank regiments went on an exercise, I would accompany them, perched on a tank, an extremely tiring and bumpy ride with clouds of dust — but excellent training for me.

At the risk of over simplification, armour tactics seem to be largely based on a few essentials. The armour, being an arm of manoeuvre must execute wide out-flanking moves to attack defenceless infantry or take the opposing armour unawares from a flank. A set piece frontal tank to tank battle is to be avoided except when own armour has had the opportunity to take up a dug-in position to take on the attacking enemy armour like it happened in the Battle of Asal Uttar in 1965 which resulted in the annihilation of a Pakistani Division of Patton tanks. Later, this knowledge and experience about armour came in handy to me when I rose to a higher command, which often involved employing armoured formations.

I Built a House in New Delhi

The interlude with the armoured division in Jhansi proved beneficial in more than one way far apart from gaining useful insight into armour tactics and their modus operandi, I was able to take advantage of the proximity of Jhansi to Delhi in a personal manner. Earlier, I had been lucky again, in that I had been allotted a plot of land in a proposed residential colony under the aegis of the Rehabilitation Ministry, south of New Delhi, called Defence Colony, to rehabilitate officers hailing from West Punjab (now Pakistan). Without giving serious thought, I had signed the form when I was serving in J&K and forgotten about it. A good few years after, I was informed that I had been allotted a plot. By the time of my posting to Jhansi in 1961, the government fully awake now, was pressing for the houses to be built at the earliest or else the allotment of plots would be cancelled. Just about then, an army munificence in the form of eight hundred rupees came to me as the "six yearly kit maintenance allowance". It seemed like the hand of God. I plunged into the venture without the faintest idea of the practical problems involved. Anyhow, like always, the hardest part is making up of the mind, for the rest follows.

I set about a frenzy of scrounging funds from here, there and everywhere. The government sanctioned a soft loan of Rs 24,000. I secured some personal loans, which was just enough to make a start. There is enormous amount of work involved in building a house. I managed to get a very good team of architects, and spent hours collecting the ubiquitous "permits" from authorities. There was scarcity of materials such as cement, bricks, et al. There always seem to be scarcities in our country — one often wonders why. Fortunately, I had the full and active support of my wife. Friends and relatives also pitched in. I could only manage short, weekend trips but my wife stayed in Delhi with her mother for months. The Defence Colony locality today ranks as one of the best in South Delhi and is highly regarded for style and elegance. It is really a monument to the industry of the army wife. It is also an example of the army penchant for excellence coupled with thrift and a make-do spirit. We have always been known for achieving "the most with the least" and in an inimitable style. My efforts to secure loans reminded me of the story of the beggar making rock soup. It goes like this — A vagrant ambles up to a housewife asking if she would allow him to make some rock soup in her yard. Intrigued, she nods yes. The hobo pulls out some rocks from his fold and kindling to light a fire. Asking for favour of a little bit of water, he carefully put the rocks in a pan. Next, ever so politely, he asks for any leftover scraps of vegetables and may be some meat. He boils the whole lot and eats the soup, puts back the rocks and goes his way. My wife and I made rock soup many times over!

As mentioned before, I always stressed the importance of stability in an officers' personal life as well as domestic, financial and emotional stability. In this trilogy, the need for having a house of one's own takes the center stage. In the present milieu of nuclear families, it is important that the officer should have a house to call his own. It comes handy when he goes soldiering, innocently called, "non-family field posting" always lurking round the corner. Should he fall in battle, an ever present possibility, it will be a refuge for the family. In any case, the officer would need a house to live in after retirement together with a financial nest egg for medical emergencies and old age.

Financial situation of officers has improved now by way of pay and pensions which keep enhancing with age and now there is "One Rank One Pension" (OROP), which bids fair to better the lot of retirees further. However, despite all our resourcefulness and my wife's excellent husbandry, we were only able to build a single story house, but truly a beautiful house nevertheless it turned out to be. Luckily, I was able to rent it out to a Frenchman for the princely sum of Rs 850 per month, which helped in paying back the loans, and as a crowning achievement, I was able to send my son Rajiv to the Doon School. Good education and proper upbringing of children is a cherished dream of all officers. It takes careful budgeting and sensible spending habits, which are imbibed by our children. In many ways, having to live within ones means and yet keeping an elegant lifestyle are qualities worth inculcating in the young at an early age.

Later, I was dragged into litigation over this house, and was forced to go to court to get a recalcitrant and greedy tenant to vacate the premises. He proved very obstinate and exceedingly well-connected but I managed to get him out in the end, though it took a lot of effort and perseverance. It also consumed a good 13 years of my retired life and I must have knocked on all doors from the President of India and the PMO, downward. It was a soul killing experience and plodding through the legal corridors, I could well imagine the plight of poor retired soldiers who often complain that they have to go from pillar to post for justice after they have retired, quite unlike the British times, when a mere handwritten letter from the Commanding Officer would open many doors and get justice for the soldiers. Unfortunately, under the present dispensation, the military gets scant respect or consideration in the civil street. This state of affairs needs urgent attention. It affects the morale of the troops and impacts on quality of recruitment. However, all said and told, my saga of house building can be said to have had a happy end, though long delayed.

Sino-Indian War 1962

The Sino-Indian War came about in1962 and it touched my life in an indirect way in the sense that the armoured division of which I was a part as a junior staff officer moved up to Punjab as a precautionary move. The war was a total disaster for India. Much has been written about it but many aspects are still unclear and subject to controversy. Some detail is forthcoming in the writings of John W. Garver who has written about the long series of events which triggered the war, namely the Chinese perceptions about Indian designs for Tibet, failure to clearly demarcate a boundary and India's Forward Policy. Australian journalist, Neville Maxwell has also written extensively about the boundary question, often faulting the Indian position. He has also managed to obtain excerpts of General Henderson Brooks Report and the famous Ten Conclusions containing severe strictures for failure of political leadership, failure of General Staff (Army) for not standing up to the government (PMO and MoD) and total failure of the Intelligence Bureau. The salient points are that we acted on a militarily unsound plan of not relying on our own strengths but rather on a belief that there would be no reaction from the Chinese. The decisions at the highest level were taken without proper military appreciation, and no overall plan was made to prepare for a major Chinese reaction. The Intelligence Bureau Chief B. M. Mullick, a Nehru confidant, was strongly of the opinion that the Chinese would not react to our establishing new posts and were not likely to use force against any Indian post even if they could, which was contrary to the military intelligence. With the advantage of hindsight, it seems strange that so many sensible people including some in the army could accept such asinine belief. How could the Intelligence Bureau deduce that the Chinese would not react when pricked? It is also unthinkable that the General Staff did not advise the Government on our weaknesses and inability to sustain the "Forward Policy". It seems that decisions at the highest level were taken without any military appreciation, and no overall plan was made to prepare for a major Chinese reaction. Lately, an after-the-event controversy has also arisen as to why the IAF was not used to retrieve the situation by providing close support to the ground forces, an obvious after-thought for there is no record of such an offer or suggestion from the IAF.

According to General B.M. Kaul, QMG and later Commander of 4 Corps (though an ASC officer but close to Nehru), later claimed that shortages of equipment were pointed out to the government on a number of occasions. General Brooks has stated that, despite all pressures from Ministry of Defence or the duo of PM Nehru and Defence Minister (the abrasive Krishna Menon), the army should have put its foot down and prevented the execution of a militarily unsound policy. He makes no bones that the coterie of Nehru, Krishna Menon, General B.M. Kaul and last but not the least, B.M. Mullick, (all favourites of Nehru) brought this ignominy on India's head. One may say with some justification that when things turn out bad, there is a lot of finger pointing, but the price is paid by the army. The stark facts are that there was a state of total disconnect between the military and political leaders. There was total failure of the decision making apparatus at the highest level. There was no system of tri service coordination and joint planning. Hence, it would be true to say that almost all the agencies involved, are culpable of a criminal folly of monumental proportions and should have been made answerable to the nation.

Apart from the trauma of a horrible defeat, the army lost 2000 dead, and 4000 prisoners. A whole division of 15,000 men inadequately clothed and in a daze of exhaustion, came tottering back out of high altitude terrain and extreme cold temperatures. Apart from the Henderson Brooks' Report, which still remains classified though the entire report has leaked to the press, no in-depth enquiry seem to have been instituted in the ministry of defence, or the infamous intelligence bureau. Or if done, nothing has come out of it. Krishna Menon was sacked and General Thapar, Chief of Indian Army, resigned.

It left Nehru a broken man, never to recover. His legacy of "*Hindi Chini Bhai Bhai*" and the lofty Doctrine of "Panchsheel" lay in tatters. Tibet lost its independence for which they had depended on India. After Tibet was 'absorbed' by the Chinese, India lost a buffer state between India and China. The Sino-Indian boundary remains unresolved with China asserting claims to the whole of Arunachal Pradesh. They have firmed up their hold on more than 6000 km square of land, illegally ceded to them by Pakistan, through which an all-weather road has been constructed, affording the Chinese access to the warm weather port of Gwadar on the Gulf, besides a land route to Afghanistan. Unfortunately, our military misadventure has thrown Pakistan into the lap of China analogous to the Pakistani blunder of the tribal invasion in 1948 which threw Kashmir in the Indian lap. It gave a heaven-sent opportunity to Pakistan who characteristically, grabbed it with both hands to forge strong bonds of an "all-weather friendship" with China. Thence China became its benefactor for nuclear technology and nuclear weapons and through them, access to the missile technology of North Korea. Indeed, the Sino-Indian War of

1962 has been an unmitigated disaster for India in every way.

The tragedy is that the war was totally avoidable and something which we brought down on our own head by a deplorable foreign policy badly implemented. We were completely unprepared and in any case lacked the capacity to fight a war in the high Himalayas. No significant national objectives were involved. No territorial gains needed to be achieved. The inescapable conclusion is that we just drifted into it, with one step leading to another in an unwitting manner, which must rank as the stupidest reason for going to war. There is some mention in various quarters including that of the Chinese that they wanted to "teach India a lesson". It is hard to believe that a country like China would launch a sizeable offensive on such flimsy grounds. In any case, whatever be the real reason or reasons, they had obviously carefully prepared and had taken time to ensure the success of the venture. Perhaps the only saving grace was that, thanks to US pressure, Pakistan remained neutral. In point of fact, there has been regret in certain quarters of Pakistan that they missed an opportunity to hit India when we were down and unbalanced. Perhaps apprehending just such an eventuality, India had moved up its forces to the Punjab Border. Accordingly, our 1 Armoured Division, of which I formed part, had been moved up to Area Jhandiala-Guru in Punjab. We did a lot of reconnaissance and planning and the kind of things that the Army does in field conditions.

Just about this time, in May 1964. I was posted back to my unit which was still employed in Nagaland. It was very much in keeping with the norms of regimental officers alternating between regimental duties and staff duties, termed ERE (Extra Regimental Employment). To my satisfaction, I was succeeded by Major Prem Hoon of the Dogra Regiment. I was happy to see that the practice of having an infantry officer on operational staff of the armoured division, had come to stay.

4

Indo-Pak War 1965

US-Pak Mutual Defence Assistance Agreement

The Indo-Pak War, the second of four such wars, came about in September 1965. I was personally involved in this war and commanded my Battalion in active operations. The tensions had been building up between India and Pakistan since after the Pakistani discomfiture in Kashmir in 1948 which sat ill with that volatile state. The fact is that anti-India orientation has been embedded in the DNA of Pakistan since its inception. The Pakistani military with an obsessive hatred-fear syndrome against India has been on a perpetual quest for military parity with its bigger neighbour, India. This has engendered a military culture and led to numerous coups or spells of military control of one kind or another over the civilian government. As a result, Pakistan has become a quintessential Praetorian State. For securing armaments and advanced weapons, the Pakistani generals assiduously courted the US military and political leaders, claiming to be potential leaders of the Islamic countries. This coincided with the height of the Cold War when the US was eagerly seeking to wean the Muslim world away from the USSR. General Ayub Khan and Iskander Mirza wormed their way into graces of the US military and political circles, projecting Pakistan as a loyal and valuable ally of the West. As the crowning achievement, Pakistani Prime Minister,

Liaquat Ali Khan was invited for a 23-day state visit to US. Next, the nimble footed Pakistan became member of CENTO, SEATO in short order, and forged the milestone Mutual Defense Assistance Agreement 1954 with the USA which opened the floodgates of arms and treasures for Pakistan. It changed Pakistan forever.

Between 1954 and 1965, the US provided armaments worth US$ 630 million, and more than US$ 670 million in concessional sales and defence-support assistance. By way of numbers, Pakistan received equipment for one additional armoured division, four infantry divisions and one armoured brigade, plus support elements for two Corps. Pakistan Air Force received six squadrons of modern jet aircrafts. The Navy got twelve ships and material assistance for the modernization of the ports of Karachi and Chittagong.

As a result non-aligned India, drifted towards the USSR, which made a rapprochement with the USA virtually impossible and further strengthened Pakistani bonds with the USA. With this order of accretion, Pakistani military capacity increased manifold, so did their arrogance and confidence, the first visible effect showing in their confrontation with India in the Rann of Kutch. In the spring of 1965, Pakistani tanks (received from the USA as part of Military Assistance Program) entered the Rann. The memoirs of senior Pakistani officers later revealed that the deployment of this US supplied new armour had two objectives — to entice Indian armour away from northern India, where an attack on Kashmir was being planned for later in the year; secondly to see how strongly the US would protest Pakistan's use of tanks that it had provided on the understanding that they were not to be employed against India. Apparently the Americans made a mild protest by way of a diplomatic subterfuge. In the military confrontation around Kanjar Kot in the Rann, Pakistan notched some gains which further whetted their appetite for adventure in Kashmir.

The Pakistani assessment was that India was demoralized after being defeated by China in 1962; that after Nehru's death, the political system was subject to great uncertainties; that the people of Jammu and Kashmir had been alienated from India as a result of burgeoning insurgency initiated and stoked by Pakistan, and the Pakistani military capacity had been decisively boosted by the US aid. Further, it was expected that under the influence of USA, the international community would not oppose Pakistani intervention. So, by all accounts it must have seemed to Pakistan that their hour had arrived. Hence, Pakistani expectations must have been that when they launched "Operation Gibraltar" (infiltration into Kashmir) on 5 October 1965 followed by "Operation Grand Slam" (offensive into J&K) the Indian response would be confined to Kashmir only. In the event, Pakistan pushed in 26,000 to 33,000 regular soldiers dressed as local civilians across the LOC. They were directed to proceed to selected points to meet up with the local insurgents with the task of creating a statewide conflagration. However, India was tipped off by the local Kashmiris and the infiltrating elements failed to ignite a full scale revolt. At the military level, India called the Pakistani bluff and aggressed into Pakistan across the international boundary.

I Assume Command of My Battalion

I had been newly promoted to the rank of Lieutenant Colonel on 28 November 1963 and appointed as Commanding Officer of 5th Bn, 8 Gorkha Rifles, the unit where I had had my professional birth. It is always the dream of an infantry officer to command his own battalion and that too, in battle. Having completed my tenure of duty with the armoured division, I reverted to the unit in Nagaland which was under orders to move for a peace station tenure in Pune. We boarded a "military special" in Dimapur from the east and made our way across India to Pune on the west. I took over command from Colonel Madan Gopal Aul, while travelling in the train — a first for the unit. A military special train is quite something. It consists of coaches for upwards of 1200 men, plus stores and vehicles, together with cooking galleys and an officer's mess. The unit adjutant coordinates with the railway staff, the schedule for halts for meals and exercise needed for a 7-10 days journey. All in all, it is a pleasurable change to soldiers' normal life and looked upon as a kind of holiday on wheels. On reaching Pune, we quickly settled down to a routine of training including exercises and marches for toughening.

Unit Moves to War

However, it turned out to be a very brief interlude for the war clouds gathered over Kashmir in less than a year of our arrival in Pune, and at a 24 hours' notice, the unit had to pack up and board a train for the railhead of Pathankot. Pakistan had launched "Operation Gibraltar" in the first week of August 1965 (some say that it had started on 24 July 1965) unleashing massive infiltration into Kashmir hoping that the valley would erupt in spontaneous revolt against India. Fortunately, alike most such ventures of theirs, Pakistan had failed to make proper preparations. In addition, India had responded with alacrity, rushing troops up to the threatened areas. My battalion was inducted posthaste to stabilize the situation in Chamb-Jaurian sector in Jammu. The forward brigade under Brigadier Master, had crumbled against a massive surprise offensive, (Operation Grand Slam) and my unit was rushed up to take up a blocking position in their rear to stabilize the situation. On arrival, we were told that we had employed our air the previous day, so we were to move forward under cover of darkness and also to assemble in wooded areas. Having tucked away my unit in an orchard (Rakh) for the night, I moved up in my jeep towards the village of Jaurian, in the morning stopping for a little while under cover of a tree to let pass a couple of Pakistani jets streaking back towards Jaurian where a battle was raging. Scouting around, I noticed that apart from the Jaurian-Akhnoor road, there was also a parallel unpaved village track, along which I saw some troops from the forward brigade straggling back.

Coming back to a place where a makeshift Divisional HQ had been set up. I met General Bhayia Rajwade and told him that, besides covering the road we must also put a unit position blocking the track, which was virtually a parallel axis and told him also about a suitable ridge near the deserted village of Fatwal with high grounds covering both axes. He agreed, so after a simple meal of *dal* and *chapatis,* my first of the day, I sped back to my unit ensconced in the grove. By now the night had fallen. So, I tasked a trusted Company Commander, Major Jasbir Singh Randhawa, to bring up the troops along the main road to milestone 33 (road edge of the Fatwal Ridge) and went back, across country in the jeep to the Ridge, where I went around to site two companies forward with the other two in reserve on a rise in the rear. It was a dark night but there was sufficient starlight. Having done my reconnaissance and citing of company positions, I went down to the road end to meet the troops marching up to lead them to their respective positions. It had been a long night but to my satisfaction, the unit was properly deployed before daybreak. The next evening, 6/5 GR also arrived to take up a defensive position alongside us on the road axis. Soon a battalion of Grenadiers also fetched up to provide depth to the brigade. So, an effective defensive position was in place to cover the withdrawal of the brigade from Chamb-Jaurian. And that is where we stayed till the end of the war despite all efforts by the Pakistanis to dislodge us.

Later, in the "after-war flag meetings", the Pak commanders told us that it seemed to them that they had come up against a full divisional defensive position. Truth of the matter is that besides intense barrages of artillery guns on our defensive positions and three or four attacks, the Pakistanis did not press an attack with full vigour. It is obvious that despite their bluster and bragging, the Pakistanis have no stomach for close hand-to-hand fighting. On the contrary their tactics seemed to comprise mainly of heavy shelling which they had probably planned to follow-up on any signs of disarray in our defenses. We also had some luck, because all of a sudden, there was a palpable lull in the operations. The enemy push seemed to have stalled for one day which gave us time to further reinforce and strengthen our defences. My unit had rushed up without our complement of anti-tank weapons like the RCL guns. The pause gave me time to collar 6-7 teams from the retreating units. We were also able to complete laying of mines and erecting wire obstacles. We learnt later, that for some reason, General Ayub Khan had taken into his head to replace his Divisional Commander, Major General Akhtar Hussain Malik by Major General Yahya Khan. It was possibly also caused by our thrust into Pakistan. Anyhow, this pause proved to be a fatal mistake because it not only broke the momentum of their thrust towards Akhnoor, but also gave an opportunity for India to carry out essential re-adjustments in other areas too. Indeed, the failure of the Pakistani offensive to Akhnoor proved a turning point as it helped India to intensify its efforts elsewhere in the Punjab. It is an altruism of war that a properly dug in and resolute infantry will repulse the most determined attack and survive the most intense shelling.

To be fair, our attempt to go on the offensive also failed. My unit was placed under command of 191 Infantry Brigade, which was tasked to advance towards Jaurian. Using the defensive position of my unit as a firm base, the 15th Battalion of the Kumaon Regiment with a troop of tanks was pushed through our positions on the night of 6/7 October 1965, but their foray failed in the face of heavy resistance. I had told my commander that our patrolling had shown that Pakistan had fully dug-in for a determined defence, and that the tactical situation on the ground contraindicated an advance. But apparently the staff in higher headquarters had decided otherwise. The assumption was that our thrust into Pakistan would have unhinged all Pakistani plans and weakened their operations towards Akhnoor. Anyhow, the Kumaons met with very heavy resistance, and fell back within a few hours. I spent an anxious night, going up and down my positions to make sure that my unit stayed firm because in the confusion at night, the enemy parties often try to infiltrate in pursuit of the withdrawing troops.

I lost a brave young officer, Lieutenant B.V.R. Rao in that night. He was awarded a well-deserved Vir Chakra. I also lost 10 soldiers due to intense Pakistani shelling. In the confusion at night, one of the tanks of the advancing column stalled and the crew panicked and ran back with the troops — an unforgiving sin for tank men. At day break the next morning, I told the troop leader to send a few selected drivers along with a patrol of my Gorkhas. They stole through the brush and found the tank standing in the same area. The drivers dived in and after a few attempts, the engine sputtered back into life. The entire party drove back to our positions with my Gorkha havildar, (Havildar Kesh Bahadur Pun), sitting on top of the tank, waving and grinning from ear to ear. He was awarded the Sena Medal for this plucky achievement. Apart from this, Lieutenant M.R. Bakshi got "Mentioned-in-Despatches" for some very intrepid patrolling to the rear of enemy positions. A high spirited young officer whom I called "Bullet Bakshi", Havildar Kul Bahadur was also awarded a "Mentioned-in-Despatches" for pluck in laying mines even when under shelling.

Coincidentally, my unit fought in the same area in the 1971 War though up ahead in the villages of Chamb and Jaurian. This time, we launched a pre-emptive attack on Pakistani positions, because it is a sensitive area for them since it abuts on to their road communications to their Punjab heartlands. It is also of vital importance to India. The "Operation Grand Slam" was launched with the express purpose of capturing the vital Akhnoor Bridge, which was not only the lifeline of an entire infantry division in Jammu and Kashmir but could also be used to threaten Jammu and the Indian lifeline to J&K. General Ayub had called it "the jugular vein of India". The operation ended in failure for the Pakistan Army as the stated military objectives of their thrust into Chhamb-Jaurian sector were not achieved and subsequently they were forced to retreat following the counter thrusts by the Indian Army into Pakistan.

Highlights of Indo-Pak War 1965

Intense battles raged all across the front for a total of 17 days including some of the fiercest tank battles — perhaps the last of such tank battles in the history of warfare. Ultimately, fortunes of war inexorably tilted in favour of India as per most neutral assessments. The Indian Centurion tanks proved superior to the overbred Pattons. The highlights of the war were the tank battle of Asal Uttar which resulted in destruction of 97 Pattons (the place has been since named as Patton Nagar); capture of the strategic Haji Pir Pass by us, and the Battle of Dograi when the indomitable 3 Jat Battalion under their fiery commander, Colonel Desmond Hayde, succeeded in establishing a bridgehead across the Ichogil Canal which brought the important city of Lahore within tank gun range of the Indians. On which, the US placed an embargo on supply/sales of US ammunitions, replacements and spares for both armies. They also asked for a lull in fighting to "allow repatriation of US citizens from Lahore airport". The inference is obvious. After a UN sponsored ceasefire, the remaining settlement was worked out under the aegis of Soviet Premier Kosygin at Tashkent which also witnessed the unfortunate demise of the Indian Lion, Lal Bahadur Shastri.

Evaluation of Indo-Pak War 1965

There have been various studies of the 1965 Indo-Pak War mostly giving credit to the prowess of Indian arms. To quote two: Devin T. Hagerty in his book *South Asia in World Politics* says "The invading Indian forces outfought their Pakistani counterparts and halted their attack on the outskirts of Lahore, Pakistan's second largest city. By the time United Nations intervened on September 22, Pakistan had suffered a clear defeat." The US Library of Congress Country Studies, states: "Most Pakistanis, schooled in belief of their own martial prowess, refused to accept the possibility of their country's military defeat by 'Hindu India' and were quick to blame the ineptitude of Ayub and his government".

India achieved many objectives. The Pakistani offensive to secure Kashmir failed, this being their last military attempt to do so. There has been a status quo for nearly half a century. Now, owing to the advent of nuclear weapons on the subcontinent, there would be no scope for a large scale military operation as such. The Kashmir dispute stands frozen as it were, with Kashmir firmly in Indian hands, unless Pakistan gets a window like the Indian debacle of 1962 at the hands of China or another superpower. The greatest gain has been a manifest Indian resolve that Kashmir is an integral part of India, as such an attack on Kashmir would be deemed to be an attack on India. Hence, India would be in its right to retaliate by an attack on Pakistani territory. It was left to a decisive Indian like Prime Minister Lal Bahadur Shastri to enunciate and demonstrate this declaration, dubbed as "Shastri Doctrine". Though diminutive and humble in exterior, he proved to have the heart of a lion. He was the true hero of the war. India owes a debt of gratitude to this great man. There is a story that at a troops rally soon after the war, he spoke in his simple way and said, "Pakistanis were surprised that a short statured small man like me could fight a war against them". Patting his chest, he is reported to have said: "but you don't need a tall stature to fight; all you need is a big heart".

Some military commentators have not been kind to General Chaudhury of India. In an editorial comment on the Indo-Pak War of 1965, *The Army Quarterly*, a British professional magazine, stated that "the Indians achieved a masterly dispersion of force". There might be some merit in the comment as the General was often quoted as saying that his strategy was to destroy the Pakistani military machine, not to capture territory. No wonder then that he aggressed on multiple thrusts all across the map, with the result that when Lahore lay open for the picking, we had no sizeable reserves to do the picking!

It was also the only war where the IAF was substantially employed, albeit with diverse claims by opposing sides. The IAF claimed destruction of 75 PAF planes with Indian loss of 59 planes against Pakistani claims of downing 104 Indian planes for the loss of 19 of theirs. Air superiority was not achieved by either side. Army–air force coordination was stated to be poor. Air Marshal Lal stated that both sides did not reveal their plans and that the overall battle plan was drafted by the ministry with General Chaudhury without specifying a role for the IAF. He was also critical of Chaudhury's patronizing attitude. This was perhaps a personality issue as in the 1971 war he seemed to have got on well with General Manekshaw. The Indian Navy contributed even less as it was largely under maintenance, though Pakistan Navy did manage to destroy an Indian Naval radio station near the coastal town of Dwarka, about 200 miles south of Karachi Port. So, it was mainly an army-air battle which may well be the pattern for future battles on the Indian subcontinent in the foreseeable future, whether against Pakistan or China or both, although in 1971 War, Indian Naval missile boats successfully destroyed Pakistani fuel installations near the port of Karachi.

That leaves the question of Intelligence, the proverbial whipping boy. Our performance on this count must be rated worse than poor. An accretion of arms and armaments of this magnitude should have been detected and reported. There must have been unusual and intense activity at all levels in connection with such large shipment arriving at Karachi Port, their trucking up north through the country and lastly, troop exercises to assimilate and familiarize with new tanks and guns. One can understand the difficulty about human-intelligence for India in a predominantly Muslim country like Pakistan but there must have been a great deal of wireless chatter, corroborated by satellite surveillance. During the operations, I had no trouble getting on to the Pakistani wireless net, so that my Gorkhas would listen into their incessant chatter about "where is Imam's (Commander's) bedding, please send it up", and so on. Their wireless discipline was worse than ours. Yet, we found out about their second armoured division only when our regiments ran into their Patton tanks in Chawida-Philora area. Our air force may have been equally surprised by the number and type of their aircraft.

The Aftermath of Indo-Pak War 1965

The war finished with the UN sponsored Ceasefire on 23 October 1965 and a subsequent agreement on return of opposing forces to their starting positions. It had been a short war lasting 17 days. Nevertheless, it had been a very intense conflict involving a large number of troops, infantry and armoured formations and possibly the heaviest tank battles between India and Pakistan. Pakistan initiated the war, with all the advantages of surprise, prior preparation and a clear, numerical and qualitative superiority in armour, artillery and aircraft, thanks to the massive infusion of arms from the USA. It may be stretching the point but it would be a valid comment that the American largesse was the spur for Pakistan to embark on this venture. It must have been obvious to the US too and their experts would have expected decisive victory for Pakistan. Then why did the US build-up Pakistani strength to such an extent. In any case, it must have been obvious to the Americans that tanks and heavy artillery would only be employed by Pakistan against India. This puts a question mark on the oft quoted US protestations of friendship towards India, a sister democratic country. Did the US wish to punish India for siding with the USSR Camp?

Be that as it may, but one can say that Pakistan may not enjoy such military edge over India again. Agreement to give up territorial gains has also been criticized by Indian analysts for Indian gains had been more, certainly in criticality. We gave up the strategic Haji Pir Pass, a large swath of their fertile land in Punjab and most of all, agreed to vacate the bridgehead over Ichogil Canal dominating Lahore. In short, contrary to views of Pakistanis themselves and a few biased commentaries, the war ended in total failure for Pakistan and not "a drawn match" as claimed by Pakistan and its sympathizers. Above all, their prime objective of the capture of Kashmir was not achieved.

Post War Activity for the Unit

Soon after the end of the war, Pakistani troops opposite our unit withdrew beyond the Munnawar Tawi and we followed to secure our territory. From a military viewpoint it was a surreal experience to be seeing "the other side of the hill". We walked over the ground which had been under Pakistani possession till a few days ago, and the ground which we could only visualize while poring over maps. I took full advantage of the situation, taking my officers and men to see the pattern of Pakistani deployment on the ground. Their battalion consisted of three companies against our four companies. I walked with my officers and men over the routes followed by them as our patrols stealthily under the cover of darkness at night. The ground looks very different at night, more so, sneaking through enemy held areas. Standing on ground held by them till a few days ago, we looked back to where we had deployed for 12 days. Our Fatwal Ridge did not look so formidable but our dogged defence had made it so. We also theoretically planned attacks on the Fatwal Ridge from the other side like they must have done for days. All in all, it was a very good learning experience. On the flip side, in one of the flag meetings prior to their withdrawal, a young Pakistani officer asked me in a shy manner, "Sir, I have not seen a Sikh officer before. Can I see one now?" I called up Jasbir Randhawa to meet the youngster.

Otherwise, life was very pleasant. In the area of Jammu, the weather turns crisp and cool in November and the countryside was flush with game. I organized a gun club and scrounged around for 12 bore cartridges and soon, we were bagging quantities of partridge, the wily jungle fowl and green pigeons. At night we would go out shooting wild hare. We trekked and hiked all round. However, it was sad to see the signs of death and destruction everywhere. The mud houses had been flattened by ceaseless gun fire. Most of livestock was destroyed. A war does terrible things to land and its people. Men and able bodied individuals flee but many women and children suffer in the panic. Chamb-Akhnoor area is Dogra country. Dogras are a very friendly and hardy people whose main occupation is agriculture and soldiering. The Dogra Regiment has a proud history of valour and discipline spanning hundreds of years. They came and quickly set about rebuilding their mud houses and plowing their ravaged land.

Posted to Staff College Wellington

In a month or so, our brigade was pulled back to a rest area near Pathankot, where we lived in tented accommodation. Soon, I got a posting as Instructor at our Staff College located in the deep south of India, at Wellington in the Nilgri hills. I handed over command of the battalion to the newly promoted Lieutenant Colonel S.L. Tugnait, an old friend with whom I had served for many years. It was a wrenching experience leaving the unit, which had been my home for well-nigh 18 years. Hereafter, I would only come on short visits as a senior officer. But of course my wife and children were delighted at the prospect of living together as a pleasant change. I went back to pick them up from Pune, where I had left them along with the soldiers' families when the unit had gone up to the war.

The usual pattern is that when the unit is in a peace tenure, 100 to 200 families of men and JCOs (Junior Commissioned Officers, like subedar, etc.) come from the hills to live with their men in accommodations, called "family lines". When the unit goes to a field area, the families go back to their homes in Nepal, sometimes to the Regimental Training Center. In our case as the unit had to leave in a hurry, I had arranged to keep them in Pune together with my wife and other officers' wives. They would often meet together to hear news of the units' doings in war and otherwise keep busy attending classes for knitting, sewing, etc. This institution, special to the army, is called Welfare Centre, as a sort of club run under the care of the wife of the commanding officer. Many officers' wives learnt Gorkhali language, so it was happy clubbing and camaraderie.

Train Journey to Wellington

We boarded the train in Pune for Wellington, a very long haul indeed, down the entire length of India. The long train journey was enjoyable giving us time to be together and see so many railway stations, each with its own flavour. One could see the facial features of people and types of food changing in front of our eyes as it were. India is a varied land, peopled by diverse ethnicities yet all very Indian in a special manner. We travelled to Coimbatore then to the station of Mettyapalam in the Nilgiri foothills where, to our delight, we changed to a metre gauge toy-like hill railway which went happily chugging through tiny hill villages. When it groaned up steep gradients, one could easily get down and walk with the train, as if ready to push if required. We were a happy young couple with two adorable children, travelling carefree in company and the world seemed to be ours. We chugged up to the railway station of Wellington, where we were received by an old friend, Colonel Manohar Chibber and his wife who took us home for dinner. In a few days we were ensconced in an idyllic wooden cottage of our own called "Crinken", perched on a hill slope overlooking a tea garden.

Tri Service Environment

The college, grandly called, Defence Services Staff College was charged with the responsibility of training specially selected officers, in staff duties at the level of a Major and equivalents in the navy and the air force — a tri service organization aimed to inculcate fusion of culture and operational procedures of the three Services. The teaching staff, called Directing Staff (DS) were accordingly selected bright and up and coming Lieutenant Colonel rank officers from the three Services. This college represented the second of four rungs of tri service training, that is, National Defence Academy at the Cadet level, Defence Services Staff College at Major level, Higher Command Course at Colonel level and finally National Defence College at Brigadier level.

One of the oldest military institutions in India, the Defence Services Staff College was founded in 1905 as the Army Staff College at Deolali (near Bombay), and then relocated to Quetta (now Pakistan). After the Partition of India, it came back to the Wellington Cantonment in the Niligris district of Tamil Nadu, India. By 1950, it was progressively transformed into a fully integrated Defence Services Staff College (DSSC), imparting training to officers of the three Services, together with some officers of the Indian Civil Services, paramilitary forces and friendly foreign countries. DSSC is affiliated to Madras University for award of MSc degree in Defence and Strategic Studies and is recognized as a Research Institute.

The concept of a staff college owes to the German genius for efficiency in professional military training and is a legacy of the Prussian General Staff System consolidated under the aegis of Von Moltke the Elder. On appointment as the Chief of Staff, he had established a system of professional training for operational and and administrative planning and creation of a special officer class to be known as "German General Staff", which was to be the most efficient and effective in Europe; an autonomous institution dedicated solely to efficient execution of war, unlike in other countries, where the staffs were often fettered by meddling courtiers, parliaments and government officials. Each year, the Prussian Army's top 120 junior officers were selected by a competitive examination to attend a course at *"Kriegsakacademie".* The academic standards at this institution were made so demanding that fewer than half of the entrants graduated successfully. From this elite, Von Moltke used to select 12 best for his personal training as general staff officers. They attended theoretical studies, annual manoeuvres, "war rides" (a form of tactical exercise without troops, like our TEWTs), war games and map exercises under Von Moltke himself. The aim was that when they would become the Chiefs of Staff of major formations, they could be relied upon to think and act as taught by Moltke. He called them the "nervous system" of the Prussian Army. This highly intense and professional mode of training proved its worth in the Prussian victories against the Austrian Empire and countries in Europe. Subsequently, most other armies in Europe, copied the concept of specially trained "general staff" in one form or another. So, it can be said that if the Romans gave the concept of regular armies and the military bureaucracies to the world of warfare, the Germans bequeathed a system of general staffs. Subsequently, the original German concept was also copied by the British though tempered with their sense of prudence and balance.

The validity of trained staff as the corner stone of military success is unexceptionable, for the success of any military venture rests on twin pillars of an excellent plan and excellence in implementation. Best of plans may come unstuck if not supported by proper preparation including desired mobilization, which is good staff work. A commander may be gifted with great strategic intuition and acumen to decide as to where to bring the enemy to battle, but it may not amount to much if he does not possess, or has not taken the trouble to possess the means and wherewithal, to move large enough forces of his in good time and well prepared to turn his dream into reality. The devil lies in the detail, as they say. When I was GOC of the Strike (Reserve) Corps in Mathura, my never ending search was to look for ways to clip days, even hours, from our mobilization plans to reach our operational areas in the north. I had my staff draw and redraw the complex "movement tables" as taught at the staff college. As an example, the speedy mobilization of vast US forces to Iraq for "Dessert Storm" was a marvel of logistical planning. History also tells us that the legendary Alexander the Great had to assemble a stockpile of 52,600 tons of provisions, enough to supply his army of 87,000 infantry, 18,000 cavalry and 52,000 followers for four months, for his longest march from home, in 326 BC, between Indus River and the Makran coast in Baluchistan, a distance of 300 miles as an example of logistical planning.. For continuous resupply, he arranged for an accompanying fleet along the Indian Ocean. Nearer our time, we witnessed as how the US operations in Afghanistan were severely impacted by the tenuous supply chain from Karachi Port up to Afghanistan. Again, the 1947 Pakistani invasion of Kashmir by Pakistani tribals floundered for lack of proper groundwork for sustaining the offensive. Similarly, on our side, our misadventure in Sri Lanka was hamstrung by inadequate staff work.

In a nutshell, that is what we attempted to teach during the course at the Staff College. The curriculum covers making of operational plans and plans for logistics along with the study of general subjects bearing on the profession of arms. The participation of officers from all the three Services teaches the larger scope and extent of operations besides familiarizing them with special features of different Services and need for joint operations involving two or more Services, sometimes also paramilitary forces and civil agencies. The broad-based teaching is conducted in syndicates of 8-10 students to ensure personal attention. There is a mass of written work as the staffs in formations would be issuing instructions mostly in written mode (this was before the IT revolution). Both students and instructors work long hours. In a manner, the instructors work even harder as preparing the lesson material, conducting classes and correcting 10 written papers submitted by students took up a lot of our time. It was quite common for us to sit till late at night correcting students' answer sheets, the students work often ending with more red (instructor markings) than black (student work). Quite often, they are taken outdoors to discuss plans for attack or defence on the ground. During the course, the entire class is taken down on a 4 week course to study operations in the plains. There are arrangements galore for extracurricular activities including golf, riding, sailing on Pykara lake close by. Being a year-long course, students are provided housing for families, making for lively parties and happy social life especially on weekends. The students and teachers alike, make lifelong friendships. We worked hard and played hard. At the same time, life was also highly competitive as the future appointments and career prospects of students depended on their performance on the course, yet there was a spirit of friendly bonhomie. For all, it was an exhilarating experience to meet and interact with high caliber officers from different services. The overall atmosphere was unmistakably cerebral and professional. Most of us qualified for MSc degree in Defence Science from Madras University. It was also an important milestone in the instructors' career as most of us eventually ended up as Chiefs, Army Commanders or three star Generals or equivalent ranks in other Services.

All in all, it was a very pleasant interlude in our life. Our families had a great time. The wives had mahjong and canasta sessions. The children took to riding though the horse lines were a long trek down the hill. My daughter Sweetie and Ritu (daughter of my friend Bhupinder) became quite good at it; Ritu in fact excelled in horse jumps. My son, Rajiv, all of five years, was not happy as being small, he had to suffer the indignity of "leading reins". We played a lot of golf, often getting the better of the commandant, General Har Pershad. His very charming wife once said to me, "Harish, he comes home whistling whenever he wins, but is glum for hours if he comes back beaten — so why don't you let him win now and then". Thereafter, he always won! He was also an avid horseman often taking part in gymkhana races. Once, my friend Colonel Ram Singh, tipped us off to bet on his ride called "Katowice". We bet on his horse but he lost. He said that nearing the winning post, he heard the commandant shouting from behind "Ram, get out of my way"! We made a lot of substandard wine in spite of the excellent "*enab-e-shahi*" scented grape of Mysore. Adi Sethna even attempted liqueurs. The Nilgiris is beautiful land with some of the finest climates in the world. The saying is, "death never comes in the Nilgiris". So, many retired British officers and planters settle down in the place. Our Field Marshal Manekshaw built a beautiful estate there after retirement, naming it "Stavka", after the higher military headquarters of the Russian army.

5

Taking Command of 114 Infantry Brigade, in Ladakh

From an instructor at the Defence Services Staff College in the Nilgiri Hills, I was posted on promotion to the rank of Brigadier, to command 114 Infantry Brigade in Ladakh. It so happened that when I received the happy news on 20 November, 1968, I was in Delhi on leave to attend the wedding of my wife's niece. On my request I was granted a short postponement and allowed to report by mid-December.

Frequent postings are a common occurrence in the life of an officer, happening every two years. Usually, an officer does two years of command and two years on staff in every rank to ensure balance of command and staff experience, and then with a bit of luck, he gets promoted to the next rank. It is a continued squeeze all the way to the top owing to the pyramidal rank structure of the Army. Simply put, from a base of about 45,000 officers, there is only one chief at the apex. There are various reasons for it. There is a laid down criterion of age to rank to ensure physical and mental fitness of officers for different level of command: Colonels must be fit and young to command a battalion in the toughest environment; Brigade Commanders should be mentally and professionally fit to plan operations and also be able to lead from the front, and so on all the way to the top (We read that in the armies of East India Company, commanding officers of regiments often became so decrepit with age that they could barely mount a horse!). Besides, the army can only have one chief and only so many generals, brigadiers, colonels. The military secretary's branch is continuously busy monitoring cadre management to ensure that the required numbers of officers are available of each rank, at any given time plus a small reserve. It is a complex exercise as there are always fluctuations in the intake and wastage rates of officers due to various reasons. Promotion up to the rank of Major (now Lt. Col) is automatic on passing of requisite tests; after that, there is a system of selection boards for promotion to each rank. The army makes every effort to ensure that the system is fair and transparent. However, the narrowing of the funnel is so pronounced that the process of selection often becomes a process of elimination. The age and rank is also linked to retirement. Hence there is an intense competition throughout the service career of an officer.

This is extremely stressful for the officers, but the service gains, as the system ensures high standards of excellence for the service. On the down side, even some bright officers opt to retire after they complete a minimum service of 20 years for earning a pension. The Chief presides on the promotion boards for Brigadier and above, with his principle staff officers as members. The proceedings and recommendations are reviewed by the Ministry of Defence (MoD).

On getting the posting orders to Ladakh, my first concern was about staying arrangement for my wife and children and for the children's admissions to schools. Initially, I thought of leaving them with her mother at Delhi so I went about the usual rounds of likely schools. I sought meetings with the principal and teachers of St Columbus for my son and Nuns of Jesus and Mary Convent for my daughter. People familiar with the system would know the painful grind, as it is a recurring problem faced by all officers on postings to the field area. Nuns and padres are a little more sympathetic to service officers but they have their own problems in a large city. I managed to get some kind of conditional promises from the schools but then my mother-in-law had a sudden flux of other guests, so I had to think of an alternative. Ultimately, I decided to leave the family in Meerut, since an old friend and ex 2IC (second in command) of my Battalion from the 1965 War, Colonel Reggie Campus, offered to arrange for their accommodation. More importantly, being a devout Christian and an ardent church goer, he promised to arrange admissions for the children to the convent schools there. He also agreed to make arrangements for their move by road from Delhi. So, on 20 January 1969, I bid farewell to my family and flew to Leh in an Air Force AN 12 plane, landing at Leh in the midst of the severe Ladakh winter at high altitude. I had to stay at Leh for three days of acclimatization at the divisional headquarters. On the fourth day, I took a rough five hours' journey on a winding un-metalled road over the Chang La pass (17,590ft high) and then "down" to my brigade headquarters located at Tangtse near Darbuk at a height of 15,400 feet.

Having been at Gulmarg in Kashmir, I was not new to the mountains but the scale of terrain in Ladakh was truly awe inspiring with scree slopes rising to thousands of feet. Ladakh is in an arid zone getting minimal rainfall, so it is quite common to encounter deserts at 15000 feet and above. At those altitudes, the winter temperature would often plummet to 20 degrees below freezing point, and at places to minus 40 degrees owing to the wind chill factor.

My brigade was a self-contained force of about 6000 officers and soldiers, for which all supplies had to move over the same tenuous "road". The pass was closed for winter months because of heavy snowfall. That left just four to five months of the short summer for stocking of a full year's requirement of basic dry rations like grains, cooking oil, sugar, canned or powdered milk, condiments plus oil for heating purposes and so on. It is amazing as to how much tonnage is needed for sustaining a garrison of 6000 men for one year for just basic victuals. Supply of war- like stores such as ammunition and replacements in war would balloon the tonnages. Fresh supplies (vegetables, fruit, and perishables like eggs and meat, etc.,) were air-dropped by parachute throughout the year, together with mail. Air dropped fruits come down frozen and does funny things to the original fruit. Oranges came frozen solid like stones. Troops would have to thaw them by putting them in hot water which would make them taste bitter. The supply chain for the entire force of a division in Ladakh was again quite tenuous. In summer the stores were trucked via Srinagar, over Zoji la, to Leh, but in winter the supply was by air from Chandigarh to Leh on AN 12 aircrafts and then onwards to forward brigades at Tangtse (mine) and at Kiari and Karu. The road to Kiari and Karu was open throughout the year. Truly war is 75 per cent logistics.

My brigade group comprised of three infantry battalions, a field regiment and a heavy mortar battery of artillery, and complementing units of field engineers and a workshop, together with a hospital under command of a Lt Colonel: in effect, an independent brigade. The battalions and artillery units were deployed on high ridges in dug-in positions covering the two axes (routes) coming from Chushul to Tangtse direct and via Lunkung, the two are separated by a ridge of high mountains in between. The forward positions (one Company position was at 19,000 ft.) would be occupied periodically but for the rest of the time, particularly in winter, the troops stayed in make-shift bunkers in the narrow valley at 15,400 feet above sea level. The living accommodations were heated by contraptions called oil burning *bukharies* (probably taking their name from the famed Central Asian town of Bukhara). It was an expensive and messy means of warming. I asked Major Koshy of EME (Electrical and Mechanical Engineers) to try to devise a better method. He tried a few contraptions but did not succeed. I recommended to my divisional commander, Major General P.Choudhury, that the problem should be referred to a group of scientists working in Leh who were spending a lot of time trying to grow greens in the short growing season at high altitudes. They had some success but ended up producing gargantuan heads of cauliflower weighing 8-10 pounds, huge radishes and carrots and so on. It had something to do with a combination of sandy soil full of minerals, the sun at high altitude (when it shone) or play of ultraviolet rays. Hence the Ladakhi diet is quite innocent of greens. Their staple is millet or barley pounded into grain or soaked. Milch cattle, like cows do not survive the harsh climate and so the only source of milk is from low yield Yak or Mare. Ladakhi children, once weaned off mother's milk, get very little milk and their diet mainly consists of parched barley with occasional scraps of meat. It's a hard existence; hence the population is sparse, subsisting near the streams.

Generally pacifist Buddhists, the Ladakhis can be quite warlike when aroused. They are enlisted in Ladakh Scouts and J&K Regiment and make good soldiers. I had a platoon of Ladakh scouts attached to the brigade headquarters and they were my constant companions in my visits to defences and forward outposts located at great heights. After we instituted the game of ice hockey at the brigade headquarters, these Ladakhi lads proved to be strong members of the brigade ice hockey team. The brigade team often won the Inter-Battalion Tournament. I also set up Inter-Battalion matches in the game of soft ball. For both the games we freely improvised the equipment such as normal hockeys and balls. We innovated for softball also, which was even picked up by other brigades. Preparing an ice hockey field was quite easy. We only had to level out a piece of ground and then divert a stream to flood it. It froze solid by the morning and then would last for days with minimal daily refilling. I also laid out a nine-hole golf course by just removing stones and boulders and levelling out the sandy ground.

I encouraged battalions to think up games and competitions to keep soldiers happy and healthy because effects of high altitude combined with extreme cold, affects morale and human spirits. People tend to be morose and depressed by the "winter blues", affecting sleep and appetite. Commanders had to watch out for troops throwing away rations. These problems intensify in Siachen. Inactivity and boredom with built-up anxiety are also experienced in case of troops cooped up in pickets along the LOC in Kashmir but severe climatic conditions in Ladakh make things worse. Games and sport apart, I made sure that units got out and familiarized with the likely approach routes and axes, by troops and officers' parties and as part of exercises. The high ridge separating the two routes of access to Darbuk-Tangtse was considered to be too high to cross. I led parties across this range at least in two places to disprove the theory.

Again, it was thought that a force advancing on Chushul axis could outflank our position at Darbuk-Tangtse by crossing over a high Pass, Horulam La, which would allow it to advance toward Shyok. To disprove this myth, I took a group of officers to the pass so that we could see the difficult terrain both up to the pass and down to the other side. In fact I arranged for a pony to take General Choudhury all the way up to the pass.

On one occasion, once while attempting a crossing, I got stuck on a ridge where the map showed a possible crossing – (the track petered out). So along with my brigade Intelligence Officer (Captain R.P. Singh), I had to seek refuge in the mountain hut of a Ladakhi shepherd for the night. They use smoke for warmth which is fine as long as you keep low. The next morning he led me through a gulley to the side riding a yak. Yaks look fierce animals but they are really gentle, nimble footed creatures with an uncanny ability to cross an ice field, avoiding the patches of shallow ice. There was an unnecessary sequel to this incident. My Brigade Major (Major Chimni) reported me as lost to the division as a routine matter. But it seemed to have caused some panic. Luckily, knowing my ability to muddle through problems, Chimni was able to calm the staff in the division HQ and dissuaded dispatch of search parties, etc.

A large number of VIPs used to come on visits in summer. They were very chary of getting stuck overnight in Tangtse, and would keep glancing over the shoulder at the clouds thickening up. From the safety of Chandigarh and Leh, a foray over the forbidding Chang La must have appeared to be a wild adventure. The pilots of the helicopter flight at Leh were all our friends so they would often check if we wanted any particular visitor frightened off. To lay it on, I would receive the visitors with my jeep prominently fitted with oxygen cylinders – just in case the visitor would have breathing problems! I also had conveniently constructed a large underground bunker close to the helipad with an impressive sand model duly marked and flagged for giving a short presentation to the guests followed by a lunch and most of the visitors would then ask the pilot if it was time to leave. But the more adventurous types would ask for a chopper flight over the cobalt blue waters of Pangong Tso lake.

Once, Prime Minister Indira Gandhi came on a visit with a large entourage in three choppers, escorted by the Corps Commander General Sartaj Singh himself. I received her at the helipad with jeeps with the usual oxygen cylinders. Welcoming her, I added for good measure that the weather had been terrible for many days but today it just cleared up as if the skies had parted for her. She seemed to like that, saying she was always lucky with the weather. Then when she was alighting, I heard a tinkling sound and looked around but she said it was nothing of hers. Anyhow, we had a good visit. I had arranged for a bevy of local women bedecked in amethyst stones studded on their head dresses – they literally carry all their wealth on their head. On returning after a sumptuous lunch, while walking up the chopper ladder, she suddenly turned round and asked me, "where is my charm that dropped while I was boarding"? Luckily, I was able to give her the funny looking metal object. Fortunately my smart Brigade Major (BM) had overheard the PM while she was alighting. So, he had found the article after conducting a search and given it to me. The

PM, squealed with delight and said: "Oh thank you, it was a Maori charm given to me in New Zealand and I always carry it for good luck". My Corps Commander, otherwise known as a fire eater, practically thumped me on the back, thanking me profusely. On getting back to Udhampur (his HQ), he even rang up complimenting me on a "well arranged" visit. So much for luck! The Naval chief came with his wife: they were thrilled by a chopper flight over the Pangong Tso lake. It is the largest salt water or brackish water lake in Asia situated at a height of 13,900 feet above sea level, 134 km long and 2-4 km in width, about a quarter of it is in India, the rest is in Chinese held area. Because of bauxite or mineral deposits, there is no life in the lake. It freezes solid in winter allowing trucks to drive over it.

During the summer, quite a few parties would come to entertain soldiers and in turn we looked after them and showed them around. On one occasion, a troupe came visiting from Gujarat, to put up shows of energetic Garba dances. They particularly wanted to visit the forward brigade at Tangtse. I was a bit chary about how they would fare at high altitude and made special arrangements for the young dancers to take whiffs of oxygen in between performances, behind the stage. In the event I need not have worried, as the spirited young boys and girls of Gujarat took to the environment very well.

There existed a very basic hut for visitors situated aside a gurgling mountain stream. I enlarged and improved it to create a posh two bedroom cottage for VIP's, calling it "Laughing Waters". Appropriately enough, the first visitor to use it was a comely American blonde, one Miss Snow or Snowstone, a supposedly famed photographer of *The National Geographical* Magazine. She came highly recommended from someone in Delhi. I drove her at a fast clip to the Pangong Tso, with barely an hours' daylight left for taking photographs. She was happy to spend an evening with my officers. Before returning next morning she promised to send copies of photographs that she had taken. However we never heard from her. May be she was struck by a bout of amnesia (the high altitude did affect one's memory). Later, I also got constructed a large hut to serve as an officer's institute, further down the same stream, also inaugurating a "First Summers Swim Club" for swimming in the freezing cold water of the stream, a foolhardy adventure with most of us emerging with pink-red skins. Luckily, nobody got frostbitten in the wrong places. Later, I heard that one of the walls of the hut just collapsed and had to be rebuilt next summer. At the high altitude, the cement does not set in the cold, which curtails the building period.

Our GOC, an alumnus of staff college, also kept us on our toes with exercises with troops called 'collective training' in both summer and winter. He asked Brig Sushil Kumar, commander of 163 infantry Brigade located in depth at Karu, to set and conduct an exercise for my brigade. Sushil was my course mate and a close friend, so I felt a bit put out that he would not divulge the general plot of the exercise to me, but we both took it in the right spirit and have remained good friends till today. The exercise required a long night march on the Manali-Leh road via Tangtse, and then to the main Upshi-Manali road after going around the Loma Bend, notorious for high winds and temperatures of minus 40 degrees, and then to advance on the main Manali-Upshi Road. My staff helpfully arranged for a sturdy pony for me to ride but I could not use it as my legs would freeze after a few minutes of riding in the cold at night and I found it better to walk to keep the circulation going.

We always seemed to be out on one exercise or another for the very good reason that in the harsh climate, it was always better to keep the troops out on the move rather than allow them to sit and mope around *Bukharies*. In fact, our biggest problem in long winter days was an onset of boredom.

114 Brigade was the proud inheritor of the force which had fought the Chinese to a standstill under the intrepid leadership of then Brigadier Tapi Raina in 1962 (he became the army chief later). I used to take groups of officers to the Chushul air field which was used for ferrying in as many as 95 air sorties, to

bring in the AMX 13 tanks which made all the difference in the battle of Chushul. There we would point out the features around which the fighting raged: Lukung Hill (24,000 ft.); Gurung Hill (25,500 ft.); Magar Hill (17,000 ft.); Spangur Gap (14,000 ft.). One could also see the famed Rezang La where the redoubtable Ahir Company of 13 Kumaon Battalion fought, literally to the last man. I hiked and trekked to my heart's content including a visit to Shyok and "Hot Springs". It was great to be young and a senior officer with the resources of my brigade. I still look back upon my tenure in Ladakh as a high point of my service life.

With Chief Gen. Krishna Rao at College of Combat, Mhow

The Ladakh economy was quite scratchy, mostly depending upon pashmina wool from the soft inner winter coat of the Tibetan goat. Rarer still was shahtoosh wool from the Chiru antelope of Tibetan Plateau (now banned for sale or spinning). The presence of the army was most lucrative for them, as we employed a large number of ponies and porters. In fact, in the villages, the size of the pony herd is a mark of aristocracy. A grizzled old Ladakhi, one named Tablang of village Tablang, owned such a large herd that he had amassed chests full of cash in his house (we could not pay by cheque as he did not have a bank account; in fact there was no bank beyond Leh). The story was that he would offer one chest, and sometimes two for a likely suitor for his daughters, number of chests depending upon their looks. It was a standing joke amongst the young officers that "Tablang of Tablang" could give them a better deal than the army.

I completed my tenure in 114 Infantry Brigade literally with a bang. One fine morning there was a flurry of excitement that the corps commander wanted to speak to me. That day I had planned to take a group of my officers to climb a high feature overlooking Tangse, so I was tempted to dodge the summons but then in the army you never dodge a call from the corps commander. Actually it turned out to be good news for me. He was ringing up to say that I had been selected to attend a course at the coveted National Defence College in Delhi. So instead of cancelling the long awaited climb, I made it into a celebration. Here was an imposing mountain with a height marked as *19,999ft* on the map (some surveyor had a streak of humour!). It would stare me in the face every morning as I got out of my bunker and I had promised myself that I would climb it one day before leaving. I used to speak to my officers about it also. So, collecting my volunteer group of 35 keen officers, including 2-3 doctors with requisite paraphernalia, we started with a light step. It was a long trudge up the mountain, often without a track but we managed to scramble up to the top in about six hours. After a short break, we dug out a large flat boulder. Then I got each officer to stand on it for a quick photograph. In the end, I formally presented them with a printed card (printed from Chandigarh months earlier), saying: "Certified that -------- has successfully climbed 20,000 ft." I am sure most of them have preserved the certificate for posterity. I picked an easier though longer route down but it seemed even harder, (it is always so) but I got them all down safe and sound. Only some medical officers were sick for a day or two and a few others complained of headache.

The National Defence College Course

I said goodbye to my officers and men, and the mountains of Ladakh on 20 November 1970 and happily went down to the divisional HQ at Leh to board an AN 12 aircraft to Chandigarh where my wife and son were glad to see me (my daughter was in a hostel in Pune Convent). We packed up house and motored down to Raksha Bhavan in Delhi where accommodation was allotted to us for the duration of the year long course. The National Defence College is a premier training institution of the MoD which is known as a centre of excellence on matters pertaining to National Security. It is the highest seat of strategic learning for Indian defence and civil service officers of the rank of Brigadier or Joint Secretary-Deputy Secretary. It is a prestigious 47-week course for a few hand-picked officers and also about 25 officers from friendly countries such as, USA, UK, Canada, France, Germany, Australia, Sri Lanka, Nepal, and so on. It generates ideas on strategic planning on national and international security matters. It also serves as a well-regarded 'think tank' on matters of defence. The alumni consists of student officers from army, navy and air force, as also officers of IAS, IFS, IPS and from other ministries and a group of teachers of similar representation.

Training schedule consists of deliberations and study of various subjects and topics in seven integrated analysed` groups of 13-14 officers, coordinated and discussed under the assigned teaching staff. The subjects for study and analysis cover all dimensions of domestic, regional, and international issues to equip the students to be informed policy makers in diverse fields. The aim is to impart a broad understanding of different aspects bearing on national policy such as economic, political, military, scientific, and organizational. Training also includes lectures by prominent persons and specialists followed by discussions. During my course, the hot debating point was the developing situation in East Pakistan, a swelling flood of refugees to India, and Indo-Soviet Treaty. Typically, one witnessed a lot of over-intellectualization on arcane aspects of the Treaty without recognizing the practical advantages of support and assurance of help from USSR. Perhaps on our part as serving officers coming from active formations, we were also guilty of a sort of tunnel vision. To my mind, rationalization of perspectives really highlighted the value of the course. Dr Romila Thapar, well known historian and author lectured to us on ancient Indian history. Other luminaries spoke on a variety of subjects. I thought the programme of lectures was a useful feature as, besides the formal lecture and a session of question-answer, the guest speakers mostly stayed for lunch which allowed for informal interaction. Coming together of senior officers of diverse disciplines and background was very productive. It was excellent exposure on how the civilian mind worked. Similarly the civil officialdom got an inkling of our thought processes. This is all the more important because the officers of MoD, the Foreign Service, the police, etc., do not have any knowledge or experience of the defence matters. Whereas the reality is that it is the civil officials who have the ear of the political leaders on military matters. Hence there is great value in such institutions of integrated learning.

The course also includes visits to places of significance within India; for instance we visited the AMUL milk cooperative which has become a byword for milk production or "White Revolution" in India. We went to Anand and met the dynamic Dr. V.Kurien who explained about the origins of the movement and his future vision. We visited Sikkim, Bhutan and Darjeeling, and so on, to familiarize with outlying parts of India. The Course visited by groups the Middle-East, and East Europe as also the eastern countries. Of particular interest to my group was the visit to Iran where the Prime Minister

Hoveyda was kind enough to receive us in his luxurious office (with a strikingly beautiful Iranian personal assistant). He spoke to us for about twenty minutes regarding the situation in Pakistan and was at pains to advise us that India should eschew any interference as it will only enrage the "wounded tiger (Pakistan)". Brigadier Chibber from our group replied that the people of East Pakistan were the real wounded tiger. Hoveyda, the consummate politician that he was, took the awkward interjection in his stride. He smiled a little and said, "We are talking about the Indo-Pak relations". We were also wined and dined at an army club. The common people seemed friendly enough to India, but at the official level, there was a distinct tilt towards Pakistan. It was a common phenomenon. Pakistan seemed to have discovered the art of becoming a favorite of all countries. They certainly had the uncanny knack of acquiring "all weather allies". Here was a Shia Iran and a non-Arab country, whereas Pakistan is largely a bigoted Sunni country which is rabidly anti-Shia, considering the spate of terror strikes against their mosques. They have been firmly ensconced in the Saudi Arabian camp. In fact, there was a strong sentiment of ultra conservative Wahabi Islam even at the time of our visit to other Arab countries in 1971. Yet, the pro Pak sentiment in Iran was unmistakable. We could see the same tilt towards Pakistan in Kuwait and UAE. Kuwait has a sizable Indian community of Hindu merchants. They invited us for tea and refreshments. They seemed to be thriving. Oil riches have made Kuwait very affluent. Visiting the market place, we found that quantities of hundreds of Swiss watches were being sold by the weight. There is also a strong US influence in UAE. The picture was different in Yugoslavia. The great Marshal Tito had died, and the country was but a shell of its former self. The communistic fervour seemed to be on the wane and the atmosphere was fast changing to western ways. We witnessed a very non-communist and tawdry cabaret show in the hotel where we were staying!

The War of 1971 and Birth of Bangladesh

The NDC course was ended prematurely by end of September 1971 so that officers could go back to service assignments. I was posted on the staff of 2 Corps under General Raina. The corps and its complement of divisions and supporting arms were concentrated near the town of Krishannagar in West Bengal. The Bangladesh War or Indo–Pak War 1971 will go down in history as the strangest war or a war that should not have been. Pakistan initiated and entered into this war with every military and civil factor stacked against them and with practically no chance of winning. Yet Pakistan embarked on this suicidal war, through monumental ego and megalomaniac ambition of one man, Bhutto, aided and abetted by inept and fawning generals. In fact, the blame rests mostly on the generals, for they should have known better and could have blocked the doomed adventure. Instead they seemed to have been blind-sided by grandiose visions of superiority of their forces over India. And yet they started the war by a preemptive air strike against 11 Indian airfields on the western front on 3 December 1971. Tellingly, they grandly christened it as "Operation Chengis Khan"!

Whatever be the greed of civilian leaders, the basic military rules seem to have been flouted. A cardinal rule of war is that the invading force should select favourable time and ground for giving battle. Instead, we see that Pakistan generals got dragged into fighting a battle in East Bengal separated by a thousand miles of Indian Territory. To crown all, there was little hope of air support to the beleaguered forces. The local population was also hostile. In view of all this, it is hard to understand Pakistan embarking on a campaign to "crush India", which was reported to have been the slogan of thousands of Pakistanis marching up and down the streets of Lahore and other cities, though they should have been familiar with military prowess of India as they had had a taste of it in 1947 and 1965 wars.

There must be a lesson in this episode for us. It is obvious that Pakistan's hatred of India is so deeply ingrained in their DNA that it makes them blind-sided to practicalities and military realities. Indeed, India would do well to remember this streak of irrational behaviour endemic to the Pakistani psyche. The advent of nukes on the subcontinent has made things from bad to worse.

The Indo-Pak war of 1971 originated out of a domestic conflict between the Government of Pakistan and its eastern wing, which rapidly assumed the proportions of a revolt and a mass guerrilla movement to break away from the union. As it is, the Pakistan state was a geographic freak with its two wings separated by a thousand miles of Indian Territory. Apart from the tenuous link of religion the two wings had nothing in common; East Bengalis were different from the Punjabis as chalk and cheese. There was difference in every sphere, be it culture, language, climate, in fact in every way. They were also looked down upon by the overbearing Punjabis. East wing was also more populous. Things came to a head when Sheikh Mujibur Rehman and his Awami League Party won outright majority in Pakistan's parliament elections and he staked claim to rule Pakistan. Bhutto refused to accept the situation and engineered a military "crack down" on the eastern wing through complicit generals headed by General Tikka Khan who earned the epithet of "Butcher of East Bengal". The crackdown also included hounding out of the Hindu minority which caused an exodus of ten million refugees to India. The Indian Prime Minister, Indira Gandhi made a tour of the world capitals emphasizing India's plight at the huge burden of millions of refugees, besides the human tragedy of people being displaced from their home and hearth. India also signed the Indo-Soviet Treaty of Friendship with Russia.

Following a horrendous pogrom by General Tikka Khan on the night 25/26 March, Bangladesh made a unilateral declaration of Independence on 26 March 1971. Both Pakistan and India mobilized their forces. However, despite mounting pressure by Pakistani actions, under astute leadership of General Manekshaw, India wisely held its hand till the ground had dried and mountain passes in the north had snowed-up (China factor). Even so, Pakistan, trigger happy as always, struck the first blow (preemptive air strike on eleven Indian airfields on evening of 3 December 1971). On that, India launched an all-out land, sea, and air assault on Pakistani forces in East Pakistan and also a limited defensive operation in West Pakistan.

2 Corps under General Tapi Raina launched 4 Infantry Division and 9 Infantry Division towards Jessore which was captured on 6/7 Dec and fanned out to the town of Jenida in NW, and then wheeled South towards the major town of Khulna. I headed a team of officers including one Mr Ghosh (IAS) with the task of liaison with Bangladesh government and giving aid to civil population. However during the actual operations, I was free to visit different fronts and forward brigades and divisions to have a ringside view of the battles taking place. The Pakistan Air Force had been shot out of the skies within the first week, so there was little risk in movement even during the day. A friend, Brigadier Rajendar Nath had just captured a Pakistani position by a dawn attack when I met him. He was happy to have captured his objective, but a bit deflated when soon after the action, General Raina came and said, "Good, after all you have captured this position". I told him that everyone in battle is a bit tense, so he should not take it to heart. General Raina always led from the front. He was very kind to me and would often chat about the operations. He thought well of me but once I made a *faux pas.* While accompanying him in his helicopter to one of the divisional commanders, he asked my opinion as to how long the war was likely to last. Never in doubt, I confidently said, "two weeks". Pakistan folded up in the next 2-3 days! Later, during a visit to Leh, he had a laugh saying even he was also surprised at the sudden collapse of Pakistan. During Bangladesh war, once

going to 9 Division at night, I met the commander, General Dalbir Singh. He was in his pyjamas in his caravan poring over the maps and busy giving orders on the wireless to his brigade commanders. He was in full command of the battle and hugely enjoying himself. He was saying, "Inder, don't worry, hold from the front and send a battalion to outflank the blighter from the left". I have often recounted this anecdote as the finest example of a natural warrior, confident and gutsy in battle.

General Tikka Khan struck again on 14 December when Pak was facing imminent defeat. The entire intellectual elite of Dhaka was eliminated; teachers, professionals, college students, in fact the cream of Bengali manhood were massacred and hundreds of women raped. Estimates vary but it is said that 3 million people were killed and upwards of 200,000 women raped. Back in1947, at the IMA, the same Tikka Khan, then a captain, was my platoon commander for two terms. He was a serious, humorless man but I never thought that he had the makings of a Chengis Khan or Nadir Shah. He seemed to have thrived on this reputation because he ended up as the Pakistan Army Chief and later a Defence Minister in Bhutto's government. The fag end of war witnessed drama of the last ditch effort by the US to save Pakistan. Then US President Nixon made frantic efforts to muster support from Jordan and Iran, who were reportedly asked to send their military aircrafts, such as F-86, F-104 and F-5 fighters to shore up Pakistan. Americans also encouraged China to lend material support plus move formations in the North to threaten India. When Pakistan defeat seemed imminent, Nixon dispatched Task Force 74, led by aircraft carrier *USS Enterprise* into the Bay of Bengal. It arrived on 11 December 1971. As the war tended to acquire international dimensions, USSR also dispatched two groups of cruisers and destroyers and a submarine equipped with nuclear armed missiles.

The Indian Army fought a brilliant campaign, employing *blitzkrieg* tactics, exploiting weakness in enemy positions and bypassing strong centres of opposition. Pakistan military capitulated in less than a fortnight leaving 90,000 POWs in Indian hands.

Pakistan suffered a humiliating defeat. They lost half of their territory, a third of their army, half of their navy and a quarter of their air force. More than 5000 sq miles of their territory in the west also lay in possession of Indian forces. The political and psychological impact was worse. Their two-nation theory lay in tatters as a Muslim East Bengal had fought and ousted fellow Muslims of West Pakistan. It also put paid to the wonted Pakistan's strategic doctrine that "defence of East Pakistan lay in West Pakistan". Perhaps their other strategic concepts would also tumble, such as the "Heartland theory" and the much touted doctrine of "Afghanistan constituting strategic depth to Pakistan's defence".

After the end of hostilities, I was involved in repatriation of Hindu refugees to their homes in Bangladesh. Ten million men, women and children, young and old were shipped back in 70-80 special trains. It was hard work coordinating with refugee camp authorities and the railway staff but there were high spirits all around. It was heart-warming to see families cheerfully sitting and waiting for the trains on railway platforms. I would often ask what they were specially looking forward to. They would laugh and shout. "*Amar sonar Bangla, Hilsa khabe*" (we are going to our golden Bengal where we will eat the famed Hilsa fish). The war does strange things to people. While we were fighting and chasing Pakistanis, the local populace rose in pent up anger against the Biharis who had come in the wake of Pakistani troops and were ready accomplices to Pakistani depredations. Now the Bengalis and their Mukti Bahini were hunting down the Biharis. At one point a large body of Bihari men, women and children was being chased by irate Bengalis. It looked like a slaughter in the making. This was near the town of Jessore; the local deputy commissioner urgently asked for my help. All our troops were far ahead, so I bundled the frightened mass of poor Biharis in the local jail which was luckily lying vacant as all the criminals had made good their escape in the confusion of war. I have never seen so many people eagerly rushing into jail and being grateful for the favour!

By the end of December 1971, I went back to Delhi to pick up my family and our belongings and headed for Mhow, where I had been posted as commander Senior Command Course.

6

Commander, Senior Command Course

I reached Mhow, bag and baggage, with wife and two children on 18 April 1972. Thousands of army officers have made this journey over the years, yet the tedium has not changed. We travelled by a Delhi-Bombay through train and switched to meter gauge railway at Khandwa or Ratlam, both connecting at the unearthly hour of 2:30 a.m., which was quite bothersome while travelling with children and sometimes also dogs. On top of that, every one of us does this pilgrimage at least five to six times or more in our service life. My appointment rated quite high in the army hierarchy as SC course was considered an important milestone in the career graph of an officer. In fact, at one time, it had a dread reputation in the army. Originally attended by officers of rank of senior majors, it had the reputation of being a test course to determine the ability of officers for promotion to command of battalion/ regiment. It was called "struck off" (original acronym being SO Course) course for those that did not make a satisfactory grade. Subsequently, around 1970-71 officers of the rank of Lt Colonel started being detailed for the course.

There is still a modicum of 'grading' on this course but in general, the overall emphasis has shifted to teaching but the need for a stringent selection criteria remains still valid. The crucial importance of this appointment is such that it remains a pivotal role. Now the rank of the battalion/regimental commanders has been upgraded to a full colonel. I thought that the old system should be retained albeit with some modification to make it less threatening with a shift of emphasis to teaching rather than testing. Pressure by itself is not a bad thing. It is good in some ways, for the students would prepare with greater diligence and hone up on the rudiments of the profession before coming to the course. More importantly, the course would have specially selected instructors, i.e., officers with a proven record of having been outstanding commanders in both war and peace.

The Unit Commanders Win Wars

There is no gainsaying the importance of a Commanding Officer (CO), any less than the importance of a CEO in the corporate world. It is his responsibility to painstakingly groom, train and nurture his young officers. He also ensures that troops in the unit are fit for war at all times. In battle, everyone in the unit from the soldier to junior commissioned officer, to the squadron/company commander look up to him. All must have confidence in his ability. He carries the life of a thousand men in his hands. In army hierarchy, he is the last link in personal command of troops. Hereafter, brigade and divisional commanders do not command troops. They only command commanders.

It is also often said that "the commanding officer is the unit." In futuristic warfare, the role of unit commander will be even more crucial. The CO also constitutes the feedstock for future brigadiers and generals, all the way up to the chief. Therefore the selection for this rank is crucial for the overall excellence of the army. Later, when I was an Army Commander, I had once suggested that the selection board for Major to Lt Colonel rank should also be presided over by the Chief. However, considering the chief's existing work load, it was found difficult to increase the number of existing selection boards.

When I went to command this Wing in 1972, the situation had changed further, in that most of the officers coming as students had commanded units in war; some had even been decorated for excellence. So, I got all my instructors together and told them that we must drastically change the orientation and thrust of our instruction because we will be dealing with officers fresh from having commanded units in war. First off, we got down to recast and rewrite all existing exercises and instructional material (a lot of it had been in vogue for long). In a way, I said, our thrust should be, both to learn and to teach. In point of fact, a common complaint in the army used to be that the teaching at schools of instruction tended to be rather bookish and often unrelated to realities on the ground. So, we even invited suggestions from the war veterans for updating our training material. My instructors, initially doubtful, soon got into the swing. All of us put long hours of work, but in the end, I think, we left our tenure at Mhow with a feeling of a "good job, well done". Indeed, through my long service, I always preached that it should be the endeavour of every officer to leave his mark on whatever he does, and make a difference.

We covered the usual ground. We taught various operations of war such as attack and defence, and so on. But, above all, I put special emphasis on leadership and on the art of command. I also stressed that after a service of 14-15 years, they would have imbibed sufficient theoretical knowledge and perhaps also practical experience of operations of war. Now they should learn the broader aspects of warfare and above all, concentrate on the all-important subject of leadership. Besides, the Commanding Officer is weighed down with a thousand responsibilities and numerous duties, so during the command tenure of two years (the norm), one cannot achieve everything, hence on assuming command, the CO should decide on his priorities and identify the main thrust of his command, as defined by the tasks allotted to the unit and the prevailing state of training of his unit. Thereafter he must pursue his chosen mission in a single minded manner. Fortunately, there is continuity of service for officers in units of infantry and armoured corps, where it also counts the most. Once my unit was relieving a battalion of Rajputana Rifles, I heard a man singing the battalion song, which among other things had this bit about how "then came Colonel Pahlajani and he tightened the *langars* [soldier's cook houses]". The soldiers know so much more than we think! They are very observant and are quick to spot the main thrust of the policies of a CO.

Visiting 6/8 GR, J&K, 1972

I noticed that while making plans in most of our training exercises, the officers had a marked tendency to play safe. There was a disturbing trend towards sameness of plans. In a course of instruction it is understandable that students would play safe so as not to make a bloomer. But I thought it showed a basic reluctance for originality and hesitation to take risks. It is a common weakness. I explained that in battle, more often than not, only the unusual will succeed. This tendency to be afraid of making mistakes has to be discouraged in the army, certainly in war. It is different in the civil services where delaying decisions or giving negative decisions may pass as wisdom and in some cases, may even prove profitable. However, any kind of dithering and negativism in war would be disastrous. Hence, in the army we must preach the gospel of boldness, risk-taking and positivism. Seeds of such traits have to be planted at the earliest stages of an officer's career.

In the services we meet officers of all type. Some are natural warriors, with a marked tactical acumen. Some are by nature more innovative. Some are sincere plodders. It is the job of the CO to intelligently judge his officers for then he would be able to employ them productively, getting the best out of every one. Through my teaching career, I have often wondered if it is possible to "teach" tactical acumen. Further, how can we inculcate aggressive instincts or teach bravery? At present all we can do is to teach the art and craft of war so as to instill confidence born of knowledge and practice. However, the commanding officer can do a lot to consciously encourage and build up the quality of boldness and initiative in his young officers and give them the confidence that it is alright to make mistakes as long as they try to the best of their ability. Leadership is essentially about setting a personal example. I have often seen that wherever the CO is of a positive frame of mind and has the go-getter attitude, this quality filters down to the last jawan and there is a palpable air of high morale in the unit.

The service can do all this but many people believe that these qualities are basically inborn, that is, either a person has them or not. The question arises: Is the science of psychology far enough advanced to make it possible to identify and gauge the quotient of courage and bravery at the selection stage? Even a partial inkling will help. This is a task for our entry-level selection boards. At any rate, whether or not we can teach these qualities, we should at least be able to recognize and record the presence of such qualities. To do that, we should suitably modify the existing proforma of performance evaluation or the Annual Confidential Report (ACR) which should contain an extra section devoted to this aspect. The commanders at all levels should be required to judge and grade their subordinate's officers for such traits. The important point is that it will be more productive to teach the grammar of tactics and strategy to a brave person than to teach bravery to an officer no matter how good he is in theoretical knowledge of warfare. This brings us face to face with the age old theory about martial races. The British subscribed to this theory and gave preference to recruiting from certain classes and certain regions. The theory stands outmoded now but one may not argue with the tally of decorations earned and battle honours won by regiments of certain ethnicity. Either way, most would agree that soldiers (and officers) hailing from rural stock usually perform better than those from urban areas. To conclude my experience about the SC Course, I think I learnt as much as I taught. I did a good job and came away with the satisfaction that I had made a difference for the good.

At Directorate of Military Operations at Army HQ

I got the posting orders to Army Headquarters at Delhi, in the prestigious Directorate of Military Operations as deputy director. So, we packed once again and took the awkward train connection back to Delhi arriving there on 12 January 1973. This time, we were able to live on the ground floor of our own house in Defence Colony. General Inder Gill was the DMO (Director Military Operations) with two deputies, DDMO-A, Brigadier M.L. Chibber (my course mate and a friend of long standing) and DDMO-B, Brigadier M.C. Gupta of the Engineers. I was to relieve Gupta who was a serious, humour less officer but very hard working and meticulous in his work. He had drawn up an elaborate programme of handing over, going through the entire list of his files. His job was long term planning, so I politely asked him to put me in the picture about the plans and that I will familiarize with all the files in my own time. Chibber was one of the ablest officers of our batch (he expired a few months ago). He dealt with current plans about which he briefed me in half a day. General Inder Gill was even sharper though a bit brusque of manner. He had me in his office for fifteen minutes and that was that.

My Experiences at Army HQ

It was my first posting to Army HQ so it took me a while to settle down. It is a whole new world with its own pace of work and its own culture. The entire ambience was dominated by officers of Ministry of Defence (MoD) and to lesser extent, the Ministry of Finance (defence). All "cases" mostly pertaining to purchase of equipment, were put up (submitted really) to MoD, which would then be discussed in a meeting and then passed or rejected. The MoD did not keep its own files, so all cases were prepared and put up by army, navy or air force who were the "supplicants". In sum, newly posted officers had to understand and learn compliance to this reality. I learnt it early. We mostly dealt with a joint secretary, a South Indian gentleman with a bloated ego. He called me up once after a conference on some subject where I had put forward the army point of view a bit too firmly or so he thought. He tried to give me a dressing down in his own way. He had no authority to do so, but I just listened and came away. Chibber told me not to mention it to Inder Gill as he would only storm into the gentleman's office creating a big row and needless friction. Indeed, Chibber and I, between the two of us, would try to attend most of the meetings because whenever the general participated, he would lose his temper in the first five minutes and the issues would only get postponed and delayed, which did not bother the ministry at all, and worked only to the disadvantage of the army. In fact, it seemed to be a common tactic of the ministry to demonstrate its art of one-upmanship, and at the same time, delay expenditure.

Another reality about South Block (where MoD is located) was the ubiquity called Upper Division Clerk. Having been there for ages, they appear to know everything and excel in "fixing" matters. The MO Dte had one Mr Santokh Singh. He was a fine individual with the ability to get things done in a very adroit manner. For instance about this time I was applying for a house building loan to the government. He helped me fill the voluminous application form and then went to different ministries concerned with the result that the loan was sanctioned within a few weeks, which would otherwise have taken months. By virtue of their long stay in the ministries and being quite at home in the corridors of power in Delhi, these people are highly resourceful. They have their own network and grape-vine to the MoD, and often to their counterparts in other ministries too. They are the masters of the world of files and with an elephantine memory they remember the antecedents and history of all cases.

The labyrinthine procedures are often responsible for unnecessary delays, and is the chief reason for the under-equipped state of the armed forces. It concerns all purchases, big and small. I had a practical experience of this phenomenon once while pursuing a minor case for purchase of special boots for the paratroopers. Here we were, myself from the army, a deputy secretary from MoD and a representative from Ministry of Defence(Finance) discussing the need for these special boots with two members not having ever seen the army boots, leave alone meeting a paratrooper in person. It took me a while to get the required approval. It is not a matter of procedure. It is all about control. It is a highly dilatory procedure, I suspect, on purpose to discourage expenditure. It is a double whammy. At the macro level, the budget for various services including the army is passed by the Government after being duly approved and processed by the MoD. Subsequently, each and every item of expenditure above a certain level is routinely scrutinized and "passed" by the ministry. This is their strongest lever of control which is exercised at their whim and fancy.

Another lever is the instrument of "conference". A conference about matters of policy would have 12 or 13 attendees and the discussion would go on for hours with most of us being none the wiser about what had been decided. Indeed, one had to wait for the minutes to know, a few days later as to what had been the decisions. I would often remark about this and say that the person preparing the minutes was the real artist. In principle, an attendee can write an objection but it will get lost in reams of notes to and fro with nothing coming out. I learnt that the real purpose of these conferences was not so much to hear views of the attendees on the subject under discussion, or to arrive at a consensus or decision. More often than not, the decision had already been arrived at and in any case the *Burra Babu* knew pretty much everything about everything. So the masterly device of a conference was meant mainly to diffuse responsibility. In other words one may say that the aim was to "balance the books", meaning that the case has to be shown to have been discussed with all stake holders, and then decisions arrived at and duly recorded as minutes on the files. The famous British TV serial titled, *Yes Minister* is a fairly accurate representation of the byzantine politics of the secretariats and the turf games that the bureaucrats play. The ministry bigwigs would usually roll up around 11.00 a.m., depending upon their position on the pecking order, spend the forenoons chatting over cups of coffee, afternoons on meetings and then sit till late working on the files.

An appointment at the army headquarters and working with the ministries is a learning experience for a service officer. Apart from the hours and pace of work, the civil officials have a different perspective about work altogether. As General V.P. Malik (retired) pointed out in an interview recently (Times News Network, 20-12-2015 with Reporter Robin David) the MoD just does not have any accountability. This is perhaps the root cause of most of the procurement troubles of the armed forces. Above all, the MoD and its subordinate offices are extremely conscious of their supreme authority over the army, navy and air force in almost every sphere, which are looked upon as subordinate services. It is not to say that all IAS officers are unconcerned about defence needs. Some are very able and dedicated. It will be fair to say that when they are good, they are very good but when they are obstructionist and egoistical, they can be formidable. Usually, officers at the level of secretaries have a balanced perspective. Later, while working in the capacity of Deputy Chief of Army Staff (DCOAS), I had very good experience of interacting with one Mr Sushital Bannerji (Secretary MoD) and found him to be an extremely intelligent and balanced officer and a perfect gentleman.

To be fair, our interaction with the MoD is a two way street and most frictions arise out of lack of proper perception about each other. The question of attitudes is there but there is also basic ignorance about each other. The armed services lack the broader perspective of issues at the governmental level (mainly financial constraints at the national level) whereas the civilian bigwigs in the ministries have never heard a shot fired in anger. Lately, attempts have been made to merge the MoD with headquarters of armed services but it has been effectively stymied by bureaucratic wrangles. The fact of the matter is that there can be no merging of two unequal entities, for besides the different domains of expertise, the main stumbling block is that of privilege and power. The MoD will not compromise on that count.

Another imposition regarding serving at Army Headquarters Delhi is the 9 to 5 hours of work. In our units, we work formal hours from six in the morning till lunch and after a short break we spend the afternoons playing games with the men. Anyway, in Delhi, all of us had to bring a pack lunch and four of us would often get together; Sunderji from MS branch, Bhupi from AG, and Chibber and I from MO. It was a lot of fun though and we would pass a very pleasant half hour discussing various things, professional and personal. As a flip side to this, once General Manekshaw proposed a five-day week in all service headquarters thus giving a full weekend off to everybody, but the strongest objection came from the army of clerks! It seems that they were happy spending the whole day in the air cooled comfort of South Block rather than to have to spend a long weekend in the heat at home.

Tackling Armed Revolt of UP Police

General Inder Gill sent me out to represent him on two occasions of importance. I accompanied a team headed by Minister of State (Home) K. C. Pant along with Ashwini Kumar of Police to Lucknow in connection with the revolt of UP armed constabulary which had spread to most other elements of the state police. It was an eye opener to see how the civil government functions. There was a large conference of about 18-20 police officials and a bunch of UP state officials. There was bedlam with everybody talking at once. There was no clarity on how many policemen had revolted, who were their ring leaders, and how many weapons had been taken. The rebels had taken refuge in an old fort with nobody knowing about the stock of their provisions of food and water. The Director General of Police, one Mr Das, did not seem to be in control of the situation.

The chief secretary informed us that the strike by UP armed constabulary had spread to civil police and perhaps also to police intelligence and police wireless personnel. Somebody said that the rebels had taken over the telephone and wireless communications so all information was suspect. Next a smaller group re-paired to HQ Central Command. The Army Commander of Central Command was firmly of the view that army required governmental approval for use of tanks and artillery to take on the PAC personnel ensconced in the fort.

Ultimately that is what worked, although not in the literal sense. Troops were employed to surround the fort and a couple of tanks and field guns brought over from Jhansi, were moved up as a show of force and that did the trick; the PAC battalion surrendered meekly. However, it took a few weeks of confusion and lot of hand-wringing and blame game between the police and civil officials before the situation stabilized. I could not help thinking that if these disparate elements had been dreamed up as an army of the Home Ministry and a possible counter to the army, their value and effectiveness was there for everyone to see.

Audience with HH the Dalai Lama, Dharamsala
(Author 3rd from Right)

Secret Mission to Sikkim

Next, I was sent on a cloak and dagger kind of a mission to Sikkim. My DMO (General Inder Gill) told me that some situation was developing in the mountain kingdom of Sikkim where a movement was building up against the Chogyal. I was to work as ears and eyes for him and represent the MO Dte. Since Sikkim lay in the jurisdiction of Eastern Command, I was to observe the protocol and meet the Army Commander in Calcutta en route to Siliguri and Gangtok, but I was not to divulge the plans regarding Sikkim. On my query as to what were the plans for Sikkim, he only smiled and mumbled, "We don't know, anything can happen".

Anyhow, I flew to Calcutta and dutifully met the Army Commander, General Navin Rawley. He seemed mystified and kept asking probing questions. I said that I was supposed to meet one Mr Avtar Singh of Ministry of External Affairs who would brief me. Sometimes a half-truth works better than beating around the bush. I met Mr Avtar Singh at Siliguri and flew with him in his chopper to Gangtok where we were met by our ambassador, Mr K. Shankar Bajpai, son of famous Girja Shankar Bajpai. I also met Brigadier Prem Hoon commander of the infantry brigade which had been moved up to Gangtok. Bajpai seemed fully in control of the situation. He said that a large faction of Lepchas were almost in a state of revolt against the Chogyal. He did not quite spell it out but it was obvious that should the Chogyal be forced to abdicate, India would not stand in his way and further, would not oppose the wishes of the Lepcha majority if they were to offer to accede to India. I got the drift. The Chogyal was also an Honorary Colonel of my Regiment, 8 GR. So I had an audience with him, exchanging the ceremonial scarves etc. As usual, he was quite drunk and his American wife, Ms. Hope did the usual pleasantries. Bajpai addressed the Chogyal in a familiar vein calling him "Number One".

Overnight, as a result of some skirmishes between the Lepchas and Sikkimese, a few were left dead and some were injured. Officially the Indian troops only kept a watching brief! The tug of war continued between the Sikkimese and Lepchas and other minorities for some time in the local assembly. Ultimately, the Chogyal capitulated under mounting pressure and Sikkim acceded to India in 1975.

There was an unpleasant sequel to the whole affair for me. While taking a return flight to Delhi, at Calcutta airport I got a phone message from the Chief of Staff, Eastern Command for me to speak to the Army Commander. General Rawley was quite angry and told me that I had been less than honest with him when I met him on my way up and had deliberately misled him about my real mission. He followed it up with a complaint to General Inder Gill and perhaps also to the chief but General Bewoor is reported to have taken the fracas in his stride. And that was the end of my foray into military diplomacy. Subsequently, I happened to meet Mr Bajpai (now retired) in a seminar at the Institute of Defence Studies and Analysis and we had a good laugh about the entire episode. I remember telling him, "It is a pity that you weren't around in other mountain kingdoms".

I feel that my Director, General Inder Gill did not quite know what to do with me. An inordinately opinionated man, he obviously did not think that he needed a brigadier to do the perspective planning for him. He was an able man nevertheless and would spend hours drafting papers in long hand with a pen, not with a pencil and eraser as we were taught since school days. He did not believe in using a stenographer particularly for classified subjects. Many a time, I represented him at meetings of the Chiefs of Staffs Committee (CoSC). In fact for some subjects, the meetings were routinely attended by the deputy directors.

The CoSC was then and still is an effete body of service chiefs who meet occasionally to discuss matters and sending general briefs or recommendations to the government on various matters. It was essentially a meeting of equals without a clear command structure, though nominally, one of the chiefs (longest serving) was designated as the chairman. More recently, the Government has decided to appoint a permanent chairman of the CoSC but an incumbent is still to be appointed and there are reports of serious misgivings from within the MoD. Quite expectedly, the ministry mandarins are opposed to a high functionary of the armed services usurping their powers of direct access to the P.M. Perhaps it is also seen as the precursor to the appointment of a Chief of Defence Staff (CDS) which is even more of an anathema to the civilian hierarchy.

After six months, General Inder Gill was succeeded by the highly decorated officer, General Zoru Bakshi as the DMO. Zoru had a very different style of functioning and was more approachable. He got into his job straightaway and asked me to put up files on perspective planning. I had to tell him that there was no such thing and that as far as I knew, General Inder Gill, carried all the perspective plans inside his head or in hand written notes kept in his cupboard. Anyhow, General Zoru Bakshi set about the job in right earnest. He instituted a study on the "War Wastage Rates". This is a concept of codifying the amount of ammunition expended in one day of active operations so as to form the basis of provisioning with the formations in the front as also of stockpiling in the depots. It is expressed in 'so-many days' of War Wastage Rates (WWR).The figure is under continuous review by the general staffs to keep abreast of the prevailing or expected intensity of operations in a given theatre of war.

Having something worthwhile to do, we got fully immersed in the study and prepared papers, the entire effort culminating in a presentation by me and a discussion in the operations room with all stake holders, mainly heads of arms attending. We had a lively discussion, sometimes heated arguments based on personal experience of operations of people. Zoru intervened whenever I seemed to be overwhelmed or outranked. He was very good and he carried a lot of respect because of his war exploits. In such studies, there will always be difference of opinion but the purpose is to arrive at an average figure for planning purposes. Besides, there is inherent flexibility in the concept because the absolute quantities are roughly quantified by specifying the number of days of WWR for a particular operation.

I had a family crisis of another sort during this tenure. My daughter had her heart set on a medical career. She slogged her way through successive examinations and interviews for admission into a medical college. She finally succeeded in getting acceptance at the Armed Forces Medical College at Pune

(AFMC) and everything looked fine. But then as a bolt from the blue, she got a "compartment" in the optional subject of Hindi in her premedical course at Sophia College Ajmer, Rajasthan (State of Rajasthan has very high standard of Hindi). The Maharashtra University under whose jurisdiction the AFMC functioned were not hung up on standards of Hindi language but mandated an outright pass in all subjects including 'the optionals'. I tried to remonstrate with both universities (Rajasthan and Maharashtra) but neither would budge. I made a dash to Jaipur where my cousin had recently retired as IG of Police in the State of Rajasthan. I went to Shimla and met the CM through a family friend, trying to get admission for her in a college in Himachal Pradesh. Nothing worked. So the poor girl had to settle for a course in English Honours in Lady Sri Ram College for Women in Delhi. Subsequently, this change of course affected her whole life in many ways. This kind of difficulty is common for service children, because they do not have the benefit of studying in one place for long unlike the children of civil officials who stay in one place and one state for long stretches.

My son, Rajiv had better luck. He was studying in Doon School at Dehradun. Around this time, I was cleared for promotion to the next rank of Major General. Brigadier Umesh Saxena, who was serving as MS (Military Secretary) to the Chief, General Bewoor, rang me up with the good news. He kindly offered to help me choose between 14 Division in Dehradun and 10 Division in Amritsar. So, to Dehradun I went to the delight of my wife and of course, my son.

Divisional Commander in Dehradun

I had come as a cadet to Dehradun on 8 August 1946. I was returning as a Divisional Commander on 8 February 1974, a professional journey of 28 years. I was 49 years old. In between, I had fought a war at the head of a battalion, taught officers

GOC, 14 Infantry Division, 1974

about the profession of arms at the war college, taught staff college, worked in the Military Operations Directorate (MO Dte) in Army Headquarters, commanded a brigade in Ladakh and attended the NDC course. I did the regulation tenure of two years at every step, sometimes moving just after earning the mandated two ACRs. In short, I had done all that a promising officer is expected to do but all this activity takes too big a chunk of time out of the life of an officer. The point is that age of 49 years is too old for a divisional commander to be really robust and fit enough to battle on the mountains and on high altitude. He would certainly be too old in a futuristic war or a nuclear environment. I think there is something wrong with management of our officer cadre. *We should aim at having division commanders at 35-40 years of age; brigade commanders of 30-35 years, and battalion/regimental commanders of 28-30 years.* These are the kind of age-groups which will ensure optimum results in a future Kargil.

I was posted as GOC (General Officer Commanding) 14 Infantry Division with Headquarters at Dehradun, arriving on the morning of 8 February 1974 by overnight train from Delhi with my wife and daughter. We were received at the railway station by the incumbent, General Harish Bakshi of 5th Gorkhas. The division with its logo of a 'Key' had a proud history of operations in Burma in WW II. Dehradun was the traditional home (training center) of a number of Gorkha Regiments (1st, 3rd, 4th, 8th, 9th Gorkha Rifles) since long. In fact, the regimental training centres and cantonments were dotted all over India, mostly in places of salubrious climate, known as "non-fan stations". All the operational cantonments were located on the North West Frontier as the army was tasked mainly to meet the threat from Russia in the north-west, defined as "the frontier". After Partition, the frontier for India moved down to the edge of West Punjab. So, it was decided to move out the training centres inland to make place for the formations which could then be moved closer up to the new frontier to ensure quicker mobilization. So the 2 Corps (under General Raina) was located at Chandimandir, and 14 Division was located at Dehradun with brigades at hand, with the operational role of guarding the Ganganagar border area of Rajasthan.

My brigades were located at Meerut (Brigadier Pran Anand), Roorkee (Brigadier Anand Sarup) and Clement Town, Dehradun (Brigadier Lachhi Chand Sabharwal). I was aghast to learn that the division had never been allowed to train in the area of its operational responsibility for some misplaced considerations of secrecy. The forward thinking and practical soldier, General Raina acceded to my request to take the division out to train in our OP area. To ensure security and as a training measure I had the division to move stealthily under cover of darkness. We mud plastered the usual formation signs on the vehicles and the troops took off the logo sign from their uniforms. The move worked with copy book precision and I was feeling quite pleased with the security measures. But, on the second day of our arrival, the Pakistan public radio rural programme had some rustics chatting that Indians were rummaging for their "lost key" (alluding to the formation sign of a key of my division) in the desert sands. And to think that we had for long hesitated to train in the area of our intended operations for reasons of security, little knowing that the hordes of smugglers and bootleggers had been regularly crossing the border manned by BSF with impunity. It goes without saying that movement to and fro of smugglers means rampant exchange of information or intelligence.

Training in sandy soil proved very useful. We learned the technique of driving through and around sand dunes without getting stuck in heavy sand. We conducted training at all levels culminating with a divisional exercise conducted for us by the Corps. By now, General Raina had moved up as western army commander and General A.M. Vohra had taken over 2 Corps. I wrote a paper on mobile defence in the desert terrain, a concept based upon a grid pattern of defensive strongholds and employment of armour operating around the infantry pivots. General Raina came and congratulated us all for utilizing our time in desert training in a very gainful manner. I think it was a valuable experience and everyone in the division came back to our locations fully satisfied.

Coming back to Dehradun after the hard training was very welcome. I did a lot of golfing, fishing and trekking with Rajiv's Housemasters, R.D. Singh, and Gurdyal Singh the mountaineer in Doon School which also allowed extra "home time" to Rajiv. My wife became very popular with the boys as she would take *aloo parathas* to them, which they would devour even after dinner in their mess hall. School boys are perpetually hungry! We did a long hike to Gangotri – Gaumukh and a glacier climb up to the meadow of Tapovan at the foot of the Mountain Trishul. Our daughter Jyoti got married in October 1975 whilst I was in Dehradun. The marriage was graced by General Raina and his wife. In fact, during the last big dinner, General Raina told me that he was sending me back to the College of Combat as Commandant to complete the good work that I had initiated on the senior command course. I would have preferred doing a staff job as Chief of Staff of a Corps, but I had to bow to his wishes. So, soon after the wedding we packed, said goodbye to our many friends in Doon School, and we were off. On a more personal note, it was at Dehradun that I lost my father who succumbed to a massive brain stroke. So, Dehradun has bitter sweet memories for the whole family.

7

Commandant Army College of Combat, Mhow

Within a few weeks of the wedding of my daughter Jyoti in Dehradun on 14 October 1975, we packed up the household and made our way down to Delhi and thence to good old Mhow by a train journey of the awkward connection at Ratlam, arriving on 10 November 1975. This time I had come as the Commandant of the College of Combat (it was correctly later re-designated as Army College of War in 2008). Mhow had not changed much since I was here as Commander Senior Command Wing except that now as Commandant of the whole College, I had the responsibility to oversee all three wings as also an elaborate logistic set up. The College consisted of Higher Command Wing, Senior Command Wing and the Junior Command Wing. These were three independent wings, each with a distinct character and student body, but had the common purpose to impart training to officers at different levels of command.

In the Army there are many schools of instruction specializing in diverse disciplines. The forte of the college of combat is tactics and strategy and allied logistics. It is a premier training institution of the army, which is also a leader in evolving and analyzing concepts and doctrines that have a bearing on tactics and strategy. Annually, upwards of 1200 officers of different ranks and disparate battle experience pass through the portals of this hallowed institution, which gives it a character and personality all its own. Students are taught by hand-picked instructors. They also interact mutually and learn from each other. It is a crucible for new thought and a vast think tank. It constitutes a significant link in the chain of continuing in-service training and process of grooming and preparation of officers to ensure that they are made fit to discharge their duties with professional expertise at different levels. Taken together with the ongoing training in the units, this step crowns the entire edifice of professionalism. It is doubtful if so much attention is paid to in-service training in other professions.

Junior Command Wing

The junior command wing trains captains and majors to command a company of infantry or a squadron of armour and equivalent level in supporting arms and services. At this level, they are taught to function as part of a battalion or regiment. To do so, they learn, practice and apply the rules of tactics. They are taught the different operations of war such as advance, attack, defence, and withdrawal and essentials of achieving surprise. It is basic, bed-rock training. They are young bucks, bubbling with energy and enthusiasm, so we encourage new ideas, originality of thought and spirit of enquiry but our task is to balance high spirits with hard realities of the battlefield. I remember attending the JC course as a student myself, full of wild ideas but being brought to earth by a very patient and wise instructor, Major R.G.R. Bali of Garhwal Rifles. In some ways it is the most difficult course to teach well. Full of spirits and ideas, I once had an argument with my instructor about the best way to site a defensive position – forward of a water obstacle or behind it. The conventional wisdom is that the defensive position should be sited behind the obstacle as the obstacle would add strength to defence. With my half-baked ideas, I stupidly argued that if the defender was to fall back behind the obstacle, it would amount to a withdrawal, and giving away the ground ahead. My instructor, instead of just shutting me up, patiently explained that the defender would deploy screens or covering troops forward of the obstacle so there was no question of surrender of any ground. The Junior Command Course is positioned at the most crucial level. It is like breaking-in of a young colt. There has to be just enough of firm handling and no more, because over control will kill the spirit of enquiry. As commandant, I used to visit their discussions and outdoor exercises very often. I also used to deliver the opening lecture and often also deliver the valedictory address. The wing commander was a cool and capable officer, Brigadier Sami Khan who rose to be an Army Commander.

Training modules comprised of straight lectures, discussions in small groups called syndicates, discussions on a sand model, a contrivance special to the army where an imaginary or real piece of landscape is reproduced which is then used to discuss various operations of war. We also take the students out on real ground to demonstrate various activities and also to "paint imaginary situations" like enemy position on a hilltop, and discuss ways to attack it. Sometimes, we divide the course with one group acting as "own troops" and another as "enemy". To lend realism, an actual infantry battalion and a squadron of armour are stationed at Mhow. So, there are Tactical Exercises Without Troops (TEWTs) and tactical exercises with troops. In short, the army spares no effort to impart training using maximum ingenuity. The course duration of three months is packed with activity, morning to evening, and often through the night. The course is divided in semesters with detailed one-on-one counseling between students and instructors at the end of each semester. The aim is to continually advise the student in a transparent manner on the aspects where more effort is required on his part. I explained to instructors and students alike that we were there to produce good officers and not to fail people. I also emphasized that this course was devoted to plant the seeds of professionalism in the young officers which was our main thrust.

Senior Command Wing

This course constitutes an important step in the education of an officer. Indeed, each course has its own importance in the officers' career in a progressive manner. However, I personally rate this course as the most crucial for two reasons. Firstly, at this step, one can discern the high flyers from the plodders. Secondly, the quality of an army is determined by its unit commanders. In my previous tenure of commander of this wing, I had given it my maximum and undivided attention. Now seeing it in perspective of the overall learning curve of an officer's career, its centrality became all the more evident. I had spent a great deal of time to upgrade the instructional material to bring it in line with the realities on the ground. We changed the remaining exercises settings to actual war settings, relative to Indo-Pak wars of 1965 and 1971, and later the US wars in Iraq to the extent relevant to our conditions. Wherever possible, I arranged to get the commanders (colonels and brigadiers) who had actually fought those battles to attend the discussions and presentations.

I introduced various other innovations. In all imaginary situations and sand model discussions, we started appointing one syndicate to act as "enemy." Both sides first presented their plans individually without the other side listening in. Then I would go through the operation by phases, following the same procedure for each phase. It generated a great deal of enthusiasm turning the discussion into a two sided battle. The point is that only one sided linear discussions assume that every plan will succeed and proceed as planned which is not what happens in real war. This new two way method underlines the uncertainties of battles, besides testing out the resilience of the plans. It also allows for highlighting the important aspects of surprise and value of doing the unexpected.

I instituted a set of studies, entitled, "How do our enemies fight and make war". We have a fairly clear idea as to who would be our likely opponents in a future war and we have also had experience of fighting against them. But there is seldom an ongoing periodical review of the changes and advancements in their armies, for meaningful analyses. To keep abreast of the situation and tactical thought prevailing in the army, we instituted a series of presentations by groups of people from different sectors. We had to keep it on a low key lest it took away too much of time of students. We collected some material and literature about the technique of war gaming. Subsequently, one of my successors, General Sundarji did very useful work in this field.

Higher Command Wing

This new course recently introduced constituted a pioneering effort of the army. It is indeed considered a showpiece. The student body consists of specially selected colonels and their equivalent officers of the air force and navy (two each). The students are handpicked. As per their record they are supposed to have 'arrived' and are by all accounts marked for high places. The course is designed to deal with higher direction of war and addresses the issues of strategy and national security. The emphasis is solely on analyses apart from teaching, training, and discussion. Hence, the system of grading performance of students on this course has been done away with, which is regarded as a welcome futuristic step, futuristic as all other courses end with a performance evaluation, whereas there is no grading on this course. It still remains as the only course of its kind. At the JC course, the students study tactics. At the SC course students study tactics and also rudiments of strategy. On the Higher Command course, students question tactics and strategy: so three courses cover the entire gamut of officer craft. The College as a whole constitutes a unique think tank, for it consists of both thinkers and practitioners of war. The college also carries the responsibility to analyze and study broader issues such as nuclear dimension, space weapons and cyber warfare.

We organize lectures by a large number of specialists, military as well as civilian authorities on their domain specializations. Sometimes, the speakers tended to get carried away, as for instance one of them stating that his job as a commissioner is to uphold the Constitution. It was politely pointed out to him that safeguarding of the Constitution is the province of the parliament and the judiciary and not that of the administrative organs of the state. We also invited a few reputed journalists from the media. Most of the guest speakers came as out of station invitees; so they were provided accommodation and entertained in the officers' mess, where the students had the opportunity to discuss matters in a relaxed and informal manner. All in all, it gave students wide exposure to the non-military world and to issues beyond their normal milieu.

When discussing specific operations, we tried to get the concerned commanders from their locations to come and sit in. In addition, we introduced a programme of battlefield tours or forward area tours, where we were able to get the commanders to describe how they saw the situation, and speak on their strategy to fulfill their mission. Many dignitaries from the army visited the College. The chief and the central army commander were regular visitors. I often pointed out to them that the presence of such a large conclave of officers of all levels in the vibrant atmosphere of the college provided ideal opportunity to feel the pulse of the army. General Krishna Rao and his team of the Expert Committee came and stayed for two days to get a sampling of the issues engaging the attention of officers of the army. During my tenure of duty, I approached our mission as teacher of the University of Military Knowledge.

The army is constantly involved in study of concepts and doctrine at different levels. The apex body is the Army Training Command (ARTRAC), one of the seven operational commands of the army, located at Shimla. It is a dedicated high level organization for formulating concepts and doctrines which are specifically applicable to our operational environment. The next rung on the ladder is the Military Operations Directorate at Army Headquarters which is followed and augmented by army schools of instruction, principally the War College, the last and the most important step is the active formations, who are the final user – practitioners and stakeholders. I spent a lot of time with Higher Command Course and participated in most of the discussions. It was a very pleasant experience to interact with bright and inquisitive minds. I think the officers of air force and navy made significant contribution, although the main thrust tended to be army oriented. Perhaps it was a natural outcome of the course being run at an army establishment but I think this bias was not resented in any way. Besides, it is a known fact that the army constitutes by far the largest component of the armed forces, though it is intimately related to the Air Force.

Now the air force and navy have instituted their respective higher command courses. It is a step in the right direction because it is desirable that all services address their respective operational problems and develop their individual tactics and doctrines. However, there would still be need for an umbrella tri-service course at the level of Higher Command Course to evolve and develop a national doctrine. Further, there is urgent need to evolve and fine tune the doctrine and thought concerning joint operations, which is an inescapable reality for the future wars. It will also engender a sense of unity among the three services because the dictates of national security make this unity a live necessity.

During my command of the War College, General Raina, the Chief paid us a visit. I discussed all the initiatives that have been introduced in all wings to make the training more meaningful. A very professional officer, he went through it all and spent a lot of time at each wing. Later, he received a personal invitation from the Chief of the Russian armed forces for a two week visit to the USSR in April 1978. He very kindly included me in his small party of three officers (General Gurbachan Singh, the Central Army Commander, Brigadier Kaul from Army HQ in addition and myself with himself at the head of the mission. He was accompanied by his military assistant, Brigadier Satish Issar of Kumaon Regiment. The Soviet Chief really rolled out the red carpet, put his personal plane at General Raina's disposal and laid out an elaborate tour programme. I had the occasion to visit Russia many times in connection with procurement of arms, but the trip as part of General Raina's party stands out as most memorable. We visited a large number of soviet army installations in addition to many places across the length and breadth of the vast country. We visited Leningrad, Kiev and the fabled Samarkand. Amidst a lot of toasts and the soviet hospitality, we were given fair exposure to the Russian army. I found their training methods to be fairly good but in no way ahead of ours except that some of their training aids were quite good; wherever possible I later adapted them in our College.

Mhow: Its Special Flavour

Mhow is a very pleasant place. Situated on the Malwa Plateau in central India, it has equable climate. It is a typical cantonment small town like many others dotted over India. These overgrown villages subsist mainly on the commerce generated by the garrison, and in this case, its life depended on the training establishments. Mhow was indeed an officer town which had a revolving population of over a thousand officers of all ages with equal number of wives at any given time. Apart from the College of Combat which was the biggest institution, there was Military College of Telecom Engineering

(MCTE), of the Corps of Signals, the Infantry School and a host of supporting units.

The town was known for its restaurants, eateries of all stripe and also some makeshift dance clubs along with the usual complement of Anglo-Indian girls that somehow always gravitate to cantonments. The most popular set of small business were a number of tailoring establishments.

They must have fitted out generations of officers and came to acquire good tailors. One could get a suit of clothes or a blazer and gray bags made in a day, maximum two. As a matter of fact, General Raina on retirement as the Chief and posted as Indian High Commissioner to Canada, came and stayed with me for a week for the explicit purpose of getting clothes made for the diplomatic assignment. Mhow boasted a fine old officers club, called Club of Central India dating back to 1900s. The nearest big town was a bustling mini metropolis of Indore, an old center of commerce and business half way between Bombay and Delhi. It was also connected by air on Bombay-Delhi route.

We built a sailing club on the Bercha Lake nearby which was a man-made lake of fair size. It was essentially the source of water supply for the cantonment. There were the usual bungalows for officers though a large number had crumbled now and were lying in ruins. One of them was the bungalow where Winston Churchill had once lived as a lieutenant. Through some administrative wrinkle the dilapidated structures could not be rebuilt. They had been built and nominally owned by the contractors who built the original set of barracks. As a part of the contract, they were obliged to build a certain number of bungalows on cantonment land, for residence of the officers of the garrison at their cost. By way of compensation, the contractors were paid monthly rental. The idea was that this way the contractors would get to cover the costs incurred by them in a set number of months. At the same time the government would get to have available, suitable bungalows for the officers of the station without any charge on the government. The contractors were never supposed to live in them. With passage of time, the original contractors died and the bungalows fell into state of disrepair. Now heirs of the original owners, though technically owners of the properties in a manner of speaking, were not allowed to sell or rebuild. The army had no money to buy back and rebuild. So there they were, eye sores, as a continuing source of frustration for the station commanders. This problem plagues almost all old cantonments in India. But the administrative hiatus still remains unsolved. I tried to resolve the matter but found the entire issue so obfuscated by red tape that I gave up in despair before I started.

The presence of a large number of officers' wives made for a lively social life. It also helped in cementing of many friendships. In fact the routine of frequent courses at the army schools gives opportunity for officers and their families to bond with other families and strike life-long friendships which forms the larger entity of the army fraternity. These friendships endure even after retirement. At Mhow the officers on the courses were kept extremely busy so the wives had to find ways and means to utilize time on productive pursuits. My wife, as the senior lady of the station, organized classes for many hobbies such as sewing and tailoring, cooking, book reading, flower decoration, homeopathy medicines, yoga et al. A service wife is a marvel of versatility, adaptability and thrift. She is an uncomplaining companion and an unfailing support system for her husband through good times and bad. She brings up the children and manages the house, often all by herself. In a sense she is truly the backbone of the army.

I invested a lot of time and effort on the officers' messes, paying special attention to nutritious meals, comfortable surroundings and comparatively quiet ambience. There is surfeit of talent among officers and their ladies, so I got a lot of artwork done for the messes. One of my instructors on the SC wing, Colonel Moti Dhar painted an enormous mural depicting the passage of successive waves of invading armies across the

Indian landscape. It is still there, filling an entire wall of the 'A' (senior) Mess. A lady made series of paintings depicting birds of Madhya Pradesh. End-of-course get-togethers put up by the student community were always a riot of fun with traditional though good natured jokes at the expense of the instructors.

I served the College of Combat for well-nigh three years, and it proved to be three very productive and satisfying years of my service. I lived in a beautiful bungalow, the only double storied house in the cantonment with a very well laid out garden and decorative ponds. At the personal level a few months after my arrival, we got the glad tidings regarding the birth of Aditya, my grandchild from my daughter Sweetie. (We have nicknamed him Uzi after the Israeli submachine gun as since even as a little tot he was very high spirited). Sweetie died early so we have brought him up as a son. Now a strapping young man of six foot three, he is the delight of our life. He got married to a lovely girl, Ritika, granddaughter of General Gurbaksh Chopra who retired as Director General of Ordnance Corps. The young couple lives in the town of Palo Alto in California, USA.

Motivation of the Soldiers

War is a competition in technology. It is a matter of big guns and munitions. To Napoleon, it was a matter of big battalions. It is a contest of national will of the contestants. In sum it is many things to many people. However, above all, it is universally accepted that the man is the lynch pin - he is the ultimate weapon. The national will manifests itself through the will of the soldiers in the front line. Similarly, big guns are important but only when handled expertly. Hence the adage, "It is not the gun but the man behind the gun that counts." So the great captains of war down the ages have striven to understand this ultimate weapon of war. If it was true in olden days, it is truer in the modern times since the battlefield has become ever more deadly and more complex. What makes this instrument function at its best? What is the primeval impulse which makes men to go rushing headlong into the jaws of death? Simply put, why do men fight? How can the urge to fight and confront danger, be inculcated and honed? How can the commander motivate and inspire his soldiers to achieve extraordinary results?

First, it must be understood that war is an intensely human activity. Human beings fight best when they are fully motivated and fighting for a cause. The cause is often manifold. They may be fighting to protect their home and hearth; "for the graves of their fathers and the temples of their gods"; "to protect the vital interests of their country; to defend their societal way of life, and in the final analysis, to follow a leader who they believe in. Indeed, the leader factor is the strongest lever to trigger patriotism and valour. Sometimes a particularly charismatic leader may prove to be the overriding influence. For instance, the Indian soldiers fought with conspicuous valour and fortitude in the two world wars even though they were fighting for the British cause but still they fought well because of the quality of the British leadership and the British inspired credo of "*Nam-Namak-Nishan*". They substituted loyalty to the cause of England by loyalty to the regiment and community (Sikhs, Rajputs, Dogras, and so on) and loyalty to the soldier's oath.

At the human level, the soldier fights best when he has confidence in himself, confidence in his knowledge of the art and craft of war, confidence in his comrades and confidence in the ability and bravery of his officer. He must also have confidence in the administrative system. In the words of Field Marshal Carriapa (first Indian chief): "the soldier should have one meal in his stomach, one meal in his rucksack and he should know where the third one is coming from". He should have confidence in the system of replenishment of ammunition and spare parts (important for tanks and guns) and should be confident that if injured, he would get proper medical care. Being human, the soldier is also affected by societal factors:

respect and prestige he gets from the society, knowledge that his family will be cared for in the event of his death, and a feeling of well-being about himself and the well-being of his country (soldiers in the front line engaged in hazardous patrolling get upset when they hear bad news of corruption, scams and other societal ills, back home). The soldier must get first rate training, should be equipped with modern and reliable weapons and a reasonable system of turnover of work and rest periods. The indigenous manufacture of weapons and equipment is a laudable objective but it must not be at the cost of reliability which is a serious concern of the soldier. At one time, a difference of opinion arose over an indigenous tank called *Arjuna,* between Directorate of Research and Development (DRDO) and the army. The armoured corps, particularly the unit equipped by Arjuna tanks (43 Armoured Regiment) was unhappy about the technical problems (bugs) and likelihood of malfunction in the operations. The manufacturing factory thought that the army was being unduly critical. In the same way the army is unhappy when its modernization schemes are being unduly delayed.

The vital role of leadership especially at the level of company commander/squadron leader and at the level of platoon commander/troop leader's level, is fully realized but often not possible due to shortages in these ranks. During the final assault on the enemy position, in the excitement and explosion of adrenaline, all reason flies away; all that is left is a fiery emotion and the urge to follow the leader blindly as it were. It is the same for squadron leaders and troop leaders of armoured corps where the tank crews of following tanks will follow the leading tanks of the commander in the headlong charge in clouds of dust and despite the anti-tank fire of the enemy. However, this kind of loyalty and confidence is achieved after a lifetime of effort and hard work on the part of the leaders. The officer has to establish a reputation for bravery and ability and then work tirelessly to train his men so that they would have confidence in themselves coupled with the belief that their leader will have made the best tactical plans and would lead them to success.

There are other factors which are equally important. Patriotic fervor is a prime motive, so is a burning religious zeal. As far as patriotic fervor is concerned, there need be no ambiguity now about what the army will fight for. The soldiers fight to safeguard India's hard won freedom and to keep inviolate our territorial integrity. We fight for *"Bharat Mata"* and hold aloft our tri-colour flag. Greetings of "Jai Hind" are most common in the entire army. In fact, the "NAM" part of the soldier's credo should be identified with loyalty to the country to emphasize that soldier fights as much for his regiment as for the nation. The religious zeal is another significant motivational factor. It should not be difficult to invoke as the Indian soldier is deeply religious. In any case, even the British acknowledged its relevance and did not object to distinctive war cries of various regiments even though most of them were linked to our gods and goddesses. A war cry is the slogan shouted by troops while assaulting enemy positions. So the battle grounds continue to resound to the war cries of *"Har Har Mahadev"*, *"Jai Bajrang Bali"*, *"Bole So Nihal Sat Siri Akal"*, *"Jai Durga Ma"*and the like. The most proud war cry is that of gorkha regiments. Charging with flashing *khukris*, they shout *"Ayo Gorkhali"* (here come the Gorkhas).

To emphasize the spirit of patriotism, the regiments and battalions recount for the new recruits and young soldiers, the regimental exploits in different wars after gaining independence. The units proudly celebrate their "Battle Honour" day which is awarded for conspicuous achievement to the Battalion in specific operations. Considering that the army has been deployed in umpteen wars and counter insurgency operations ever since 1947, there is no dearth of such shining examples of valour and signal success. The motivational aspect of each unit is commented upon by the formation commanders in their annual inspection report. In addition, the unit commander's annual report itself has to comment upon the state of morale of his unit. The concept of *morale* is a distinctive feature of the army. It connotes an amalgam of self-confidence, self-esteem, confidence in the leaders and comrades, pride in the unit and country and a spirit of general well-being.

Appointed Colonel of the Regiment, 1972

Farewell to 14 Infantry Division

8

Deputy Chief of the Army Staff, Delhi

Towards the last months of my stay in Mhow as the Commandant, College of Combat, I was informed that I had been appointed as Deputy Chief of the Army Staff at Army Headquarters, New Delhi. It was good news by all accounts as the deputy chief is an important member of team of the select group of officers who are appointed as Principal Staff Officers (PSOs) to the army chief. In fact, it will be correct to say that the PSOs are the key staff officers of the chief through whom he exercises command of the huge edifice called the Army Headquarters, and by logical progression, command of the entire Indian Army of 1.12 million. PSOs (seven such officers) carry the rank of Lieutenant General but in the army hierarchy, they are considered a notch above all other Lt Generals of the army except Army Commanders (there are a total of 90 Lt Generals in the army as of today). The PSOs are not graded amongst themselves as such but traditionally the general staff used to be 'first among equals', and considered an important functionary. Earlier, his position was even higher because he carried the title of Chief of General Staff (CGS). The oft retailed story is that this appointment was "cut to size" during the tenure of General Mucho Choudhary as the chief. It is said that, when General Choudhury was on a formal visit to USA, he took along his chief of general staff (CGS) Lt General Moti Sagar who was on occasions taken to be the senior of the two by the hosts (in American hierarchy the CGS was the top man at that time). Be that as it may, the CGS of the Indian Army was re-designated as the Deputy Chief of the Army staff (DCOAS). Further, in my time, the post of Vice Chief was created who became senior to all the PSOs. After my tenure, the office of Deputy Chief was further bifurcated into two.

As part of continual restructuring the subjects of "operations and intelligence" were taken away from under the CGS and put under the newly created appointment of the vice chief. This step was widely seen as a retrograde move as on principle it is considered bad to split the general staff. In other words, the departments (called Branches) dealing with operations (DMO), intelligence (DMI), training (DMT), weapons (DWE) and "staff duties" should be the domain of one officer. Anyhow, personally I felt elated to be chosen to serve directly under the chief, General O.P. Malhotra, a thorough professional and a kind man with impeccable manners. It seems that during his last visit to the College of Combat as the chief, he had told me in confidence that he was taking me to Delhi as his deputy. By mischance, I missed that bit of our conversation (I was perhaps preoccupied with something else or missed it because my hearing was becoming weak). Anyhow, it is a measure of his innate goodness that he did not take offence. I came to know of my *faux pas* when Major General Sapra, the then director of weapons and equipment, told me later that the chief had mentioned to him that Harish did not seem to be keen to come to Army HQ as the deputy chief. This seems to have raised quite a few eyebrows, among the army hierarchy and the community of touts dealing with acquisition of weapons, for this appointment is considered a choice posting by all standards. I am happy to say that throughout our association in service as also after retirement, General Malhotra was exceptionally kind to me and both he and his gracious wife were a source of great comfort and support through the worst period of personal tragedy in our family. Both have passed away now.

As Deputy Chief with Chief Gen. Krishna Rao (Author is 3rd from Right)

I was considered as the chief's right hand man and had direct access to him. Other PSOs also had the right of direct access but I think they had to seek an appointment through his personal staff, possibly because their offices were located at a distance or on a different floor. My office was close to his and he granted me the courtesy to walk in unannounced. Besides, my professional duties, my responsibilities were to organize (with MS) the Biannual Army Commanders Conferences. I also had the ceremonial task to pick up the Prime Minister (the redoubtable Indira Gandhi) from her residence and escort her to the biannual conference of the army commanders. It was for me to make small talk while travelling in the car. Sometimes I did well and delivered her to the meetings in good humour, sometimes not. Once I goofed, remarking that NT Rama Rao (of Andhra Pradesh) had reportedly taken "sanyas". She just flared up saying that his *sanyas* was nothing but a charade as he remained as devious a politician as ever. I quickly changed the subject but the damage seemed to have been done as through the conference she was a bit glum.

Indigenous Production of Armaments

The acquisition of weapons and equipment took a lot of my time. India's indigenous manufacture of arms was extremely limited despite an elaborate structure of Director of Research and Development Organization (DRDO) and the Ordnance Factories Board (OFB). I often dealt with Secretary of Defence Production, the highly regarded Mr K. Subrahmanyam and we had a running tussle regarding delays (and resultant cost over runs) of our indigenous production and the unacceptable standards of the manufactured items. Mr Subramanyam and his people complained that the services were being unduly critical and were only keen to import equipment from abroad. This was in the year 1979 when our manufacturing capacity was in infancy after hundreds of years of neglect. Indeed India was just waking up after centuries of slumber because owing to foreign rule, India had been denied the knowledge and capacity to develop and manufacture indigenous arms in the country. Leave alone weapons, there was almost total lack of manufacturing capacity except of the most elementary kind. Indians had for ages been confined to the dung heap of basic agriculture and what had been described as "hewers of wood and drawers of water". The renaissance, sprit of scientific enquiry and innovation had slipped past India by a wide margin. Interestingly, the design of the present bullock cart has largely remained unaltered, even down to the hard wheels, for thousands of years. This state of affairs prevails in spite of strenuous efforts by the government to modernize the nation and setting up of many institutes of science. The development of nuclear technology is a rare example. We perhaps owe it to the genius and farsightedness of Dr. Homi Bhabha, supported and reinforced by Nehru's vision.

The roadblocks are many. The foreign powers jealously guard secrets of their research and development. Why would they part with drawings and designs and thereby risk losing their slice of the arms bazaar? We have also been handicapped by our own Gandhian philosophy and impractical idealism. For a long while we have suffered under qualms about manufacturing and selling of arms which was considered immoral and against humanity. We did not realize that armaments constitute a major part of global commerce and account for a significant part of economy of nations. In sum, for a variety of reasons, India still lacks an industrial base of any magnitude. The next and perhaps, the biggest road block is our hallowed preference for the public sector. In this regard, we have a very elaborate apparatus of manufacture but without matching effectiveness. The private sector is looked down upon as corrupt, self-serving and untrustworthy. In point of fact, the reality is that if the private sector is blamed for acting without scruples, the chief culprit for that has been the infamous "permit raj" devised and operated by corrupt politicians and civil servants. We seemed to have missed the point that although there is corruption in both the public sector and private sector, the private sector is at least efficient for the simple reason that a private business has to be competitive and productive otherwise it will fold up.

To top it all, India has suffered from a national paranoia of corruption and has added layers of procedures and multiplicity of agencies dealing with a proposal, forgetting that big corruption takes place at high places, whereas at the operating level, the problem is that of only petty corruption. The upshot is that India imports almost 80% of its requirement of weapons and warlike equipment at enormous cost. In marked contrast, Pakistan is smart enough to get these either as free aid or purchases them at highly concessional rates (at book value in case of USA). And they get them from both USA and China. During my time, the bulk of our purchases were perforce sourced from Russia. Their prices were eminently competitive and besides, they extended substantial credit terms. Most of the large purchases were offered on basis of deferred payment spread over 15 years: the first payment starting two years after commencement (in some cases completion) of supplies. European and American arms were more sophisticated but pricey. In addition, the US arms deals were heavily affected by political considerations and came with many legalistic and conditional clauses.

On one occasion, I went to the USA in quest of anti-tank missiles for our infantry battalions. At the last moment, our delegation was reinforced by a lady from our legal department (to read the fine print in the contract documents) with the result that the American negotiating team was also buttressed by a formidable legal person, also a woman. We came back empty handed as between the two ladies we did not make much headway. The Americans were very cordial and friendly but they said they had their regulations. They demonstrated the firing of the anti-tank missiles (I was permitted to test fire one on the simulator), but they offered complicated supply schedules and non-matching figures for launchers and missiles. Similarly, we were interested in their 155mm howitzers (I had our top artillery officer, to accompany me). Again, their response was outwardly positive but they would not agree to supply the best type of ammunition. On an earlier visit for buying unarmed aerial vehicles like drones (UAVs), we had identified a system but the manufacturer stated that he would need release from the US Government which would entail a long drawn protocol. The fact is that the US attitude was not very helpful as a result of their pronounced tilt towards Pakistan.

The Bofors Gun Controversy

Most of the purchases made were on government to government basis (G to G deals), but sometimes the deals had to be made with commercial companies. The Bofors controversy and its aftermath commenced in my watch in December 1986. Basically, it was a straightforward case of acquisition of medium guns which the army had been seeking since long (we are still searching the market for them). As mentioned earlier, we had gone to USA to investigate a US 155 mm Howitzer but the proposal did not fructify chiefly owing to the US reluctance to supply special AP (Armour Piercing) shells. We were actually looking for a self -propelled (tracked) medium gun for employment with armoured columns. The Russians had a 155 mm howitzer but it did not match all our specifications. The French had a gun in the same category which was considered a "possible". We were very impressed by the literature put out by a Swedish arms manufacturer called Bofors AB. So, I headed a team to Sweden to evaluate this gun. It promised to be a major purchase; hence I took along my Director of Weapons and Equipment, Major General K. K. Hazari and Director Artillery, Major General Jaggi Chand and a few others. We spent nearly a week in Sweden and saw the gun being demonstrated in various configurations including firing on the range. By all accounts the gun suited our requirement. It was also a howitzer, that is, it was suitable for deployment in the mountains (it could fire at a high angle; in *upper register* in gunner jargon). It was not fully self-propelled, but it was mounted on a wheeled chassis and it could move under its own power for short distances. In other words, it had a "shoot and scoot" capability (useful for avoiding counter shelling by enemy). In short, we came back satisfied. As per the normal practice, I discussed the comparative merits and demerits of the equipment with my colleagues who had accompanied me and put together an after-visit evaluation report for the chief (and ultimately the MoD). The report summed up a full cross evaluation of different guns on offer, but by a sixth sense, I did not append a final recommendation as per the usual procedure. (Actually I was alarmed at a lot of loose talk about the entire project). The chief read through the report but was mystified that I had not given a final recommendation. He asked me about it, but I demurred by saying that as he was the senior most artillery officer of the army, it would have been presumptuous on my part to write the final recommendation. Anyhow, he must have given his recommendation while forwarding the report to the Ministry of Defence (MoD) because, soon after, a few guns came for field trials by an appointed trial team at our School of Artillery at Deolali. After the exhaustive negotiating process at various levels, a contract was signed on 24 March 1987. However (lucky for me) before the contract was signed,

Delegation to Bofors, Sweden, 1979

I had moved on to my next assignment as GOC 1 Corps after handing over to my successor, General Sundarji who steered the proposal in the final stages. It was a USD1.3 billion deal for supply of 410 guns followed by indigenous licensed production in India of double that number in a phased manner. Later, around May 1987, reports started appearing in the media that kickbacks of the order of USD 10 million had been paid to the higher ups in India starting with the Prime Minister Rajiv Gandhi. Subsequently, on 27 October 1989, the CBI charge sheeted Quattrocchi (an Italian middleman alleged to be close to the Gandhi family), Win Chadha (Indian middleman), Rajiv Gandhi, Mr. S. B. Bhatnagar, the then defence secretary and a few others. Such is the state of our judicial processes that nothing much came out of the furor except that the follow on numbers got interrupted. All the principal characters died off, Quattrocchi, Chadha, Rajiv, Bhatnagar and few of the others. Later the same Bofors gun gave sterling service in the Kargil conflict.

The upshot of the entire scandal was a hectic controversy about the procedures that were being followed for acquisition of arms. Since then, the process of purchase of arms has been made highly complex and more to the point, the mandarins at the MoD have got an opportunity to enhance their power and authority at the expense of the military. The revised Defence Procurement Procedures (DPP) was promulgated by the MoD on 1 June 2013. The very laudable and ostensible aim of the DPP is to expedite capital procurement and develop a strong indigenous defence industrial base by creating a level playing field for the Indian industry. The procedures are designed to ensure highest standards of transparency and probity. Further, the DPP or procedures are aimed to be dovetailed into other desirables like the Defence Production Policy (DPrP) 2011 and the offset policy, which is meant to help India build a defence industrial base through joint ventures and acquisition of foreign technology. Another principle laid down is the desirability of making deals based on multiple vendors which is often not always possible. For example, in the last 40 years, except for the solitary incidence of the deal for Bofor guns, all other contracts have been concluded on single vendor basis or have been government to government deals.

Make in India Initiative

In furtherance of "Make in India" initiative of the current BJP government, the defence manufacture has been thrown open to the private sector. However, the progress has been extremely slow. The Directorate of Indigenization has since been placed under the MGO (one of the PSOs) under the Army Chief. But despite all efforts, till now the fact is that bulk of our requirement continues to be imported. The performance of Defence Public Sector Undertakings (DPSUs) as also the ordinance factories is woefully behind schedules or is not up to the required quality. It is obvious that there has to be greater reliance on the private industry which demands assurance of a level playing field, simpler and stable procurement procedures before the private sector invests huge funds. The private industry will also want a commitment or a reasonable assurance for the long term patronage. Nevertheless, the requirement is that services must have support of a vibrant industry and advance technology not only in defence armaments but in all segments. India has a long way to catch up to make up for lost time. General V.P. Malik, who was the army chief during the Kargil operations, said in an interview to TNN on 20 Dec 2015, that India cannot be well prepared for future high tech wars as long as 70% of the sophisticated equipment was imported. Without total self-reliance, national security would always be subject to whims and fancies of outsiders. At the same time, the DRDO and numerous ordnance establishments need to be made accountable. General Malik pointed out that he felt the pinch of dependency during the Kargil war when urgent spares, ammunition and other equipment were refused by the manufacturers/exporters on one excuse or another.

It is therefore imperative that we must draw up a perspective plan for industry for ten, twenty and thirty years and then pursue the stated objectives with a single minded focus. It will be pointless to get lost in the morass of procedures and red tape. We must prioritize, keeping focus on really important aspects. As it is, we have managed to evolve dreadful and dilatory procedures which confuse and confound all parties. The Defence Procurement Procedures (DPP) was daunting enough; thereafter the numerous amendments have added layers of regulations rather than simplifying matters. At present, the procurement goes through eleven phases to the contract stage, requires seven committees for evaluation, and has thirteen different departmental organs to execute and vet the process. Further, all the agencies report to different financial heads. There is no central agency to monitor the overall process and not even a central file tracking system. This is deeply unsatisfactory. We need to evolve simple and practical procedures with a view to produce results. Subsequently, if there is corruption or culpable delay or wilful mistakes, heads should roll.

Counter Productive Procedures

Have the new procedures produced the desired results? Have they succeeded in wiping out corruption or have they only resulted in delay? It is difficult to say but the IAS lobby has certainly added to their authority and control. It does not make sense. The important point is to ensure that the modernization needs of the services are taken care of in time. Ever since the ancient times, the army is the one to have borne the brunt of fighting. Even in the case of Kashmir, the army is the key. Indeed, without denigrating the importance of navy and air force in any way, one cannot overemphasize the centrality and importance of a strong and modern army. The weaknesses of the present system are easy to identify. At my level of deputy chief of the army staff, I repeatedly highlighted the unsatisfactory state of army's modernization. For some reason, the air force and navy seem to fare better (ministerial bias!); they get a larger share of the capital budget to begin with, yet consume over 80% of their allocation, whereas the army, the least modernized service is forced to surrender/re-appropriate its capital budget for its inability to procure equipment in time due to obstructions from the MoD. There has not been a single big ticket acquisition on capital account for the army for the last 40 years, in spite of representations by respective chiefs. The other important point to be borne in mind is that in any procedures for acquisition of arms, the final say must belong to the principal stakeholder, that is the service concerned and not the ministry nor the DRDO because in the final analysis, it is the soldier, naval rating or the airman who will go to battle, not the IAS official, or the DRDO. In other words, *authority must go together with accountability*. Next, we must understand that procedures alone will never eliminate corruption. The wrong doer will always be a step ahead. What will discourage or lessen corruption is the certainty of punishment on getting caught, but this happens to be our weakest point. The focus should be on effectiveness and results, not corruption or procedures.

Is Our Military Capability of the Desired Kind?

India spends billions of dollars on defence. Yet for years ever since independence, we do not seem to have found a viable response to the never ending Pak transgressions. The question often arises: is the country getting the right returns from the resources expended? We maintain a huge military apparatus: a very professional and well equipped army of a million plus: a well-regarded air force, and a navy boasting an aircraft carrier and nuclear powered submarine capability. We are a nuclear weapon power at par with Pakistan. Ours is a much larger economy expected to top a Rupees trillion mark in the foreseeable future. We are a stable democracy. Our bureaucracies are supposed to be stacked with brain power. In sum, India is bigger, better and mightier than Pakistan. But for some reason, all our superiorities have not deterred repeated Pakistan depredations; Jihadist attacks, bomb blasts, plane hijackings, the attack on our Parliament and the infamous commando assault on Mumbai. Currently, Pakistan is instigating and stoking a virulent anti India insurgency in Jammu and Kashmir with the yearly drama of infiltrations in summer. Worse, there are disturbing signs of their latest efforts to subvert our Muslim community making some headway through Indian Mujahideen movement. Their hand is seen behind the fake currency racket and in almost each and every insurgency or uprising in our country.

To crown all, they make no secret of their animus against India. Instead they proudly proclaim their designs "to make India bleed from a thousand cuts". Recently, in 2015, their army chief has gone on record to claim Kashmir as "unfinished business of partition". Pakistan strenuously denies India a space in Afghanistan affairs. It has ceded thousands of kilometers of our territory illegally to China. Where does the problem lie? True, an all-out war between the two nuclear powers may be out of the question. But what kind of punitive action, or surgical strike would be still possible within the bounds of a nuclear threshold. Is this going to be the face of new wars? If so, are we preparing accordingly for tailor-made military capabilities, so that the military can offer viable options to the political leadership?

There is too much of loose talk, mostly out of ignorance, to the effect the government lacks the guts to retaliate against provocations. The fact is that on several occasions our leadership has responded to adverse situations with courage; witness Lal Bahadur Shastri's bold decision to aggress across the international boundary into Pakistan in 1965. Similarly, Indira Gandhi went to war against Pak genocide in East Pakistan in 1971. Perhaps we can say that on both occasions India had the priceless advantage of politico-military accord. In sum, political leadership can only be as good as its military capability and readiness. The reverse is equally true. Therefore, it is imperative that India should figure out security procedures and structures which will make possible viable strategies to retaliate against any transgressions by hostile elements. Clearly such responses will have to be properly prepared and rehearsed in different scenarios. The targets and force structures would need to be worked out in great detail. Then the strikes will need to be mounted and orchestrated in a professional manner. We will also have to take into account and prepare for counter strikes by the enemy. The nuclear bogey needs to be faced fair and square. After all, Pakistan had no hesitation in launching Kargil offensive despite the advent of nuclears on both sides.

Such capabilities will perforce have to be integrated, tri service solutions, which brings us face to face with the prickly issue of integrated operations under a CDS for single point coordination within the different services of the military as also for the politico-military interface. Operations of this nature and sensitivity demand secrecy of the highest order. Indeed, we have to be careful that there is no careless chatter on this subject by a wise restraint on the subject by politico military leadership and media alike. A case in point is the "Cold Start" strategy evolved by the Army as a possible form of response to certain situations vis-à-vis Pakistan. There was a lot of talk and braggadocio in the army circles including the schools of instruction. There was open controversy with the Indian Air Force. Consequently, the Pakistani military and its ISI claimed that any such initiative by India will be met with a matching counter force. For good measure they claimed that Pakistan had already planned for counter response and that they were on the verge of developing or acquiring tactical nuclear weapons for just such an eventuality. The doctrine of "Cold Start" was put in Cold storage! In the same vein, there was a lot of talk in all circles about India's plans to raise a new corps for deployment in Arunachal Pradesh to counter threat from China. For some reason, this proposal also seems to have been put in on the slow-burner. In contrast, the Chinese plans for modernization and development of new weapon systems are characterized as "developments for peace".

Soon after I assumed charge of the appointment of deputy chief, I had a mighty jolt in my personal life. My daughter, Jyoti died on 19 August 1979 leaving a baby boy of barely two years of age. She had had a turbulent marriage, a wayward husband and non-supportive in-laws. I have never forgiven myself for not taking firm action in time. The signs were there. After child birth I had taken her away to Mhow but stupidly, I relented and allowed her to go back after 3-4 months. Parents are in a quandary in such situations. We often take the conciliatory line for the long time good but it sometimes proves to be the wrong choice. My wife and I would constantly worry and discuss the options. Divorce seemed such a dire solution with unforeseen impact on our daughter and the little boy. I was also deeply involved in my professional life and onerous duties of deputy chief. The stark reality is that I dithered. Consequently, she just withered away and died in my arms. We were all heartbroken. The chief and other colleagues, General Sushil Kumar (my DSD), General S.K. Sinha (AG) and many others gave us unstinted support.

Later, I got embroiled in a nasty legal battle with her husband and more so, his very obstreperous parents. I was determined to bring up the child myself, unhindered and totally segregated from their evil influence, whereas his father wanted to assert his right to custody of the child, as the surviving parent. I fought tooth and nail and knocked on all doors. The case dragged on (on purpose, as per advice of my canny lawyer). The inevitable happened; the father got married to a foreign girl, and ultimately agreed to concede the child's custody to me, but the case consumed a good five years of our life. But, life is full of compensations. Bringing up of the delightful child exposed my wife and I to joys of parenting and making us a young couple all over again. We were able to bring him up as a son and give him excellent education including graduation at Georgetown University in Washington. Settled in USA, he is the love of our life and he and his wife give us more happiness than can be imagined.

Awarded Param Vashist Sewa Medal

In February1980, I was awarded the Param Vashisht Seva Medal (PVSM) in recognition of meritorious service in the post of deputy chief and as Commandant College of Combat. The services set great store by medals and honorifics, which count more than monetary awards. It is a part of service ethos that soldiers will risk limb and life for recognition and fame. Monarchs have exploited this urge since the dawn of time. The awards are invested by the President in person in a grand ceremony with a host of dignitaries from Prime Minister down attending. The investiture is held in the grand Durbar Hall of the Rashtrapati Bhavan and followed by a reception when the all and mighty mingle with the awardees and their close family members in an informal manner. There is a flurry of photography by family and by professional photographers at hand. Another welcome feature of the ceremony is that the awardees are granted the privilege of inviting their close relatives like parents and wives. The out of town guests travel at government expense and are appropriately housed. My father had passed away, so it gave me great pleasure and pride to invite my oldest brother and his wife to come for the occasion from Pune. In a way it was appropriate as he had been instrumental in my joining the Army. They were both thrilled and suitably impressed. My wife escorted them and they all proudly witnessed President Sanjeeva Reddy pin the medal on my chest.

Around this time, my Masters Degree for "Defence Science" also arrived from the University of Madras. It made a nice brace of achievements. In April 1980, I visited the Mountain Kingdom of Bhutan in my capacity of deputy chief. We had a special relationship with Bhutan. India gave full material support to the tiny Royal Bhutan Army (strength varying from 6,000 to 8,000 soldiers) for training and equipment. We maintained a training mission, Indian Military Training Team (IMTRAT) at Thimpu, capital of Bhutan. The deputy chief chaperoned the budget for the force through the Parliament, so an annual visit by me was an important occasion for them. Officially, I was the guest of the chief of the Royal Bhutan Army, then General Lam Dorji (his rank kept in step with the rank of the officer-in-charge of our commandant of IMTRAT). My wife, son Rajiv and young Aditya accompanied me.

On the first day of my arrival, my party and officers and ladies of IMTRAT were entertained by the queen mother (the king was not married then) to a performance of Bhutanese dragon dances in her palace grounds. The performance was interrupted by a sudden shower, half way through the show; so the queen graciously invited us to step into her palace. The ladies were ushered into her private chambers and offered new sarees to change into. We all trooped back out after the shower had stopped. It transpired that after the show and light refreshment, our ladies asked to go back to change into their, by now dried sarees, but the queen mother said that the sarees given by her were to be taken as a personal gift. The IMTRAT ladies were of course thrilled. Uzi was in his elements playing with some palace children. The next few days were given to meetings with our training team. The important part of my visit was a ceremonial call on the young king in his ornate chambers. I exchanged scarves with the king, and after a cup of Bhutanese tea and some small talk, I was bowed out. The Chief of Bhutan Army, Lam Dorji had some problems about the supply of molasses from India for their distillery which I promised to sort out. Bhutan distillery is a venture of the Royal Bhutan Army and makes rum and a good Pan liqueur with an uncanny taste and flavor of "Pan". Lam Dorji became a personal friend and we have kept in touch till now.

On 12 May1980 was little son Aditya's third birthday which we decided to celebrate at the cantonment hill town of Sabathu. We drove up in my car to the tiny but a typical Inspection Bungalow, found all over the Himalayas. After the 4 GR Centre shifted from Bakloe to Sabathu, it became the home for the combined training center for 1st and 4th Gorkha rifles. True to the army tradition, the commandant called on me and offered all help to make our stay comfortable. Then to my surprise, he said that they would be honoured if I agreed to take the salute at their forthcoming 'attestation parade' (passing out parade) to mark culmination of the training of recruits and their induction into the army as soldiers. As the serving Colonel of the 8 Gorkha Rifles, I could hardly refuse. But not having brought my uniform and trappings, I had to telephone my staff officer in Delhi to scramble up the necessary things which he did. So I was able to perform the required ceremonials including an address to the newly inducted young soldiers. It was interesting viewing for my wife, more so for my sons, Rajiv and Aditya.

Next, there was a pleasant interlude for me and a good change from the hot-house atmosphere of Army HQ, when the chief asked me to go to take the salute at the Passing Out Parade of the cadets at the Officer Training Academy, Chennai. The Indian Military Academy in Dehradun, trained and commissioned regular officers for the army. The Academy in Chennai was established on 15 January 1963 to train officers for the short service commission for the army. Now it has developed as a full-fledged Military Academy at par with IMA Dehra Dun: producing a large number of officers who have performed with distinction in peace and war. I was quite pleased at the prospect of being the inspecting officer of a ceremonial passing out parade, as against being a cadet at the other end. I went to Chennai where I was received by the commandant who briefed me about the procedure with which I was quite familiar. I enjoyed reviewing the Parade the next morning. The cadets were smartly turned out and their drill movements were of a high standard. In my address, I complimented the cadets, congratulated their instructors and emphasized that they were fortunate to command some of the finest soldiers in the world and that their mission will be to be worthy of the soldiers that they would command. I think it was an inspiring message to impart. Later, I met General Inder Gill my old DMO, who had retired by now and settled down in Chennai. He complimented me on my speech. Coming from him that was high praise indeed!

Next, I moved up the ladder to the command of a corps. It held the same rank of a Lt General but was higher in importance. Besides, it indicated that I had been considered fit for elevation to an Army Commander. As per the rules, a prospective army commander should have done a graded staff appointment and the command of a corps and still have about two years of service left. An officers' career in the army is a long and arduous journey which does not forgive the slightest slip. One also needs enormous luck. I was on an inspection tour of the Military College of Telecommunication Engineering (MCTE) at Mhow when there was a call for me from the Chief, General Krishna Rao. He told me that my appointment as GOC 1 Corps had been cleared by the MoD. It was good news because 1 Corps was the premier corps, designated as the "Strike Corps" of the Indian Army. So, I rang up my wife at Delhi telling her the good news. Being the practical army wife, she set about packing and worrying about school admission for Aditya. Meanwhile, my son Rajiv had also been able to get an offer of admission in Claremont College in USA for a course of MBA. What is more, he had also secured the all-important US visa for the same. So, after a disastrous run of luck in 1979, things seemed to be working out well for us again.

9

Command of 1 Corps, Mathura

I was appointed General Officer Commanding (GOC) 1 Corps in early August 1981. Mathura is situated close to Delhi, so we moved by road in my car, with the baggage following in a truck. However the usual rigmarole of packing and opening up at the destination had to be borne by my wife; by now she was a veteran of moves and had worked out a drill. I once suggested to her to write a booklet of guidance for the officers' wives. She said that it was something that each housewife learnt by doing. This time she also had the help of my son, Rajiv who had secured his admission for an MBA course at Claremont College in California, USA. To fill the waiting gap, he had also picked up a short course at Delhi University. Like the wives, the army children had also perfected a drill for the regime of frequent moves. We were received by General Tirath Singh Oberoi, a decorated veteran of the Parachute Regiment, whom I was to relieve. A fine soldier and a perfect gentleman, he had very thoughtfully vacated the flag Staff house and moved into the corps guest house. There is a flurry of activity on taking over of a new assignment apart from the usual social occasions of farewell and welcome; so it was very helpful to settle down quickly in the permanent accommodation.

1 Corps has the distinction to be designated as the Strike Corps of the Army. That is why it has been stationed at Mathura in the interior of the country. It is also appropriately located

so as to be suitably placed for access to the Northern, Central and Southern sectors. It has a very interesting and versatile role and I was happy to be given the opportunity to handle the very many issues involved. Soon after bidding farewell to General Oberoi, I plunged into the operational milieu. The first task I addressed was to make a thorough examination of the mobilization plans of the Corps because, as I saw it, the Corps had to get to the required area in quick time and properly organized to accomplish the required tasks. In such scenarios time is of essence. My brigadier in charge of administration and his staff were taxed to the hilt with their patience stretched to the limit. Every morning I would arrive with fresh questions or new ideas and back we would go to the movement tables. I explained to my team that if we could shave off a day in the total time factor, or even by half a day, it would be worth the trouble. Apart from the movement schedule of the columns, the composition of the individual groups was also important. To make matters more interesting the inter se priority of arrival of different elements had to be flexible, contingent upon the evolving operational situation. We war-gamed various contingencies. All in all, I think we did a lot of good work. At least it made us all aware of the complexities of the problems.

The Corps had to have flexible approach to operational tasks. Our primary role was to undertake offensive operations often to exploit the success achieved by formations on the ground. That scenario would dictate strategy and tactics of rapid follow on and pursuit of the enemy who had been ejected from his defensive position. The emphasis would be upon risk and bold action. In case the enemy defensive system had not been fully broken into, the pace and nature of operations for the strike corps would be of a more deliberate nature; in other words, instead of a headlong pursuit of withdrawing enemy, we would have to first reinforce the formation in line. In either case we would have to negotiate the next line of obstacles before a full break out. The Corps had also to be prepared to shore up defensive posture of the formations in contact, if our defensive system appeared to be in danger of collapse. If that was not complex enough, such permutations and combinations had to be worked out for each sector. It also involved familiarization with terrain and existing lay out of the formations in different sectors. So a great deal of discussions and coordinating conferences were needed. I was constantly on the move. I visited XVI Corps in Jammu- Shakargarh Sector where I Corps had distinguished itself in the Battle of Basantar River in 1971, for discussions with General Ashok Handoo (we had been instructors together in Staff College). I also had a long and productive visit to HQ Northern Command under General Smoky Malhotra; his chief of staff General Bhupinder Singh was an old friend from IMA.

The Corps Exercise

Another priority of mine was to hold a Corps exercise. The Chief, General Krishna Rao, approved the idea of an exercise but would not allow the Corps to move up to Jammu area. So we had to organize it in general area of Mathura–Vrindavan. As far as I know this was the biggest exercise held by the strike corps for a very long time, if ever. I discussed the matter with my divisional commanders including 31 Armoured Division which was a part of the Corps. Everyone was quite enthusiastic and gave many good suggestions for the exercise. I appointed a drafting-planning committee headed by Brigadier Shakti Singh, Commander 50 Parachute Brigade and set aside three hours every afternoon of my time to work with the Team on the settings, narratives, tasking of divisional commanders and schedule of the exercise. I had written many exercises in my service at different levels and had held exercises in all formations that I served in, but this was by far the biggest venture that I undertook.

The setting chosen was the most appropriate to the role assigned to the Corps, namely a break out battle after a hole had been punched through the defensive system of the enemy. The corps was to pour through the gap created in the enemy positions, break out enlarging the gap and race to objectives deep inside the enemy territory by fluid offensive strikes, by infantry armour columns under the cover and close support of own air force. For realism, we posed an obstacle of a defended canal, which the corps was to overcome, by way of a water obstacle. To ensure that momentum of the advance was maintained, we worked in a parachute drop of a battalion, behind the supposed enemy holding positions on the canal. We planned the para drop to take place at night with limited help from moonlight in the second half of the night. Having completed the paperwork and reconnoitered the ground with my drafting team, I gave the final finishing touches and was satisfied that we had prepared a very good exercise without any flaws or loopholes. I explained the overall layout and main profile of the exercise to the Chief who gave his approval after suggesting a few changes. A true blue blooded professional that he was, he promised to attend a good part of the exercise including the para drop at night and said that he would bring along the Northern Army Commander too.

Next, I briefly explained the aims and general sequence of events of the exercise to my commanders who were to participate in the exercise. Traditionally, all large scale exercises with troops are held after the April harvesting season to avoid hardship to farmers and to minimize monetary compensation to be paid to them for any damage to the crops. So, we scheduled the exercise to start in the last week of April 1982 and to go on for 2-3 weeks. Mathura area warms up mid-March onwards but fortunately the weather gods smiled on our efforts and a few unseasonal showers cooled the temperatures. The exercise progressed flawlessly and the Chief was especially pleased to witness the night parachute drop, with the troops coming down accurately right in front of the spectator stand. He complimented Brigadier Shakti Singh for high standard of training of the 50 Parachute Brigade. The canal crossing too went off very well and so did the break out inland. On conclusion of the exercise, we carried out a series of discussions and analyses so as to synthesize our experience into a nascent concept which generated a great deal of interest. So we can say that the aim and purpose of the exercise was achieved.

Ancient Mathura

Meanwhile, I made a number of improvements in our surroundings as was my wont in all cantonments that I had the opportunity to serve in. I laid out extensive lawns in the flagstaff house compound including building of a tree house to the great delight of my little son (Aditya). I improved the Corps headquarters area and built up a beautiful office complex. I also improved upon the main park in the cantonment. Mathura is the abode of Lord Krishna, and his legendary dalliance with the Gopis. My wife, a Krishna devotee, was very happy to see the fabled landmarks of the landscape, like Radha's village Barsana, and the mountain of Goverdhan which, as per legend, was lifted by Lord Krishna on his little finger to provide refuge to the people drowning in a cataclysmic flood.

We got a lot of visitors including foreign guests. They would want to visit some of the ancient temples. I used to be hesitant about taking them to the decrepit and ill-kept temples, so I would take them instead to the Hare Rama Hare Krishna temple which was at least kept spotlessly clean. Once the commissioner of Mathura Division, Mata Parshad came calling on me. I suggested that he should persuade upon the temple authorities to clean up the storied temples. He laughed saying that if he tried anything of the sort, he would get his transfer orders the next day. I realized that, being of Dalit background, he was skating on thin ice in this center of Hindu orthodoxy. However, I do think that the wise men of the Hindu religion should put their mind to constructive initiatives such as restoration and proper upkeep of the ancient temples some of which are more than 800 years old. There was the usual good convent school in Mathura. I think the nuns must have been mystified to have to give admission to my little son Aditya who by all appearances was the age of my grandson (which he was). My wife and I were once invited to the usual 'tiny tots' show at the convent. On conclusion, my wife was asked to give away the prizes. When Aditya's name was announced and he came to receive the prize, he was dumbfounded to see his mother giving him the prize. Mathura also has a first rate museum of artifacts and statues of the Kushan and Kushak period.

Annual Leave in USA

After the successful completion of the Corps exercise, I decided to go on annual leave to USA to visit my son Rajiv, who had got a job in a small east coast town called Greenville. So, my wife and I along with Aditya (or Uzi) took off in first week of July 1981. Before finalizing the programme, I wanted to check with my friend and batch mate, Lt General Raj Kumar Jasbir Singh, who was then the Military Secretary (MS) to the Chief as the air was thick with rumours about my impending promotion to army commander and I did not want to have to return half way through my leave after incurring a lot of expense. So, one Sunday, I motored down from Mathura to RK's house in Delhi. On meeting him, I enquired about the rumours. His was a sensitive appointment, so I only enquired if I would have an uninterrupted holiday for full two months. He thought about it for a few minutes but said that I could plan on two months in the States. That seemed quite positive so off we went. We had a great vacation, in Claremont and drove up to San Francisco where my wife's sister lived. We drove on the most scenic Highway One which wends its way from Los Angeles to SFO (San Francisco), along the celebrated route all along the coast, with Pacific Ocean on one side and beautiful pine country on the other, dotted with very pretty small towns all the way. We made a grand picnic day out of it, getting to SFO in the evening tired but happy.

The next few weeks were wonderful. We enjoyed visiting the very many sights of the big town which is considered the most touristic town of the west coast with quaint network of roads and avenues straight up and down the steep hills. The Golden Gate Bridge spanning the Pacific Ocean is a wonder of engineering. It is long and high enough to let fair sized ocean going vessels to pass under. We did the usual tourist places, a delightful tour of the China Town, a day at the Fishermen Warf, rode the quaint and famous tram ride and saw the fearful Alcatraz prison on an island surrounded by the shark infested sea around, which only a single successful jail break took place in its entire history.

It all seemed too good to last, and sure enough, one fine morning, I got a phone call from the Chief of Staff of Central Command Lucknow, Major General Nimmi Puri (an old friend) who broke the happy tidings of my promotion to Army Commander Central Command. The incumbent, General Wag Pinto had retired and gone. Nimmi was anxious to know as to how soon could I return. News of this kind coming amidst an idyllic holiday can be a bit disconcerting. But a promotion is a promotion, that too for elevation to the Command of Army. It is welcome news by any standards, and after the initial shock, the whole house rang with shouts of congratulations. There were frantic calls to the airlines for change of bookings and so on. My brother-in-law, being in the tourism department of the Indian Consulate, helped us. First, I had to go to Mathura to handover charge of the Corps and thence proceed to Lucknow, with my wife following after all chores of packing and moving the family. Many years later, when both Jasbir and I had retired, reminiscing about the incident, Jasbir apologized saying that apart from confidentiality of the matter, the Chief's recommendations had been sent up to the ministry, and since appointments of army commanders required cabinet approval, it was hard to forecast the time lag involved. The incident shows the army ethics which over-ride the ties of friendships and personal relationships.

Army Commander, Lucknow

I assumed the appointment of GOC-in-C Central Command, Lucknow in August 1982. To be elevated to this post is the fulfillment of an officer's ambition. I was to join the elite of four army commanders just below the Chief. In point of fact the appointment of army commander signified that the officer is fit to be the Chief. Thereafter, the final step to the chief is usually by tradition, only a question of whoever would be the senior most in service, when the incumbent retires. In our case, after General Krishna Rao's retirement, General Arun Vaidya took over. Thereafter, Sunderji was the senior most followed by General Chibber and myself. In the event when General Vaidya retired, Sunderji succeeded him as the next chief, and Chibber and I retired on completion of our tenures as army commanders.

The Army Central Command had a huge sprawl. It included the States of Uttar Pradesh, Madhya Pradesh, Bihar and Orissa (since renamed Odisha). I oversaw the Army units and installations located within these States. My interaction with the governments in the respective states was confined largely to courtesy calls on the respective Governors and Chief Ministers, excepting when the Army was called upon to provide assistance in cases involving law and order, disaster relief (flood and other natural calamities) and affairs concerning ex-servicemen. Since, the headquarters of Army Central Command was located in Lucknow which was the capital of UP, the civil military cooperation was very intimate. Through my stay at Lucknow, I developed cordial relations with the Governor, C.P.N. Singh, an elderly gentleman of the

GOC-in-C Central Command, Lucknow

old world courtesies, who was very kind to me. He had made a name for himself when, as Indian ambassador in Nepal, he played an important role in the Nepal revolution and end of the rule of the Ranas, who as prime ministers were the real rulers. The kings had been reduced to the position of mere figure heads. Towards the end of 1950, King Tribhuvan revolted against the unjust system and escaped to India through the Indian Embassy in Kathmandu. C.P.N. Singh thereafter was rewarded by important governmental assignments for his adroit handling of the entire incident.

At Lucknow, he graciously accorded me the status of an equal, though way senior in age and rank, and extended all courtesies. For instance, for the presidentship of the Mohamed Bagh Club in Lucknow, an old prestigious institution, he agreed to a system of rotational presidentship between the Governor and the Army Commander. I was frequently invited to the Governor's house whenever some dignitaries were visiting the State. On the Army side, I had the pleasure of hosting him at my house (Flag Staff House) and also at the Command Officers Mess. My staff and I also developed excellent working and personal relations with the Chief Secretary and other secretaries of the State. We organized annual cricket matches and so on. A big occasion was the annual civil-military conference held at Command Headquarters to which, the invitees were the chief secretaries of all states involved. I worked very hard on this event and to make it really meaningful, I arranged to call up a group of ex-servicemen from the concerned states so as to give the official an opportunity to mix with them and interact at a personal level. Many of the officials admitted that they had not seen, leave alone spoken to ex-servicemen, on a one-on-one basis. I emphasized that we were missing out on high grade

With Governor CPN Singh in Command Officers' Mess

material for lack of a proper understanding of the situation. The point to understand is that by employing these fine men, we are not doing them a favour but that in actual fact, they would be doing the system a favour. My intention was to drive home this message to the state officials who controlled a number of industrial units set up for promoting government or quasi-government industries, in the various states. Later during my tenure, and in fact throughout my career, I never missed an opportunity to promote the re-employment of ex-soldiers in the corporate world.

The operational responsibility of the command was to guard the UP-Tibet border which was taken care of by a mix of regular forces and units of armed police forces, and units of Scouts with headquarters at Harsil and Joshimath, which gave me an opportunity to visit these exotic places as also to visit the fabled temple of Badrinath, and the "Valley of Flowers". I dodged the arduous climb up to the pilgrimage site of Hemkunt Sahib at 17,000 feet above the sea level, by flying up instead on a helicopter. This part of Garhwal Himalayas is revered as the abode of gods and lies en route to the pilgrimage to Kailash Mansarover (the latter in Chinese territory).

Harsil village has a colourful history. A British Army deserter (officer) named Wilson in his wanderings to the upper reaches of the Harsil river saw tremendous commercial value in the dense forests of pine and deodar (cedar) trees. So, the legend has it, that he came back to the Court of Rajah of Tehri (Garhwal) and offered a bag of 400 silver coins, requesting grant of logging rights along the Harsil River. The Rajah and his courtiers, bemused at the sight of a bedraggled mad white man, accepted the 400 rupees and nodded his assent without realizing that he had given away the untold wealth of timbre by a perfunctory wave of his hand. Subsequently, Wilson became a legend in his lifetime. He hired local loggers to chop the trees and float them down the fast flowing river. In the end, it was Wilson Sahib who had the last laugh. He set up a thriving timbre business and amassed great wealth and status, and was treated as a minor Rajah, even minting his own currency. He married a local woman (or women) and built a massive log palace in Harsil. Apparently, even PM Indira Gandhi was once put up in the Wilson Sahibs palace. I had no intention to live in the huge gloomy structure, probably haunted, but the Scouts wing stationed at Harsil made use of it as a guest house.

The command area contained a large number of stations or cantonments so I was out on tour for 15 to 20 days of the month. Apart from the field formations such as divisions and brigades, there were static units like the army instructional establishments like the IMA, War College, Infantry School, and very many teaching establishments of arms and services. Then there were depots and other store holding units for the army like ordinance, electrical and mechanical engineers, supply depots and so on. We had as many as fifty or more cantonments. A cantonment is an army establishment; a fair sized town administered by an elected Cantonment Board under the sub area commander. Initially these started as exclusive military stations for the soldiers, but most of them had mushroomed into fairly big towns with bustling bazaars and civilian houses. The army had striven to keep out the predatory community of "builders and developers", with the result that even today the cantonments remain as havens of cleanliness and bungalows with gardens and hedges, though there are frequent proposals to throw them open to "democratic forces" which in effect means uncontrolled building activity. I made it a point to visit the posts in snowbound areas in winter, including the "strays" like posts of armed police and ITBP, taking them baskets of fresh fruit and vegetables and *mithai* (Indian Sweets), making it worth their while to have worked hard to clear the snow from the helipad. To help me to get about I had the facility of aircraft and helicopters from the air force. In addition, I had the luxury of a private railway saloon, an old world relic and the envy of other army commanders. The Command House was a grand edifice, possibility the best among the commands. It had extensive gardens, fruit orchards, even a large fish pond for growing edible fish. The command house always won the annual prize for the best garden layout and potted flowers. The grand manor house had two wings, the main wing for my personal residence and a separate guest wing with five bedroom suites: both linked by a grand colonnaded corridor. In the army, these official residences are usually well maintained, with successive incumbents making improvements. The pity is that the senior officers themselves are so busy visiting outlying stations that they get little time to enjoy staying in them. This happens more and more as one moves up in rank and position. During our stay, my wife thought it unfair that all the time and effort lavished on the command house and the gardens should go unseen. She wanted to throw open the gardens and lawns to the ladies of the station. So, she organized an at-home (tea and *samosas* etc.) for all the officers' ladies of the station plus guests from the civil side, when the flowers were in full bloom. She also requested the horticulture specialists to be at hand to explain and describe various plants. I believe that upwards of 300-400 ladies turned up dressed in all their finery. She told me afterwards that the occasion proved to be a great success. The men were not invited but she had arranged to have a video shot of the party. We still have the video cassette and often screen it for our guests.

IMA Golden Jubilee

Indian Military Academy had started as a fully functional officer training institution on 1 October 1932. So it was decided to celebrate its golden jubilee on 1 October 1982 in an elaborate ceremony. The PM, Indira Gandhi accepted the invitation to be the chief guest and to take the salute on a special Golden Jubilee Parade as a highlight of the programme. The Chief, General Krishna Rao was to be the chief host. Since the IMA Dehra Dun fell in the jurisdiction of central command, the chief asked me to be the ceremonial escort to the PM. The guest list included a large number of civil and military dignitaries starting with

C.P.N. Singh, Governor of Uttar Pradesh. The PM's own party was quite large. She was accompanied by her son Rajiv; I met him for the first time, a fine young man still unspoiled by the courtiers and flatterers. He had a natural charm and dignity. Later he was to be catapulted into the national arena after Indira Gandhi's assassination. Indira Gandhi was her usual self, palpable self-assurance and a tremendous air of authority. As her escorting officer for the occasion I had the opportunity to see her various incarnations. I found her also supremely intelligent and perceptive.

I received her and her entourage at Saharanpur air base, where we had her shifted to a helicopter for the flight to Dehra Dun. The Russian helicopter was extremely noisy and she was quite busy talking to Rajiv, so leaving them to themselves, I sat in a separate row. Sometime into the flight, she wanted some

PM Indira Gandhi at IMA Golden Jubilee, Oct. 1982

information, like to ask if they were on time. Lost in thought and deafened by the helicopter noise, I did not hear her. Next I was rudely shocked by her snapping of her fingers to get my attention. Nobody had dared snap fingers at me in my living memory. It was on the tip of my tongue to tell her that even the PM is not supposed to snap her fingers at her army commanders. I did not tell her that, though I wish I had, but it certainly put me off for the rest of the flight. Later, ruminating on the incident, I felt that her unmannerly gesture was symptomatic of the malaise of our society or the lingering vestige of the feudal characteristic of the Nehru dynasty because they had ruled India for years. Perhaps it also showed signs of decline of the Nehru era. There is a telling story, probably apocryphal, that when the great Mughal Empire was dying and the British had finally broken the Indian mutiny, a young British officer at the head of a small detachment entered the Mughal palace. He found the palace totally abandoned. Going into the kings' chamber, he was amazed to find a decrepit old man who was identified as the last Mughal Emperor, Bahadur Shah Zafar. Mystified, the British officer asked, how come, the king did not make good his escape while all else had run away. The Emperor is said to have wailed: "how could we (royal plural!) leave when the official responsible for helping me to put on my shoes had run away"! Nothing could be more depictive of the rot setting in. It is perhaps an over-simplification but the fact is that the decades-long run of the Congress party rule did not survive long after her demise. It also exemplified the cavalier attitude of the government, and equally to blame, its acquiescence of it by the military. It is said that Pandit Nehru was often heard to say that "these generals have to be kept in their place".

At Dehradun, Mrs. Gandhi was put up in the guest cottage of the very elegant house of the commandant. I briefed her on the parade next morning and asked her to study the booklet on her night stand which explained the sequence of events of the parade and so on. For the first evening of her arrival, she was to have a quiet dinner in her quarters. However, the Chief and I were invited for drinks with the commandant, General Mathew Thomas in the evening at his house. We were just into our first drink, I think, and who should walk in but the PM with Rajiv in tow. General Krishna Rao, known for his *sangfroid,* greeted her and carried on with the conversation with the drink in his hand without breaking his stride. I must say that she was also the picture of graciousness, showing a very different facet of her complex personality. I was to see another Indira Gandhi the next morning when I escorted her to the parade in the ceremonial buggy. She asked quite simply as what I thought she should say while addressing the Parade. I replied that the cadets would be really thinking about the parade to be over. She laughed and said that she agreed, and recounted how once going to address the girls in her niece's school, she asked her the same question. To which she was advised, "auntie just keep it short". In point of fact, she was very good at the parade and gave an excellent speech, emphasizing all relevant aspects important for future leaders of free India.

New Breed of Cadets

There were a number of other events. A digital musical show was put up by the cadets, which the PM seemed to enjoy. I couldn't help thinking about how things had changed from our time. The boys were so much more computer savvy and comfortable with the electronic media. I also noticed that more and more of the intake seemed to be city oriented as against the greater number with rural background in our time. There was also a visible democratization process at work as more cadets belonged to middle and lower middle class families. Quite a few were sons and wards of clerks and supervisors and such like functionaries. Many were sons of soldiers or junior commissioned officers. It was all as it should be. In the British times, preference was shown to sons of chosen Subedar Majors

(SMs), by way of rewarding them for loyalty and valour. In fact, another institution nearby was the Royal Indian Military College (RIMC) Dehradun which had produced many fine brigadiers and generals for the British Indian Army. Now another and better facility had been established in the form of a tri-service National Defence Academy (NDA), Khadakvasla. I heard that there was a problem of under subscription as also a misplaced clamour for lowering of standards which was being resisted by the saner heads in the army. Clearly, the reasons for the fall in the numbers of candidates should be identified elsewhere and remedial measures should be instituted rather than accepting lower standards.

Indira Gandhi: Her Many Facets

While climbing the stately stairs to one of the halls, I saw Indira Gandhi slowdown in deference to an older CPN Singh, she said that one has to show consideration for the advancing age of old stalwarts as they tend to be touchy about such matters. This was the consummate politician in her. Later, whilst in a pensive mood during one of the journeys, she showed an insight into our political landscape saying that people often forget that India was made up of countless ethnicities (*Jaaties*) and peoples from diverse regions, and all were important in the larger scheme of things. It seemed a bit of loud thinking but I later realized that she was in fact speaking about the long-followed Congress formula of ensuring the support of Dalit and Minority vote banks, which had kept the Party in command of the country for over sixty years of its existence. Once while returning at night from a function with just her political handyman and myself in the car, she espied some people lined up along the road. She promptly got the car to stop, changed places with her man sitting in front with the driver. Her man quickly produced a portable neon light which she beamed at her face so that the bystanders could see her face. This went on for the rest of the drive. Later, she told me in all seriousness that in the villages there was a strong belief that she was the incarnation of Goddess Durga. It was an eye-opening experience for me to see a politician at work. On another occasion I asked whether she had ever experienced the luxury of walking down a street or in a market as an ordinary citizen. She just gave a fleeting smile but that was all. She could also be a very private person.

A New Cantonment in Odisha

The small state of Orissa (since renamed Odisha) had very few central government establishments. In fact, the East coast is devoid of national installations with the exception of the Naval Establishment at Vishakhapatnam. So we scouted a likely area, located somewhat inland from the ocean which is notorious for cyclones and heavy rain.

With successor Gen. Bhupinder Singh

About this time, General Rocky Hira, Hony Colonel of 11 GR asked for their regimental centre to be moved to Lucknow from Jalapahar Darjeeling. I tried to dissuade General Hira, who was an old friend, saying that the hot Lucknow was hardly a suitable place for Gorkhas, but he had made up his mind and as he explained, he had announced this move at the Regimental Durbar, there was no changing the decision. Besides he had obtained the approval of Army Headquarters. So, I did a lot of work to arrange accommodation for them. I did everything to make their move as comfortable as it could be done in the short space of time. It turned out to be the last good deed of my tenure. That just left the final Farwell Parade and handing over to my old friend and batch mate, General

Bhupinder Singh. I laid down office on 30 November 1983 on attaining the age of 58 years. The IAF arranged for a plane to fly my wife and me to Delhi and that was that.

Farewell Parade, Lucknow, 1983

Life after Retirement

A retired Army Commander is virtually unemployable as Field Marshal Manekshaw once told me. So I looked around for suitable employment through a friend, Inder Gajra an industrialist of Indore making automotive gears. However my request for an appointment in his company was turned down by the MoD on the grounds that automotive gears had a possible application for the armed services, although the company had never supplied any. I thought it rather unfair since almost everything from a needle to a truck had potential connection to the military. Fortunately, my son, Rajiv was well established in a thriving company as the chief financial controller, later a vice president with access to the company jet, so my unemployed period gave me full freedom to enjoy life in the salubrious climate of California USA. Indeed, it turned out to be a second life of frequent holidays in Europe and stateside. By now, he had also acquired a beautiful house in the ski resort of Kirkwood. So, my retired life was a dream existence of skiing, fishing, hiking and camping. In between, my son took over as president of Skype which gave him a year in a luxurious flat in Knightsbridge area of London. So we were able to spend an enjoyable summer in London. My younger son, Aditya is also settled in California with a beautiful home. We have been spending summers in California and winters in Gurgaon, Delhi. I am a life member of the USI and an active member of the IDSA, having written a fairly large number of articles on professional subjects.

God has strange ways of his own. When life for us humans is going too well, He has a way of bringing us down to our knees. Our moment of nemesis came when our son Rajiv was struck down by cancer, leaving behind a wife, and a daughter and a son, apart from a shattered brother. My wife and I spent a whole year with him in the palatial house that he had just built up. It was heartbreaking to see him melt in front of our eyes as it were. He put up a brave fight but ultimately succumbed at 7:30 in the morning of 31st January. His company, PAY PAL bade him farewell in a grand function, attended by all his colleagues and his many friends from the Indian community in the San Francisco area. The whole family was invited to attend and say a few words. Very appropriately they conducted the function as a celebration of his life and his outstanding contribution to the company. He has left behind his wife, Sumita and two extremely talented children, Sarina, and Arjun. Sarina graduated from Princeton University and is preparing for a medical career. Arjun has just graduated from the TUFTS College and is planning to work for a few years before embarking on a masters' degree. My younger son, Aditya has been prostrated with grief since he was very close to him. My wife and I are trying to patch up our life as best as we can but the trauma of losing both of our children, our daughter Sweetie and then our son, Rajiv, has broken us, only being kept alive by the love and affection of the remaining members of the family.

10

Problems Confronting the Army

The Indian Army is the least modernized amongst the three services of the country. It has been taken for granted, though it has always carried the heaviest burden in all wars, insurgencies and national emergencies. It has been in the forefront to counter any danger or threat facing the country. Historically, all foreign invasions into India have been land based onslaughts originating from the North West. Hence through the centuries, the land armies of India have been the national mainstay. Such is the geography of the sub-continent that the huge land mass and the fertile Indo-Gangetic Plain have been the main target destinations of most invading armies. India has not been a maritime power excepting for short periods affecting short stretches of our long coast line, and history of extensive maritime trade with the Middle-east and Gulf countries. In recent times only, with the emergence of China as a maritime power, posing a perceived threat to the commercial sea lanes, India has started thinking in terms of dominating the vast expanse of the Indian Ocean, though it would entail a national effort of considerable magnitude.

However, as things stand, till date, the Army constitutes the largest, and arguably, the most important component of our national security edifice. Such may well be the most likely pattern in the foreseeable future. The centrality of the land based operations in the counter insurgency operations is even more pronounced because most of such operations are heavily army oriented with the solitary exception of the recent menace of piracy on the high seas The Indian Army has a proud history of steadfastness and bravery. It was the pride of Indian arms in the two world wars as part of British Indian Army, where British valour and professionalism of the Indian soldier earned worldwide acclaim. Since after Indian independence in 1947, as part of the armed forces of free India, the army has lived up to its fame and acquitted itself with unfailing excellence and dependability in all wars. It has had to fight against Pakistan in four wars, in 1947-48, 1965, 1971 and the Kargil Operations in 1991. In all encounters, Pakistan has had to face defeat; dramatically so, in the Bangladesh operations which cost them the loss of half of their country and over ninety thousand prisoners in Indian hands. Since 1980s Pakistan has fomented and relentlessly stoked an insurgency in Kashmir. The Indian Army has countered this "proxy war" also with unceasing vigilance, untiring patrolling and by sealing the LOC against infiltrations. The insurgency has had its ups and downs but the army has not allowed it to get out of hand. As a result, Kashmir continues to be governed by an elected representative and progressing like other states of the country. During this period, Pakistan has inflicted or attempted all manner of terrorist attacks and depredations on India. The army had also operated successfully for the annexation of Junagadh (1947), Hyderabad (1948), Dadar and Nagar Haveli (1954), Goa (1961) apart from later securing Siachin in 1984. In addition, the army has been the proverbial "dogsbody" — assigned all and sundry tasks, perhaps because it is the largest in numbers and is always there and is the most efficient entity available. In sum it will not be an exaggeration to say that if it had not been for the professionalism of the army, the territorial integrity and safety of the nation would have been in jeopardy and faced grave danger. Certainly, without its constant vigil, Kashmir may have been lost long ago. All this has made the army as the lynch pin of our national security apparatus.

The Army's Urgent Needs

Modernization

Unfortunately, it has not been the most privileged service, in fact it can be said to have been the most neglected. The picture today is that the army soldier lacks the basic essentials such as bulletproof vests, night vision devices, state of the art weapons et al. For its armoured corps, the programme for acquisition of 1,657 Russian T-90s tanks is still barely half way to completion. Major operational gaps are: besides the basic modern gear enumerated above, the army needs new-generation assault rifles, close-quarter battle carbines and light machine guns. No modern artillery gun has been inducted ever since the imperishable controversy concerning the Bofors howitzer arose 40 years ago (controversy was regarding the manner of its purchase not its quality as a weapon system). The Army Chief is reported to have written to the MoD on 13 January 2015, identifying seven critical projects which need to be pursued on priority to equip the Army with advanced fire power and enhance its mobility. He highlighted the need for 814 artillery guns, 8,000 third generation anti-tank missiles and197 battle field helicopters. He also emphasized requirement of upgrading of tanks and BMP vehicles and night vision devices and new assault rifles for infantry and mechanized forces. Post the 1962 debacle, the Henderson Report highlighted the fact that the inadequacies in the state of the Army's equipments were represented by the army to the MoD on a number of occasions before the war but these seem to have been ignored. Yet during the war, the soldiers had paid with their lives. The Defence Minister was sacked. The army chief had to resign but no heads rolled in the Ministry. The army is the most underfunded service with regard to modernization. For example in the last budget for the year 2014-2015, about 74% of allotment on capital account (for modernization schemes) went to the air force and navy with the army getting a meager 26%.

Also, nearly 75-80 % of the allocation on capital account for acquisition of advanced weapons was eaten up by committed liabilities for ongoing schemes.

Firing from Arjuna Tank

The problem is that the labyrinthine procedures and diverse bureaucratic tactics are used to scuttle a proposal at any stage. Then, there is always the bogey of corruption. Admittedly, corruption does exist in the civil and military, too though not as rampant as in the former. Many retired defence officers as also retired civil service officials from the MoD join the ranks of "agents" of arms dealers. One may recall the sting operation by *Tehelka* reporters in 2001 named "Operation Westend" wherein two reporters posing as agents of a fictitious arms dealing company, secretly filmed politicians, retired Ministry babus and ex-army officers accepting cash and other favours for helping the company get orders for its products. This led to a storm in the press and parliament. Bangaru Laxman and George Fernandes were forced to resign. A witch hunt was started by the ruling NDA government against the *Tehelka* magazine. Subsequently, only Laxman and some officials were convicted and put in jail but this led to a new brand of sting journalism though many questioned its ethics. The whole incident is covered graphically by Mark Tully and Gillian Wright in their book *India in Slow Motion* (*see chapter* "Corruption from top to tail", Penguin, 2003, New Delhi). Corruption as in that case and many others is mostly the by-product of the "Neta–Babu" nexus. But nothing can justify the cumbersome procedures and dilatory tactics that the MoD practises which cost the lives of brave soldiers.

In sum, the services are at the mercy of the MoD and have to seek its sanctions in all cases. This leads to a bidding war at the beginning of the year with final allocations depending upon the canvassing ability of different services. The pity is that the system is theoretically quite fair. The senior bureaucrats are mostly officers of intelligence and have a genuine desire to utilize the funds available in the best manner possible. However lacking adequate military expertise, they have no independent frame of reference to correctly assess the comparative merits of various proposals of different services, and hence judgment of true priorities. Indeed, apart from unfortunate absence of a Chief of Defence Staff (CDS), the country does not have an authorized and up to date "National Security Strategy" (NSS) apparatus laying down the parameters of the kind of war the country will need to fight. So the day goes to the service that has done its homework and has taken the trouble to select a good "presenter", (if they have also done some preparatory canvassing work, so much the better). In short, there are plenty of good men in the services and the ministry but there is a systemic failure. The result is that poor soldiers get sent to high altitudes without proper weapons and equipments. The lopsided allocations apart, the system breeds mistrust between the services, whereas the need is to generate unity and a spirit of cooperation and mutual trust. *Above all, we must realize that the army is actually engaged in active operations NOW, whereas the modernization schemes of Navy and Air Force only relate to estimated future needs.*

Shortage of Officers

A number of other problems confront the army. Apart from the neglect regarding modernization schemes, the army faces other equally urgent problems. First and foremost, there are serious shortages in the officer's cadre, especially in the junior ranks which matter the most in war. Out of an authorized strength of nearly 48,000 officers, there is a shortage of 9,642 officers at present. The numbers apart, there seems to be dilution in standards and warlike quality whereas the war environment is turning deadlier and riskier owing to the malaise of *jihad* and tactics of terror. Next, more and more officers are opting for premature retirement as soon as they complete the mandatory 20 years of service to qualify for pension. Unfortunately it is the brighter officers who want to go, which will impact adversely on the army's performance in future. The considerations of conditions of hardship, prolonged separation from families and the problem of children's education, were always there but these have now been aggravated by short tenures. The pyramidal slope is so steep that even brigadier rank officers, who have come up this far, showing promise, have to go home at age 52-54. The officers then are at the peak of their mental and physical ability; their familial responsibility is also at its peak, and it is hard to find a suitable job in the civil market. In short, the services offers only "half a career". In sharp contrast, the civil service officers, plus those in paramilitary forces and police serve till age of 60 years. Besides, as the saying goes, the IAS officers never retire. Most of them serve till the age of 60; thereafter they get absorbed in the large number of sinecure appointments such as comissions, boards and tribunals, etc.

This is a serious lacuna which must be addressed on priority. Prior to the Third Pay Commission, this hiatus was partly addressed by grant of higher scales of pay and pension to the armed forces vis-à-vis their civil counter parts to compensate for the shorter career and hardship factor. Since then a state of parity prevails. The problem of short tenures applies equally to the soldiers who go home between the ages of 30-35 years. Till now, owing to widespread unemployment in the rural sector, we do not feel the pinch but in the none-too-distant future, once the industrialization gathers momentum and the industry starts mopping up manpower, the services, particularly the army will have a serious problem. Minor tinkering with the system will not do. Instead, we will have think out of the box to devise new initiatives, to make a career in the army worthwhile and attractive for officers and soldiers alike.

One option is to institute considerably higher scales of pay and pension or a hefty gratuity so that people on retirement go home with a substantial nest egg to help them when they are looking for a new job, or to come in handy as seed money for starting a business. The monetary option will put severe pressure on the exchequer whether on account of higher scales of pay and pension, or a lump sum payment (golden handshake) hence may prove to be nonviable. The other option is reemployment in the government, such as in Public Sector Undertakings (Public Sector Units), Ecological Task Forces and so on. Yet another option could be to allow the armed forces to set up captive industrial units or businesses of their own, employing the ex-soldiers, in such ventures as trading houses, military farms, dairy units and the like with credit facilities and tax concessions. The Chinese (PLA) and Pakistani armed forces indulge in such activities in a big way. The PLA dabbles in industrial manufacture and export of military equipment and is known to run profitable export businesses, whereas the Pak Army is a veritable empire. Their 'Fauji Foundation' is engaged in all manner of businesses and has set up the largest business conglomerate in Pakistan having 18 industries with diversified portfolio including oil refineries and fertliser units. It also covers health care and education and training including a network of 100 educational institutions, 65 vocational centers and technical training centers across the country under an umbrella organization of 'ex-servicemen welfare'. Obviously, Pak retirees are fully taken care of. No wonder, selection for service in the army is eagerly sought after. If such ventures are allowed to be set up for the Indian armed forces, especially for the army, they will no doubt open up vast opportunities for absorbing retired personnel. However such activity could become a seedbed of corruption and illegal practices. Hence in the long run it may create more problems than it would solve. The PSU route also looks nonviable. It is doubtful if the PSUs can absorb such large numbers. Besides, the new trend is towards disposing off most of such ventures, especially those running at a loss (most of them are). There are reports that in the context of the contemplated reforms of the PLA which would lay off lots of soldiers, the state owned firms have been ordered by the government to reserve 5% of jobs for the retiring veterans. However, a democratic India may not have the luxury of such peremptory legislation.

Perhaps the only viable way out then would appear to be through lateral reemployment of retiring officers and men of the army in para military forces. At present there are as many as 246 battalions of Central Reserve Police Force (CRPF) and 150 battalions of Border Security Force BSF) besides 120 battalions of CISF and over 70 units of SSB, mostly manned by police and administered by Ministry of Home. On the face of it, these "private armies of the ministry of home", were meant to be back-up auxiliary forces for the regular army (was it as a counter foil to the armed services!). Hence, these could be profitably utilized for lateral placement of army veterans. It would not only solve the problem of "short careers" for officers and soldiers of the regular army but the infusion of these highly trained and experienced veterans in the para military forces would also give a tremendous boost to their quality and performance. Further, in an emergency situation, these units would be readily available as a trained force of up to 40 additional divisions to the service which would be a potential "game changer". This bold option of lateral emplacement of army retirees in the paramilitary forces would demand radical restructuring of the security system and may stir a hornet's nest of controversy. Hence it can only be accomplished by a firm and resolute decision at the highest level. Perhaps there will be need for another "Group of Ministers" (GoM) or a special Committee like the Naresh Chandra Committee to cogitate and make recommendations on the subject.

Inter-Service Anomalies

The army has another problem and that is the doctrine of parity among the three services, which works to the detriment of the army. The Indian Army, by far the largest service has a strength of I,129,900 men including about 48,000 officers, The Indian Navy has 58,350 men including 8,945 officers and the Indian Air Force 127,200 men including 12,120 officers(Source: Article titled "Forces battling shortage of fighting rank officers" Rajat Pandit TNN Dec 1, 2004). So, the officer cadre of Navy and Air Force is much smaller than that of the Army. However, to the seven Army commands, the Air Force has also got seven commands (same number as Army), headed by Lt. Generals and equivalent ranks. The smallest service, the Navy has three commands. In all probability, there would be a cascading effect all the way down, so the numbers in other equivalent ranks would be similar, which means a much steeper promotional curve in case of the Army officers as compared to that of the Navy and Air Force.

Social Prestige Factor

There is a psychological hurt in the mind of the services. There is a perceptible lack of respect and loss of prestige of the services in the society. It is not about the money. The young men primarily join the armed forces for serving the nation and not for amassing wealth. In any case it is known all around that the officers always live on a tight budget. In my time, we never aspired to compete with officers in the corporate world nor was there a sense of inferiority compared to the rich elites. We were contented, even proud to live with dignity and style despite limited resources. But a life in the services had prestige and carried great respect in the society. When I joined the service, I was advised by a grizzled senior in all seriousness that I should always remember to send a X-mas card to my bank manager every year. I must have looked nonplussed; so he explained, "because you will often be asking for an overdraft". As young bloods, we lived a life of elan and style to the full limits of our resources. This went with a life of sports, and out-door activity like hikes and hunting wherever possible, extracting the maximum out of life. Contrary to popular belief, we never over-indulged in alcohol. In fact, being seen drunk was looked down upon as coarse and ungentlemanly. Any case of drunkenness and indebtedness was dealt with very strictly by the commanding officer. So, whether as officers in the cities or soldiers in the villages, the services were always looked up to and admired as the best of the society. This made all the difference and made us accept hardship, danger and inconveniences such as separation from the family and problems about children's education. We were totally above politics, despite enjoying all shenanigans of the politicians. We were and still are largely, above the taint of religion or regionalism. It is noteworthy that the army runs a school of training the "Religious Teachers" at Pachmari, Central India where the curriculum emphasizes that the core values of all religious is the same. In a mixed class regiment, for instance, the Mandir, Gurudwara or Masjid often share accommodation in a large tent, and the big day of each community is celebrated together by all soldiers of the unit. I am sure similar spirit prevails in Navy and Air force.

We as officers are devoted to welfare of our soldiers forging bonds of friendship and loyalty. Unfortunately this culture is not understood by the civil officers. As a case in point, when I visited my old unit near Dharamsala in June 2012 a young Major narrated a horrific story. He had written to a young IAS officer who was a district magistrate, about a soldier's problem in his village. The officer was hauled up by the divisional commander because the young IAS officer had made an official complaint against a mere Major having the temerity to write directly to him, contravening the provision of the 'warrant of precedence'. I spoke to the General commanding the division who was equally angry about the incident, but true to the army tradition he was against making a counter representation. I mention this incident as symptomatic of the malaise. A young officer once told me that life in the services has lost the old shine and aura. This has affected the quality and quantity of new entrants. The task for us all then, the armed forces, the society and the nation is to make a career in the services attractive and worthwhile and to put back the old prestige to the service. To do that, we have to address all factors, material as well as psychological, and enlist the cooperation of all segments of the society. And it must be done, because in the final analysis a nation is only as strong as its armed forces. One of the many ways to put back the prestige will be to reward services of the chiefs and army commanders and equivalents and other senior officers by appointing them as ambassadors, governors and so on, on retirement. They will also do the country proud. The social media has a vital role to play in this endeavor to make the armed forces popular and secondly to attract the bold and aggressive material. We should exploit the lure of adventure and patriotic zeal to attract the right type of youngsters. Surely it should be possible to exploit the positive instincts of patriotism, to attract our young men to a life of danger and hardship in the noble cause of defence of the country.

The Army Needs Committed Air Support

The most serious problem confronting the Army is the unsatisfactory state of air support during the operations. This is the most serious; the Army has had to fight most of the battles by itself with only spasmodic support from the air. The IAF has no doubt accepted the task of providing close support to army's operations and they duly include it in the list of their responsibilities. They have no doubt also given valuable support in some battles where the airpower has been a battle winning factor, but to the army it has never been seen as "committed support" as from their own artillery. Perhaps it is a function of the preoccupation of air with their own air battle against enemy air. Possibly the air force is handicapped by lack of adequate resources to fight both air battle and provide close support to the ground battle. Whichever way one may rationalize the situation, the fact of the matter is the army has had largely to fight its battles alone, with the possibility of air support as a bonus only. It is necessary to change this perception. In other words the air force has to *own* the ground battle as much as the army. There must be full coordination and integration in planning and fighting the land-air battle, and the supporting procedures and wireless protocols should be ironed out jointly.

Preparing for Future Wars

The military is often blamed for preparing for the previous wars. The militaries are notoriously unwilling to improvise new tactics and techniques. Only infrequently some bold innovation is tried out and adopted such as the battle technique of *Blitskrieg* developed by General Rundstedt of

Germany before the WW II. Such radical new thinking has special validity now as the new face of future war is likely to be vastly different not only in a matter of "degree" (more of troops and weapons) but a difference in "kind", owing to new generations of weapons such as, nuclear weapons, missiles, Precision Guided Munitions (PGMs) and a revolution in communication technology which would facilitate a wide networked state, ensuring largest numbers being on grid. All these advances will accelerate the pace of operations and make possible (and necessary) instant tactical and strategic responses. The new developments have been characterized as a revolution in military affairs (RMA), which as the Americans say is a whole new ball game. It stands to reason therefore that this new war would demand new methods and capabilities. In sum, the new warfare will need fast moving operations by agile combined army-air battle groups supported by all resources of integrated theatre commands – in other words a joint army-air ownership of the battle. *In case such close integration is not possible for some reason, the only viable alternative would be for the army to have its own integral air effort or an air wing on the pattern of what has been instituted for the Navy.* It would be a second best alternative but still an advance over the present situation. It is said that in the recent past, when the army was debating a strategy of making an initial push into enemy territory, dubbed as "cold start", the air force declined to give a commitment of necessary air support as "all their resources would be committed to the larger air battle in the first 4 or 5 days". Be that as it may, the army must have dedicated and totally committed air support for its battles in future wars. Any prevarication on this requirement will be inviting failure.

Integration of Three Services

Much has been written and said about the need for integration of the services for future wars. The nature of the future war is likely to be vastly different. However, two imperatives would remain as relevant as ever, if not more. These are, firstly, the need for joint or integrated operations, and secondly, the need for unity of command. India has put in place, maximum number of Tri Service institutions to bring about the required closeness, if not fusion, of the three services but we have still not been able to achieve true "jointness" of operations.

We have a National Defence Academy (Khadakvasla) at the cadet level, Defence Services Staff College (Wellington) at Major and equivalent level, Higher Command Course (War Colleges) at Colonel level and the National Defence College, (New Delhi), at Brigadier and equivalent level. The officers of army, navy, and air force train and interact with each other at different levels. It generates a lot of bonhomie and friendships but that is where the cooperation stops. The Staff College boasted the collection of best minds in all services. If it was true of the student body, it was truer still of the Instructor group. It was the most appropriate platform conducive to professional thought and a crucible for generating futuristic ideas. I often wondered as to why the subject of tri service integration was not discussed there. Perhaps it was far too

ahead of times or the input from service chiefs was lacking – whatever the cause then, time is ripe now to do so. The need for tri service thinking cannot be ignored; not just theoretical knowledge or familiarity but a personal, lived-in experience. Air and ground are parallel domains and there has been so much specialization and sophistication over the years that they have started thinking of themselves as being fundamentally different. We used to speak of ground battle with air support or air battle with accompanying ground operations. Now, in the new milieu of joint operations, it will be joint ground-air operations (air-heavy) or (ground-heavy) analogous to the lexicon regarding infantry-armour operations. The question is, is such a total fusion possible, or will it amount to underutilization of the air asset, as often postulated by the IAF? I think the point is overstated because the range and flexibility of air power is such that it can provide "dedicated" support to more than one integrated battle group provided the two or more battle groups are operating in concert and under one theater commander. In any case these are the sort of questions which will be addressed by the joint training command. That is where the nuts and bolts of such operations will be hammered out, such as communication frequencies, codes, operating protocol and other details of the command architecture required to ensure seamless operations. Besides, the broader concepts and doctrinal aspects will need to be discussed and examined at fora like the Defence Services Staff College (DSSC), war colleges and the like.

At present, the individual services think, plan and work separately. They have their own doctrines and projections for future growth including acquisition of advance weapon systems. There is no unanimity about the kind of war that will need to be fought and what kind of capacity will need to be built. There are also anomalies such as that operations against one enemy (say Pakistan) are not coordinated by one theatre commander or even sector commander. The services operate like Satraps or warlords commanding their own kingdoms. They have their empires and fight for their slice of the defence budget with their individual shopping lists. India has a total of 19 commands: seven Army commands of which six are operational; seven Air Force commands of which five are operational, and three Naval commands of which two are operational plus joint commands. None of these are co-located and their geographical zones of responsibility have little commonality. It is an unbelievable situation. How have we ended up with such a large number of commands? Do we really need so many permutations and combinations to meet threats from just two known enemies? Whichever way we look at it, it must rate as a classic case of blatant empire building. It is pointless to discuss as to why and how we have arrived at this situation though the main instigators may be obvious. Is it possible to undo the damage in one fell swoop by an act of Parliament on the lines of the "Goldwater- Nichols Act" of the USA. It is tempting to hope that this kind of a bold decision could be taken and enforced in our context, only if it were possible in a ponderous democracy.

The surprising part is that the need for jointness of operations and integrated fighting capability is basically accepted by all; civilians and military alike. All professionals recognize the compulsions of fusing the competencies of individual services to optimize the national war-making capacity in view of the awesome complexity of the future battlefield. Our operational experience in previous wars emphatically endorses this need. There was valuable air support to the army in 1947 war which routed the tribal lascar when they were threateningly close to Srinagar, but the picture in 1962 and 1965 was unsatisfactory. In 1962, the air force did not participate at all, although it would have made enormous difference. Records don't speak of the reasons why, though much later, Air Marshal Arjan Singh airily expressed an opinion that the air force should have been used. The 1965 war saw the services pretty much fighting their individual wars most of the time. The institutional framework was rudimentary. There was no coordination and the tasks were projected and taken on, in an ad hoc manner. The air force blamed the army saying that its senior officers showed poor knowledge of limitations and capabilities of air force. The army complained that the response by the air was patchy and unreliable. The Indian Navy was given a limited role during the war. The 1971 operations, a resounding success, showed considerable improvement in joint planning, but more-so due to the personalities involved than to any institutionalized system. Even in that war, the air force could have given more effective support since the Pak air force was virtually non-existent after the first few days. Immediately after the war, Field Marshal Manekshaw, speaking at the Staff College Wellington, stated that the present system of Area Commands in India was dysfunctional, and that they needed to be reduced to joint commands operating under a CDS.

During the Indian Peace Keeping Force Operations in Sri Lanka in 1987-89, the Overall Force Commander (OFC), an army general, was initially provided with Component Commanders subordinated to him, from Eastern Naval Command and Southern Air Command respectively. However, it did not take long for the Navy and IAF Chiefs, to get their Component Commanders re-designated as liaison officers with no role other than to act as a via-media between the OFC and respective naval and air force commands.

It was the Kargil conflict in 1999 which really gave the wake-up call for a major overhaul of the existing system. The Parliamentary Standing Committee on Defence noted that it was lack of synergy among the three services which caused difficulties to the armed forces during the Kargil War. It resulted in the establishment of the "Kargil Review Committee" comprising of former diplomats, military leaders, and defence experts which made many far-reaching recommendations and set the ball rolling for many institutional reforms, after years of inertia. This was followed by a meeting of GoM, which *inter alia*, made three important recommendations, viz, (1) integration of the services both with each other and with the Ministry of Defence (MoD); (2) the creation of a Chief of Defence Staff (CDS); and (3) setting up of joint operation commands. However, the implementation was done only in a half-hearted manner amid a general lack of consensus. Only a pro-forma restructuring of the MoD was done. Similarly, the injunction regarding establishment of joint operational commands, was fobbed off by creation of the Andaman and Nicobar Command (ANC) only. For good measure, it was stated that creation of this joint command was to evolve, from first principles, and meant to provide a framework for a unified formation to test the working rules, standard operating procedures and doctrines, which would then be codified for use for other unified commands. A Strategic Forces Command (SFC) was also set up, but that is where the matters seem to have rested for long. More recently a fresh initiative came in the form of recommendation of the Naresh Chandra Committee for appointing a Permanent Chairman of the Chiefs of Staffs Committee (CoSC), perhaps meant as an incremental measure or as a compromise solution to the raging controversy regarding the appointment of a CDS. An incumbent is yet to be posted so there is no knowing if and how the new measure will work. However it would seem that like most compromises, this initiative may also prove still born. In any case, at best it appears to be a half measure which may fail the entire concept, (which is perhaps the sinister motive). Even this half measure is reported to have met with tremendous bureaucratic opposition from within the MoD. Indeed, under pressure, the then Defence Minister had to clarify that it was yet to be discussed by the Cabinet Committee of Security (CCS).

So, the situation is that although most people accept that in view of the radical nature of warfare and the vast changes in the battlefield of the future, and the reality of very belligerent neighbours, the Indian militaries will have to reinvent themselves. However there is near total lack of consensus on measures to be taken by way of implementation. Almost all stakeholders seem to baulk at swallowing the bitter pill of sweeping reforms at both operational and organizational level. The fact is that the military bureaucracies do not take to radical reforms easily any more than the civil bureaucracies. It is said that, in no profession is the dread of innovation as great as in the armed forces. The problems are; firstly the services have to change to entirely new set of operating procedures, codes and protocols and secondly, they have to adapt to those of other services. The individual services are also loath to give up their turfs and egos. A whole lot of perks and privileges will go, along with the sense of self- importance built up over years. For example, a switch to integrated commands will reduce the present chiefs to mere "chiefs of respective staffs", responsible for administering to the integrated commands, which would operate directly under the respective theater commanders who will operate under the CDS. It will have a cascading effect all the way down as the present architecture of divisions/ brigades and squadrons/wings etc., will be replaced by that of battle groups/battle teams and so on. Similar changes will occur in staffs. In short, we are looking at sweeping reforms and total restructuring of the armed forces. There will be need to update all our structures, technological, doctrinal and organizational. Above all, there will be need to change our mindset and orientation in keeping with the changing geopolitical environment and the threats facing the country. A similar exercise will need to be undertaken with regard to strategy and tactics. Sweeping changes of this magnitude will demand great courage and wisdom on the part of individual services and the government.

In general, there is desire for reform at the governmental level in principle at the higher level, but that of dogged resistance within the MoD at the bureaucratic level. Among the services the support is variable. The Army and probably Navy generally support the measure. The Air Force may not be in favour. It has principally become a matter of attitude and prestige. Another problem is that, the army being vastly superior in numbers is looked upon with suspicion. In truth, considering the past experience, the army will continue to be the biggest stake holder and will again carry the main burden of war and heaviest human casualties in any land-air war. As for the bureaucrats of MoD, the general feeling is that they will perhaps constitute the biggest stumbling block as they will not easily surrender their primacy of the interlocutor role between the services and the political leadership. Right or wrong, they are often suspected of playing favourites among the services in the matter of budgetary allocations, sanction of big ticket purchases and so on. For instance, a common belief is that most of the purchases for army modernization were shelved during the tenure of General V.K. Singh, because he had incurred the ire of staffs in MoD on the personal question of his age. Be that as it may, the truth is that some of the most urgent requirements of the Army have been put in cold-storage for many years for one reason or other.

Urgent Need for Integrated Commands and Appointment of a CDS

The case for integrated commands and appointment of a CDS is unexceptionable for operational reasons. It has also resonance for higher perspectives of integral planning and prioritization in purchase of equipments and advance weapon systems. Once appointed, the CDS will have the responsibility to draw up a master plan or a National Security Strategy (NSS). In sum, there will be a proper National Operational Plan as also a National Budgeting Plan as against the present system of ad-hoc budgetary allocations. It will also engender coherence and convergence in doctrines and competencies of individual services. The new measures will in fact systemize the entire process. Hopefully, selection and appointment of the CDS (or at least a permanent chairman of the CoSC) will be effected at an early date. There is bound to be opposition from some quarters but with Narendra Modi as the Prime Minister, the government would hopefully be capable of taking tough decisions.

The detail of the joint formations at different levels of the armed forces will be subject of discussion. It will be the first task for the CDS to hammer out with the existing armed forces, with the government and with some of the better think tanks. We have a long history of hostile intent from two quarters which may manifest in some degree of collusive action. We also know by experience that in most cases, the conflict will mainly comprise of land-air battles for some time. Lately a threat from the North has also manifested. There has been no invasion as such from the Indian Ocean except that byway of trade and intrusion of culture and ethnic bodies, the recent incident of terror in Mumbai, notwithstanding. In short, the most probable scenario in foreseeable future would be that of a land-air war on the subcontinent with threats emanating from the west from Pakistan and from the north from China, or both. Chinese threat from across Indian seaboard may also emerge in the future, although it may not take the form of an invasion per se. Instead it may take the form of interfering with our maritime trade. Anything beyond this is likely to invite a strong response from the USA. In any case, considering the constraints of resources, India will not be able to address the naval threat in entirety for some time. Notwithstanding, there will be need to dove-tail Naval plans for contribution to the overall national plan,eg, a naval blockade of Karachi Port and Gwadadar port and attrition thereon, on the lines of the attack on Kiamari, Karachi Oil farm by naval missile boats in 1971 War.

The subject of jointness of operations among the services has been admirably discussed by Mr Vijay Singh Rana, a Research Fellow at IDSA, New Delhi. He has examined the various issues in great detail showing as how the UK and USA have instituted far reaching reforms in their security services by firm and purposeful legislation. Pointedly, the author quotes US President Harry Truman. Following the experience of WWII, mainly alluding to the war in the Pacific Ocean, the President had stated that:

"We must never fight another war the way we fought the last two. I have a feeling that if the Army and Navy had fought our enemies as hard as they fought each other, the war would have ended much earlier."

A Possible Integrated Command Structure for the Future

A suggested configuration of theatre commands and functional and special purposes commands is given below, which may serve as basis for discussion.

1. Four fully integrated operational theatre commands;
   a. Northern Theatre — Comprising of the existing northern army command and requisite elements of western air command, mainly to look after J&K sector.
   b. Western Theatre — Comprising the existing western army command, western air command and south western air command primarily oriented towards Pakistan. Requisite naval complement will also be allocated if and when required.
   c. Eastern Theatre — Comprising the eastern army command and eastern air command mainly oriented to Chinese threat, also for borders with China in Himachal Pradesh, Uttarakhand, Uttar Pradesh and entire North East.
   d. Indian Ocean Region Theatre — It will encompass IOR (West) and IOR (EAST), comprising elements of southern army command and southern air command, western naval command and ANC for ops in IOR and for maritime threats.
2. Seven Functional/Special Purpose Commands
   a. Reserve Command — Primary role: OOAC tasks. Comprising elements of central army command, central air command and southern naval command.

May also have a strike Corps, airborne division and amphibious elements from existing resources.

b. Joint Logistics Command — Logistics of three services to avoid duplication
c. Joint Training Command — Training for integrated operations
d. Joint Cyber and Information Warfare Command
e. Special Forces Command
f. Aerospace Command
g. Strategic Forces Command

Naval Aircraft Carrier – INS Virat

The four operational theatre commands will operate independently, or in concert and in a mutually supporting configuration, depending on whether the threat is single or collusive. In addition, we will retain the present Strategic Forces Command and set up another six Functional or Special Purpose Commands as detailed above. The entire structure will be under the CDS who will be the overall commander of all forces and constitute a single point advisor to the prime minister and be answerable to the government on all matters pertaining to defence. As a possible amendment, a separate

Maritime Theatre may be considered in view of the recent prominence given to the naval domain. In any case, the entire organization, tasking and allocation of forces will be decided by the government and subsequently fleshed out by the CDS in consultation with the existing service chiefs and other stake holders.

Apart from the structure of theatre commands and functional commands there will be need for a phased programme for setting up the suggested structures. Considering the wide ranging restructural changes envisaged, there will be need for an elaborate implemental machinery and an appropriately high ranking minister or a GoM to oversee the progress and to iron out the many wrinkles which are bound to crop up from time to time. In some quarters it has been suggested that a bureaucrat of the rank of cabinet secretary should head the steering committee.

11

The Indian Security Edifice

India maintains a large security apparatus. It has the third largest regular army in the world after China of over a million soldiers. It has a sizable air force and a substantial navy. It is backed by an enormous mass of para-military forces. India is rated to be the largest importer of military hard ware. It is a nuclear weapon power. In sum, it is a regional player of some stature. However, in spite of the impressive credentials, India is said to be punching below its weight, or as some commentators put it, "India does not get the bang for its buck". The reasons are not far to seek. Firstly, there is imbalance and dissonance in the top power structure. Secondly, there is limited interplay between the major components of the military that is the army, navy and air force. Thirdly, civil- military relations are fraught with distrust and mutual suspicion. Fourthly, the military lacks direct access to the political leadership. Fifthly and as a result of the first four reasons, the higher defence control organization and the decision making architecture is faulty.

The Soldier and The State

On attaining Independence in 1947, India inherited a first rate military, fully wedded to the principle of supremacy of the civil authority and the concept of an apolitical military. Unfortunately, the army of India's neighbour Pakistan chose the other route. The Pakistan Army took control of the country soon after independence and since then the generals have ruled Pakistan directly or indirectly for most of its existence. Similar patterns emerged in Burma and Cambodia and African countries. What is of concern to India is the fact that the developments in our neighbourhood, have created deep mistrust in our bureaucracy and political leadership with regard to the Indian military for no fault of its own. Since then, the Indian armed forces have shown exemplary loyalty and subservience to the civil authority with never a whiff of rebellious spirit. It has been a model of patriotism. At the professional level, it has performed flawlessly and done the country proud. It has never been found wanting in patriotic fervor. It has been a shining example of Indianness, untainted by religious or regional passions. Inspite of it all, it has not been able to root out the worm of suspicion from the mind of political masters and the bureaucrats. The Nehruvian prejudice and mistrust of the army and his reported penchant to keep the armed forces "in their place or at a distance" have made matters worse. Nehru's bias against the armed forces has been well documented. Neville Maxwell describing post 1962 events, has quoted Nehru's letter to Bertrand Russell where he talks about "the danger of the military mentality spreading in India, and the power of the generals increasing". This undeserved mistrust has led to many distortions in higher defence management in India, and in civil-military relations. The Asiatic model of military control has no doubt been bad examples, so there may be some justification for worry and alarm. However, it was equally wrong for the civil bureaucracies to go to the other extreme. Nature abhors imbalance. So, we see a spectacle of *babu-neta* nexus, corruption, scams and paralyses of decision making processes. Above all, since the political leadership was devoid of military experience and chose to deny itself the benefit of military advice, the bureaucrats happily inserted themselves as interlocutors between the military and the leadership, substituting the fundamental concept of loyalty of the military to the civil authority by that of subservience of the military to the bureaucrats of the Ministry of Defence (MoD). The status of an "interlocutor" was bad enough (it is a wonder that the leaders do not find it irksome), but the MoD has gone on to perpetuate this "through me" protocol and has become a mouthpiece for the armed services in all matters. They present all cases of the services to the cabinet and other fora. Pertinently, they represent the service's case to the pay commissions, alongside their own which should rank as a classic case of conflict of interest. The system has given rise to many ills. Clearly, accumulation of excessive power in any one organ of the state leads to imbalance. In short, if it was wrong of the militaries in some emerging countries of Asia and Africa to have usurped power, it was no less unworthy of the bureaucracies in India to have cornered undue authority for themselves.

Civil and Military Relations

The Ministry of Defence (MoD) has used all strategies to perpetuate and further enhance their position of pre-eminence. They have often played favourites among army, navy and air force thereby encouraging building of competing empires. Playing favourites is always bad for a healthy team spirit. Hence, it has engendered unhealthy rivalries between the armed services. Worse, the budget allocations on capital account (for modernization schemes) to different services and then approval for individual schemes, seems to be done on the basis of personal bias, rather than the criteria of national priority. The bureaucrats of the MoD are totally lacking in professional military expertise. This has spawned the spectacle of canvassing by different armed services. To compound matters, persistent demand by the armed forces, notably the army for the institution of the CDS system has not been conceded, even though this system will obviously help to ensure properly prioritized acquisition of advance weapon systems and prioritizing of modernization projects on a professional basis and according to a holistic all-services operational plan.

Indira Gandhi at Chetwood Hall, IMA Dehradun

The ad hoc acquisition of military hardware is wasteful, which the country can ill-afford. The system (or rather non-system) is such that there is little overall synergy between the services, hence the individual services are tempted to aim and bid for unrealistic capacities beyond the pale of a country with a non-existent industrial base and limited resources. Each service is making its own war strategy whereas the need is to work on an integrated basis, aiming at integration of services and setting up of integrated commands so as to be able to fight integrated battles. All this will only be possible if a CDS system is in place. All we have till now is an "announced" government plan for the post of a permanent chairman of the Chiefs of Staff Committee (CSC), which is also still to materialize and which is reportedly meeting stiff opposition from within the MoD.

Hence, we see a situation whereby the ship of state is wobbly and unstable owing to a flawed dispensation of power between the different components. The reason is that as stated, somewhere deep within the system lurks an irrational phobia about the dread possibility of the Indian military posing a threat to the civil authority. Unless this irrational fear is addressed once and for all, discussions on all downstream issues will be unproductive. In fact, the services suspect that this transparent bogey is being perpetuated by vested interests.

To be fair, this kind of unease is not uncommon to democracies, indeed to governments of all stripe. Through history, nations have wrestled with this problem by diverse stratagems. Simply put, the conundrum is that nations *like a strong army in war but prefer weak and pliable forces in peace.* Excepting when the monarchs took to the field and personally led the troops in war, the empires sought methods to keep their militaries on a tight leash, erecting a system of checks and control. At the same time, the rulers had to have a military which should have essential requisites of fighting quality as well as total loyalty, a combination often hard to find in solely mercenary bodies.

History gives examples of failed experiments of control of militaries by the kings and monarchs. They tried to structure captive militaries which ultimately turned rogue and became a threat to themselves. In the 9th century AD, the Abbasid Caliphs of Baghdad unwittingly created such a monster. To vouch safe their hold over their armies, the Caliphs created a special corps of slaves from the nomadic Turks of Central Asia, owing allegiance to the person of the Caliph only. These slaves were formed into special military units, known as Mamelukes. As expected, these professional mercenaries distinguished themselves as fearsome warriors in the service of the Caliphate and consequently, and hence often came to be given positions of military authority. In time and after a number of campaigns, they became a formidable center of power within themselves. They took control of Egypt by 877 AD, and conquered the Mediterranean coast through Palestine and Syria. Nominally they still ruled on behalf of the (weak) Caliph but they had the natural strength of a small, self-aware, Turkish speaking military elite. They were a veritable genie out of the bottle. Ultimately, to the relief of the Caliphs, they died their own death, in that, their power was broken by the Mongols mainly owing to their own stubborn refusal to adapt to the use of firearms.

The Ottoman Empire (1517-1831) committed a similar blunder. They resorted to the system of Janissaries who were founded on a corps of young boys taken from the Christian communities of Baltic States by way of tribute. These young boys were brought up in the Muslim faith and so indoctrinated that they were left with no memories of their families or native language. They were not allowed to marry. These young boys were imparted training to be fanatical fighting machines for personal loyalty to the Caliph and as a military over other militaries, a vast enterprise of human engineering. Subsequently, General Zia of Pakistan replicated this experiment in the form of Pakistani Taliban. However, ultimately this experiment also failed as the selfsame Janissaries revolted against the Caliphs and the state. They had a turbulent history and after a numbers of revolts they had to be destroyed by the Turkish cavalry. Moral of the story is that a strong military force with loyalty only to itself or to one individual, without a leavening of patriotism is little better than a band of adventurers. Indeed, warriors must be "warriors of state", otherwise they become a threat to their creators.

The Romans, the originators of the system of modern armies also employed methods to control the militaries by keeping them away from the capital, forbidding them to "cross the Rubicon", a small river near Rome. The famed Julius Caesar did precisely that which triggered a civil war with disastrous consequences for the country. As mentioned earlier, Britain also had a brief taste of military rule under Cromwell (Rule of the Generals), but ever since then the English have followed a system of a national army subservient to the parliament. This is the system they bequeathed to India which has worked well for us for the past 68 years. *All that is needed is rationalization of the power structure between the armed forces and MoD, which will happen once the MoD is fully merged with service HQs and a system of CDS and integration of services is put into effect.* The Pakistan army on the other hand, has found a simple solution to the problem. It has just swallowed up the country. Hence, the common jibe is that: *Pakistan is not a country with an army; it is an army with a country.* It is in fact a Praetorian regime. It is to be seen as to how long will this system endure.

A state of imbalance has created problems and mistakes of the other extremes. The reverse examples (bureaucratic authority with undue influence over the political leadership and disregard of military opinion) are not far to seek in our own past. India gave away Tibet to China without solving the Sino-Indian boundary dispute. The Indian debacle of 1962 at the hands of China in the high Himalayas under scored perils of political interference and excessive influence by civilian and intelligence bureaucracies. Again, we made a mess of the situation in Sri Lanka, mainly owing to naïve and inept politics. Hence, the historical perspective clearly favours a healthy equilibrium between the different elements of the state. In sum, there should be national armies subservient to the state, and there should be judicious balance in inter se authority and responsibility between the military and other organs of the state. The soldier has to give total loyalty to the state and the state has to give due regard to the professional advice of the military. In fact the system should promote proper relationship between the two, thereby facilitating joint planning. In short, both wings should be accorded due recognition and prestige, especially so for the military because the soldiers are going to put their life on the line. War is an intensely human activity. So the military will fight with courage and dedication if its morale is high. There is a place for control by the leaders but bureaucratic control will always be resented and prove counterproductive.

I had practical experience of how direct encouragement impacts the soldier in war at the unit level. During operations in Chhamb-Jaurian Sector in 1965 war, my unit was occupying a defensive position; so we were doing vigorous patrolling to know what the enemy was doing and how his subunits were deployed. I found that reports by our patrols going behind the enemy positions tended to be just routine without meaty intelligence. So I took it upon myself to brief every patrol going out. I would give a pep-talk, telling the leader and soldiers that they will be carrying out a very crucial task with direct bearing on the well-being of the battalion. Hence, they had been handpicked by me for the important task and we all depended on their performance. I could see a palpable sense of self pride in the soldiers and the patrol would step out with spirit and verve. Again, I made a practice of debriefing them myself on their return. This small effort on my part made a world of difference. The point is that soldiers will move mountains if they know that the nation is behind them and that they have the love and admiration of its citizens and leaders.

The pity is that individually, the senior bureaucrats of MoD are outstanding officers with years of distinguished service, but the system has been so badly skewed and attitudes so hardened that rational thought has become difficult and various stake holders, least of all the bureaucrats, are loath to surrender undue power. At the same time, political leaders, embroiled in the day-to-day wrangles of party politics, and preoccupation with winning elections have no stomach for taking tough decisions. (Military is also not a very promising vote bank). However, things can only be put right by a top-down decision by the central government. Till then, the country will limp along with a system of security management which is basically faulty and inefficient, with the result that the country does not get the full benefit of its vast investment and energies.

The deep seated mistrust of the military has also led to other distortions. It has spawned hordes of para-military forces as armies of the Ministry of Home, Ministry of External Affairs, Cabinet Secretariat, NSG and others. They are stated to be forces of reserve, but are widely suspected to be a counter foil to the regular army, should it show signs of "getting out of hand!" It leads to dissipation of scarce resources. These are exclusively manned, administered and officered by the police. The personnel have different terms of engagement. They are semi-police forces which will have limited value as reserves in war, though they may be useful as a backup for the police. It specially applies to 248 battalions of Central Reserve Police Force (CRPF) and 150 battalions of Border Security Force (BSF) which would substantially enhance their effectiveness if manned by army reservists and reemployed army officers. The way they are staffed now, they will not be fully effective even in a counter insurgency role.

It is in the nature of bureaucracies to be self-propagating and proliferative. So, by diverse stratagems, they have assured steady expansion. For instance their cadre has expanded from 18 secretary level departments at the center in 1947, to 150 today. In addition there are as many additional secretaries or equivalent, and a host of joint secretaries, deputy secretaries and so on. The overall strength of the cadre has mushroomed from a total of 1,230 in 1951 to 6,150 now. The governments have often preached the mantra of paring off the work force at the center in the interest of efficiency and economy, but in effect their actions have been in the opposite direction. The Fifth Central Pay Commission, for instance, recommended reduction of 30% of central government jobs over a period of 10 years, reduction of secretary level posts from 90 to 30 and abolition of 3,50,000 junior posts lying vacant. The Pay Commission also recommended pruning of the current administrative layers from five or six to two. Expectedly, the recommendations got a quiet burial.

Parity in Pay and Emoluments and OROP

The MoD has been extremely self-serving with regard to the inter-se relationship of pay and emoluments of IAS and the armed forces. Prior to the third Pay Commission, the armed services were accorded higher pay and pensions than the IAS, to compensate for short tenures and hardship. That changed with the Third Pay Commission which brought military salaries equal to that of the civil services. It goes without saying that the representation regarding pay and pensions of all central services including the armed forces is done by the IAS. What logic compelled such a sweeping change is not known or understood. In one fell swoop, the conditions of service of bureaucrats were equated with that of soldiers though there were vast differences of length of tenure, conditions of hardship, family separation, and above all, the element of danger to limb and life.

Even today, the militaries in most other countries are favoured over comparable services of the government. The British soldiers have a 10% edge over others: US soldiers have 15-20% edge; Japanese 12-29% edge, and the French have an edge of 15%. A similar differential obtains with regard to pension scales: against the norm of 50% of last pay drawn for Indian soldiers; it is 50-75% for Americans; 76.5% for Australians; 70% for Japanese, and 75% for the French. The UK has also accepted the concept of "one rank, one pension". Now, the One Rank One Pension (OROP) issue has spiraled into an ugly row between the military and the government in India, which is bound to have profound effect in the entire country and impact civil-military relations for all time to come. All kind of rumours are aswirl, mostly imputing blame to MoD. This issue has gained such salience that even the PM had to dwell on it in his address to the nation on Independence Day on 15 August 2015. The retired soldiers had to go to the extent of surrendering their medals, and lately going on a hunger strike. According to reports (*Times of India*), the police used excessive force against the fasting retired officers and soldiers on14thAugust, 2015. Realizing the dangers involved, as many as ten retired chiefs of Army, Navy and Air Force were impelled to write a strongly worded letter to the government.

The Announcement – A Half Measure Solution

Finally in a move to break the impasse, the Defence Minister Manohar Parrikar on 5 September 2015 finally announced the government sanction. However, it turned out be a disappointment as the veterans claimed that a diluted version of the OROP was announced. Though the indefinite hunger strike was called off as a "mark of respect or acknowledgement", the relay hunger strike still continued. The veterans complained that a few key issues were not addressed, mainly with regard to premature retirement. Though government officials including the PM claimed to clarify that all pensioners would be covered, a written word has still not been received. Hence, leader of the movement, Major General Satbir Singh (retired) called for a national mega rally to protest the shortcomings in the scheme that was announced. The mega rally saw nearly 100,000 veterans in attendance. The veterans also criticized the media for blacking out the entire mega rally. They also claimed that hundreds of buses carrying veterans were stopped at the Delhi-Haryana border and were asked to go back by police officials who as they said, were acting on "orders from above". The protest continued which finally forced the government to set up a Judicial Commission under a retired judge of the Patna High Court to examine the pending grievances and give recommendations.

Generalists vs Specialists

The concept of generalist civil bureaucrats is a relic of the erstwhile cadre of Indian Civil Service (ICS) whose officers were supposed to be able to handle multifarious departments from law and order to administration to political departments. The fact of the matter is that the age of "generalists" has gone with the proliferation of functional disciplines. We are now into the age of "specialists". At present, the IAS cadre officer is supposed to be able to handle a wide variety of portfolios. When I was serving as deputy chief of the army, I often dealt with one Mr. Sidhu who was serving in MoD as additional secretary. On a number of occasions, we were both engaged in very involved negotiations with visiting teams representing a British manufacturing consortium on matters of technical specifications of military equipment and comparative price structures. A few years later, I happened to meet him, in fact I called on him for a cup of tea. He was then functioning as additional secretary in aviation and dealing with purchase of aircraft spare parts and perhaps juggling with figures of sorties etc. How can one person be expected to have expertise in diverse technical areas remains a mystery. As we become a more modern state, the appalling paucity of domain expertise in operating systems works to our disadvantages. As a result we find ourselves falling short in trade negotiations, or flubbing complex defence acquisitions, because it is entirely possible that before evaluating the specifications of a fighter jet, our official was perhaps doing roads in West Bengal! This may not be far-fetched in any manner but something which happens all too often. Indeed, to augment the bank of government talent, it should be quite in order to induct temporary specialist talents from trade or manufacturing fields for short periods.

Advanced countries like the UK, the US and Australia, all resort to inducting domain specialists at least as a temporary measure. They serve in the government for a specific task and then go back to the private sector. For reasons of prestige or patriotism it is also considered attractive for noted specialists to serve for short spells in the government. It works extremely well on all sides and this cross-fertilization of talent proves beneficial to the country. We hear of an effort by the Ministry of External Affairs (MEA) to extend an invitation to persons of eminence in diverse fields to join the ministry on contract basis. This is a step in the right direction because at present the MEA is also woefully under staffed. The lack of domain specialists affects the MoD even more, because of a bewildering array of fields that its officials have to handle, only if the IAS were to acknowledge the need. In fact, specialization in MoD should take the form of a merger with service headquarters. This merger of IAS talent and military expertise will be welcome to the armed services also, for then we would find it easy to deal with officials who will have some knowledge of military strategy and defence equipment. At the same time, it would serve the country better if the MoD had a permanent cadre of its own instead of the present system of temporary attachment of officers from the states or other ministries.

Merger of MoD and Headquarters of Armed Forces: Towards Complete Integration

By logic therefore, the Ministry of Defence should mainly consist of specialists in matters of defence (warfare, counter insurgency operations, national security and intelligence) with direct interaction with ministry of foreign affairs. It should be staffed by civil officers specializing in administration of army, navy, air force and para-military forces. In addition, there should be serving officers from army, navy and air force of different ranks, having the professional expertise. In other words, a complete merger of military and civil talent. This organization would also be able to provide proper staff support to the CDS as well as the defence minister. A merging of such a nature has been suggested by a number of authorities such as the Naresh Chandra Committee and the Group of Ministers (GoM). However, the MoD has been fighting this logical step, tooth and nail or only implementing it in a half-hearted manner. Indeed, it would be appropriate to re-designate the MoD to a Ministry of War (MoW).

The merging of service headquarters and ministry of defence should be accompanied by integration of armed services (army, navy, and airforce) into integrated theatre commands, integrated task forces and integrated battle groups and supporting specialized commands. The integrated theatre commands will be headed by officers of army, navy or air force depending upon the tasks or their expertise. The entire force will be commanded by a CDS who will be responsible for the conduct of all operations and also serve as a single point adviser to the Prime Minister on all military matters, and having the right of direct access. Such arrangements are extant in most modern countries. It will be required all the more in our case as our leaders lack experience of military operations. For the same reason, it will be advisable to have representation of ranking retired military officers in the council of ministers. Ideally, the defence minister should be a distinguished senior officer such as a retired CDS or one of the chiefs.

In conclusion, our entire security structure needs urgent review. According to the late K. Subramanyam, our present system is such that:

"Politicians enjoy power without responsibility;

Bureaucrats wield power without accountability, and the military assumes responsibility without any direction".

Apart from the problem of MoD providing the only interface between the three services and the government, another strange fact is that India is one of the few countries which does not carry out "after-war analyses" and public debate on the lessons learnt from our experience of the past wars. There may have been some effort in this direction, but these remain classified. Yet this is the only way for nations to learn and the only way for nations to mature.

That the system requires reforms urgently is known to all stake holders, but all we get are voluminous reports, analyses and very wordy notes on files (our bureaucratic specialty) but no action. In the final analysis it is not such a complex matter. In essence, the need of the hour is as follows:

(a) Military must have direct interface with political leadership (government), NOT through the MoD.

(b) Army, Navy and Air Force should be integrated with integrated theatre commands. All efforts should be made by the armed services to foster unity among themselves.

(c) CDS system must be instituted, who should draft and implement National Security Strategy (NSS) under the direction of the PM.

12

The Need for Formulating National Security Doctrine

India does not have a national security doctrine even after more than six decades of its existence as a sovereign republic, even though since after gaining independence in 1947, the country has been embroiled in several wars, border conflicts, and umpteen insurgencies, civil unrest and other crises, starting with a calamitous Partition. On top of it all, for years India has been at the receiving end of jihadist attacks from Pakistan that included highjack of aircraft, attack on Indian parliament and commando raid on Bombay 26/11. In sum, the Indian armed forces have been kept very busy and fully occupied. Currently, India is fighting a virulent insurgency in Kashmir where our army has been in a state of full and continued mobilization for decades.

We seem to have managed reasonably well, but by knee jerk reactions or no reaction and only by diplomatic representations. Till today we have not been able to respond with a counter strike. The situation has been further obfuscated by Pakistan's description of Jihadi attackers as "non-state actors". India has somehow muddled through by legalities such as evidence showing Pakistan's complicity and foot-print of its spy agencies and the jihadist organizations. We have also appealed to foreign powers. Pakistan's response has ranged from outright denial, to asking for concrete evidence and conditional promises to give satisfaction. The country has overcome the conventional challenges such as wars and conflicts by brilliant improvisation and professionalism of its armed forces. Time and again, the country has been saved by sheer guts and valour of the army and the air force, with a few exceptions such as in the 1962 war against China and our misadventure in Sri Lanka (IPKF operations 1987-1990). The surprising part is that India triumphed on most occasions even in the absence of a well thought out set of principles or procedures about response to threats to security and a framework within which the security and foreign policies should be constructed and implemented – in other words a National Security Doctrine.

One view is that since India has managed reasonably well without a doctrine on national security, getting into it now will only stir up a lot of unnecessary controversy. However, a national security doctrine must be drawn up and promulgated for a number of reasons: it will enable efficient preparation and conduct of operations; it will help us to focus on basic principles and broad tasks through which our armed forces, diplomatic corps and intelligence organizations will be required to achieve the national goals, and lastly, in a diverse country like India, a doctrine will provide clarity of action for the large and disparate political, social and different government organs which it would help to weld together.

Identifying Core National Interests

There is need to have clarity regarding the security lexicon and various elements of the security architecture. First and foremost, there is need to define the "core interests" of the country. These are the interests which the country will not compromise under any circumstances, relating to essential concerns and aspirations of the country such as territorial integrity, economic well-being and its legitimate place in the world. The "core interests in specific terms" would translate or reflect into goals – short term, medium term, and sometimes, long term. For example, these could relate to territorial goals such as: safe guarding of our territorial integrity; repossession of our lost territories (example: the entire state of Jammu and Kashmir, including the areas currently under adverse possession of Pakistan and resumption of areas illegally ceded by Pakistan to China). Similarly, the goals may include security of Arunachal Pradesh and an equitable settlement of the Sino-India border issue. An important goal could likely concern political stability and internal security.

President Bush (junior) promulgated a theory of the right of preemptive strike by the US on areas beyond the physical boundary of USA in certain situations – a Bush adaptation of the Monroe Doctrine of President Monroe of 1823. This concept may also have resonance for India with regard to developments in our neighbouring countries like Nepal and other Himalayan mountain kingdoms, Sri Lanka, Bay of Bengal and island territories of Indian Ocean. Clearly, if centers of power inimical to Indian interests are allowed to develop at our doorstep, it would impact on our security and we should have the military (and socio-conomic) capacity and political will to combat such threats. Threats may also manifest in many other forms such as diversion or blockage of rivers (e.g. Brahmaputra) which would adversely affect our economic well-being.

The identification of the core interests, or the ultimate aims and objectives should be finalized after due deliberation and after incisive debate and extensive consultation with important national leaders including responsible leaders in the opposition as the interests and goals of the country must be bipartisan not just that of the political party in power. Further, the aims and objectives of a nation must be realistic, achievable and 'just' in keeping with the norms of world order. The same considerations should apply to the methods to be employed to achieve the objectives. Indeed this exercise on "ends and means" should be addressed with due caution and judicious strategic restraint.

Next, the security calculus would take into account the threats to the core interests and identify from what quarters they are likely to emanate, and in what form are they likely manifest, the entire exercise defining the contours and contents of the national security doctrine. Deliberations on the national security doctrine by the assigned agency such as a Chief of Defence Staff (CDS) will culminate in a "National Security Strategy" (NSS). The NSS will take into account the threats or obstacles in achievement of goals and finally, plans to achieve the same. The course of entire deliberations should involve all the stake holders such as the chiefs of the armed services, the national security advisor, chief of intelligence and a group of ministers (GoM) and, in some cases, also the concerned chief ministers of selected states. The designated apex body would also debate the desirability or otherwise of the whole or parts of the National Security Doctrine (indeed even the core interests) to be declared or to be kept classified for all time or for stipulated length of time as the case may be. For instance, it is argued that had India declared that Kashmir is a "core interest" of India, Pakistan would have had to think twice before launching of their "OP Gibralter" and "Grand Slam" for the capture of Kashmir. If so, it could possibly have prevented the Indo-Pak War of 1965. It is true in hindsight that Pakistan's thrust towards the vital Akhnoor Bridge was halted in its tracks when India launched a counter offensive into Pakistan across the international boundary. However, other experts hold that Pakistan had acquired so much treasure and arsenal from USA after their agreement in 1954 that it was encouraged to think that political situation and level of their military capability (together with low morale of India), favoured a final throw of the dice. Even so, the important point is that certain core interests if declared would serve to put likely opponents "on notice".

Another important core interest of India may well be regarding its desire for a veto-wielding seat at the UN Security Council. Considering its geographical size, population of a billion people and its status and record of being a responsible nuclear power, makes India a legitimate claimant for elevation to a seat at the Security Council. So, India would be well within its rights to consider any counter propaganda as an unfriendly act. Incidentally, Pakistan is already ahead of us on this issue and has been busy, building a lobby against India's case. Certain large countries, principally the Big Five, are also expressing reservations on the issue of enlarging the list of veto-wielding powers. Many other core interests may not be declaratory but that should not stop India identifying them for itself. The important point is that the stake holders (specially the top leadership) will have them to use as a yardstick or a touchstone for reacting to developments and a form of template for planning, decision making and implementation in specific situations. It will be more important in fast developing situations, especially of the kind likely to develop in the nuclear context, as there may be no time for elaborate considerations and discussion.

Shimla Conference 1972 between Indira Gandhi and Bhutto is an example of the need for clarity on core interests. Bhutto of Pakistan was in a tight corner with over ninety thousand of his soldiers in Indian hands as prisoners (POWs). However, Indira Gandhi agreed to their repatriation to Pakistan with only a joint declaration for converting the existing line of cease fire of Pakistani and Indian troops on the ground, into a formal "Line of Control" (LOC). It appeared that our redoubtable PM had lost her nerve for she could have pressurized Bhutto into converting the Line into a "permanent boundary" between the two countries, thereby resolving the Kashmir dispute by a modus vivendi. I must admit that initially, I also tended to subscribe to that view but subsequently, on mature thought, I appreciated the true significance of an "LOC" versus a permanent "Boundary". The latter would have amounted to

India abrogating its rights to vast portions of Kashmir including Hunza-Gilgit-Baltistan under adverse possession of Pakistan, for all time, whereas this way India had emphasized (and still does) that the entire erstwhile state of Jammu and Kashmir belonged to India by virtue of the instrument of accession, duly signed by the Maharaja. As things stand now, at least in principle, India retains the right to reclaim the entire State by force of arms whenever the situation would permit. This is a graphic example of clarity and validity of a "core interest" on the part of India.

Earlier in 1948, the selfsame Bhutto gave an excellent example of the enunciation of "core interests" of Pakistan. In the UN debate on J&K in 1948, when things were not going to Pakistan's liking, he made a great show of tearing up the papers of his brief and reportedly shouting, "Pakistan will possess the atom bomb even if we have to eat grass." Since then, Bhutto has died by hanging by General Zia-ul-Haq in 1979 and Zia himself is dead and gone (He died in a plane crash on17August 1988), but the stark reality is that today, Pakistan boasts of a nuclear arsenal larger than that of India. There could not be a more striking example of the "selection and maintenance of the aim", or enunciation and adherence to its "core interests" by a nation. The moral of the story is that a nation should have the clarity of vision regarding its core interests and goals, which it should have the character and determination to pursue with a single-minded focus.

Concept of Security

National security may be defined in a number of formulations. For instance, it has been stated that if a nation has to avoid war when its core interests are threatened, it lacks security. Put differently, "a nation should have the capacity to wage war rather than compromise on its core interests". Either way, the country must build the requisite military capacity, "even if it has to eat grass". Intellectual elites may find fault with this 'bare bone' definition but the fact remains that a nation must have this basic security and should be prepared to make sacrifices of one kind or another, and it must do whatever it takes to protect itself. In contrast, it is often argued that in today's complex and interdependent world faced with many non-traditional and non-military threats like famines, pandemics, climate change issues etc., national security must be seen in a more holistic manner. Such an all-encompassing view of national security emphasizes that determinant of security is not just the military power but its "comprehensive national power". Such a broad view of security would include many factors across the board like economic security, food security, health security, security of environment (threats to ecological system, carbon emission etc.); well-being and security of people, not just territory, and security of all its people everywhere and so on. It would cover an enormous canvas of human condition into a wide context, defining what is commonly called "soft power". It is held that "total security" for a people would include anything affecting their happiness and prosperity. Richard H. Ullman, for instance, has propounded a much broader concept of security than just military. He argues that over-emphasis on the military aspect is likely to cause states to concentrate on acquisition of military strength to the detriment of a balanced approach. He gives examples of Russia and Pakistan, where excessive preoccupation on military strength has resulted in the break-up of the country (Russia) or the country becoming a failed or near failed state (Pakistan). Similarly, the 1994 UNDP *Human Development Report* by Mehbubul Haq takes the concept of "human well-being" in its broadest sense and argues for "Human security through development not through arms". Such a broad view may be going to the other extreme including almost all facets of human activity which may make the definition too diffused in focus bordering on the impractical. Clearly there is need for a balanced approach and to prioritize and sort the essential from the desirable. The essential or as an irreducible minimum, a nation must have is *"military strength, sound economy and unity of its people: military strength being at the top of the triad"*, for surely no amount of sophistry will avail a nation when confronted with an invader, if it has neglected military capacity. History is replete with examples of nations succumb to hardy and warlike invaders, if they had failed to build strong walls. The bedrock principle is that a nation without a clear concept of military force may fall prey to stronger foes. Further, the focus of imperatives may fluctuate with time and the state of a nation: a big nation which has already attained a well-armed status will have different set of core interests, whereas a weaker nation would prioritize differently. Then again, a country beset by a predatory neighbours (think Pakistan and China) will need to accord greater emphasis on defence. Situations would change as the nation gains prosperity and economic clout. This would demand a continuing review of 'the ends and means' calculus.

Henry Kissinger once stated that the purpose of a security doctrine was to translate power into policy. India has spent vast resources to build up sinews of military capacity but without a properly enunciated 'policy' or precise aim. It has been said that 'India arms but not aims'. Hence there is need to identify the nature of threats, so as to prepare and execute responses in a targeted fashion. India therefore needs to make sure that it devises a clear policy and then ensure that it is understood by the armed services and political leaders as also our adversaries and friendly countries. These must also be known and accepted by the people of the country who should know what the country is planning to do and their own role in the endeavour and what sacrifices would be expected of them. A policy or "doctrine" should also help us to develop capacity which is tailor-made to the perceived needs. This is important because till such time as our industrial capacity is developed and we achieve self-reliance in advance weaponry, we have to learn to cut our coat according to cloth and plan on targeted and tight budgets. Hence the country needs a national security doctrine as much for the armed forces as for various organs and agencies of state. We may have got by without an articulated doctrine so far but it has now become all the more necessary because India is a nuclear weapon state and is confronted by adversaries who also possess nuclear weapons.

A security doctrine is also needed to aid policy makers and concerned agencies to carry out the tasks with speed and efficiency during crisis. Witness the confusion and dither that gripped the political class and the decision-makers during the incident of high jacking of IC814 to Kandahar as also the agitated response of the public. A similar paralysis of decision-making was seen in 26/11 Pakistan sponsored raid on Mumbai. So it is necessary to devise clear-cut and practiced responses for emergency situations. It is also required to lay down "red lines" which will give warning to the adversaries of the likely cost to them of any misadventure: warning backed up by a demonstrated response.

A properly thought out doctrine will make it easier to adjudicate competing claims by individual armed forces on our limited resources. As it is, all three services have formulated overly ambitious war fighting doctrines. According to Walter Ladwig, lecturer in International Relations at Oxford University, "in the Indian context the Army seeks to leverage advanced technology to fight short-duration wars in a nuclear environment; the Navy seeks a potent blue water role with nuclear armed submarines; the Air Force wants to extend its reach from the Persian Gulf to the Straits of Malacca." (*National Security: The Need for a Doctrine* - Manoj Joshi and Abhijit Iyer-Mitra Special Report Issue # 4 – Observer Research Foundation). Obviously, there is a requirement for an overall and a coordinated national doctrine for the much needed prioritization and a joint approach. To this purpose, I have always emphasized the urgent need for a joint, tri-service approach to the subject of security and have stressed the necessity for integration in operations.

Insurgencies in India

The Third Enemy

India has experienced too many insurgencies of all kinds within 68 years of its existence. So much so that internal threats to the security of our Republic, feature as prominently in the media and other forums, as external threats. *Indeed, it would not be an exaggeration to state that India has Three not Two Known Enemies: China; Pakistan, and The enemy within.* This reality of internal dissension and disunity consumes enormous amount of national resources besides being a drag on our progress. Internal disquiet and strife is debilitating. It shows that all segments of the society are not pulling together and that the ship of State is cruising on "half throttle".

This does not add up. Independent India is often hailed as a triumph of democracy in a poor, multiethnic society. Yet, numerous internal armed challenges to the Indian state have erupted with worrying frequency. Insurgencies have been motivated by religious, ethno-linguistic, and leftist ideologies, reflecting the heterogeneity of our peoples. Worse, separatist conflicts in Punjab, Jammu and Kashmir (J&K), Nagaland, Assam, Manipur, Mizoram, and Tripura have turned many of India's border regions into war zones for years and even decades. Insurgency and counterinsurgency has inflicted a heavy burden in terms of human suffering, economic costs, and social dislocation. Indeed the internal threats to nation's security have been a common, if under-addressed, part of India's political experience.

A number of questions arise. Are pluralistic and heterogeneous societies predisposed to unrest and phenomena of insurgencies, or is it that certain ethnicities are antagonistic to assimilation in a society at large? Are these religious ethnicities more prone to bigotry and violence? Or is it a common malaise for the newly independent nations alone? Is the democratic system of government more vulnerable to factional uprisings?

Democracy may be synonymous with discussion and dissent but it should not spawn fissiparous movements or violence. Does the presence of sizable minorities in a country pose an inherent threat? These may be questions for social scientists to ponder at the intellectual level but at the practical level, India has to find viable answers to the problems, which pose serious internal threats to the security of the country, and which demand effective counter measures. Factually, India has had seven or eight insurgencies, mostly of the type based on social dissent but two have been of the secessionist type: one, the Sikh struggle for Khalistan in Punjab which was ruthlessly put down by the army and police forces. The other is the movement for "Azadi", in J&K instigated and stoked by Pakistan, raging ever since 1988, which started on the heels of Pakistani failure to annex Kashmir by a tribal invasion. It is being kept alive by support of Pakistan including frequent infusion of infiltrating jihadists.

India needs to formulate a coherent doctrine for preventing and combating insurgencies of all kinds. We have had enough experience and we have the institutions for the task, namely the Army Training Command, the War College and a highly regarded Counter insurgency and Guerrilla Warfare School. We need a proper doctrine to cover multiple scenarios and broad range of remedial action. At the governmental level, we have to understand the broader political factors and compulsions. People do not take up arms against the state unless there is severe provocation or dire compulsion. And this sort of situation does not develop overnight. It takes months, sometimes years of festering dissent. So, in essence, it is a failure of governance, lack of resilience in the political system, and inability of the petty politicians to balance national interests with personal gain. It is also failure of the intelligence apparatus and failure of local administration. We boast of a brilliant administrative cadre. We have a multi-tiered intelligence set up. We have a competent and experienced military and masses of paramilitary forces. In short, we would seem to have all the necessary tools to foresee, prevent and nip the trouble in the bud. Then what is the reason for the rash of insurgencies and violent movements?

It is axiomatic that it is far easier to prevent an insurgency than to fight it. It takes much less effort and does not leave behind bruised egos and scars of death, destruction and legacy of hatred and animosity. Social unrest is spawned by injustice and excessive use of force. So, a heavy handed approach, before, during or after the insurgency are counter-productive. The most glaring example of the use of excessive force and tragic result thereof, is that of the Pakistani attempt to crush the revolt in East Pakistan in 1971. Religion based unrest, puts the heaviest burden of responsibility on political leaders and religious leaders. India may be more vulnerable to unrest and dissent due to enormous diversity of language, culture and religion. We also carry a past legacy of agitations since the British times. In addition, there is a long history of communal riots and sectarian strife. Communal strife is almost always caused and fanned by the politicians and it is entirely preventable. It is easy to read the signs of trouble brewing and an alert administration can nip it in the bud by firm handling. After a communal riot the district magistrate should be the first to be removed.

Ultimately, all insurgencies get quelled or contained as the state possesses enormous power of persuasion, prevention and kinetic resources to crush them except such as are continuously infused with fresh blood and succour from across the border, such as the insurgency in Kashmir. Then it becomes a larger question of inter-State relations, as also of over all military capability and political will.

J&K Imbroglio

Following the cease-fire at the end of the Indo-Pak conflict in Kashmir after 1947-48. The final resolution of the UN Security

Council (Resolution No. 47 of 21 April 1948) recommended that Pakistan must vacate its aggression in J&K and withdraw its forces, after which wishes of the people may be ascertained in a suitable manner. Pakistan, did not comply to withdraw its forces from the State, which in fact, it has not done till now. At the same time, the Pakistani media, and subsequently its government, has converted the reference to "ascertaining the wishes of the people in a suitable manner" into a "plebiscite". In any case, the exercise of ascertaining the wishes of the people was made specifically contingent upon the withdrawal of Pakistani forces from the state of J&K. The fact is that Pakistan till today remains in wrongful occupation of major part of the erstwhile State of J&K. Furthermore, it has settled Pakistani nationals in the so called "Azad Kashmir" in vast numbers. It has also ceded a huge chunk of "disputed" territory (over 6,000 square meters in Shaksgam valley) to China.

On our side, the accession of the state to India has been ratified by the J&K Costituent Assembly in 1954. Since then numerous free elections have been held but peace has continued to elude the state. Also, there is lack of unanimity among various political leaders called "separatists". Some advocate accession to Pakistan, whereas a large and growing faction favours "Azadi". The present elected government of J&K is a coalition of PDP of Kashmir and BJP faction of Jammu. So, generally, the political situation favours India. The fate of the Resolution 47 is also somewhat doubtful. In March 2001, the then UN Secretary General Kofi Annan, whilst on a visit to India and Pakistan, made it clear that the Resolution 47of the UN Security Council was passed under Chapter VI of UN Charter and that such resolutions are of the nature of being "advisory and non-binding" on either party. Further, much to the chagrin of Pakistan, the UN excluded the J&K from its Annual list of unresolved international disputes under the observation of the Security Council in November 2011.

Notwithstanding the legal position which clearly favours the Indian point of view, Pakistan continues to stoke a virulent anti-India propaganda. Worse, it has fomented and aided and abetted a violent insurgency in Muslim majority Kashmir for decades. The present chief of Pakistani Army, General Raheel Sharif has stated that Kashmir is in the DNA of Pakistan, which reflects his state of mind with respect to India. Be that as it may, the Indian Army supported by para military forces, keeps an unceasing vigil on the LOC and continuously thwarts persistent Pakistani efforts at infiltrations. It is obvious that the Kashmir insurgency will wither without regular infusions of life-blood by infiltrations. Therefore, India has put emphasis on controlling the infiltrations. India has built a strong fence across the entire LOC at great cost and labour, which it mans day and night and through summer and winter. It has reduced the incidence of infiltration to a considerable extent with corresponding impact on the state of insurgency in general. Pakistan makes no bones about their hostile activity. So, in a way, it boils down to a war of infiltration. The fencing has done a part of the job. If we can figure out other solutions to the problem of infiltrations, then we will be well on the way to defeat the insurgency. We can wrack our mind to think up some tactical improvisations. However, in the final analysis probably the answer lies in technology and it will be worth putting our best scientific minds to dream up out-of the-box solutions. As it is, the Pakistan's ISI boasts that a relatively small number of jihadists tie down many Indian divisions in Kashmir. India condemns it as a "proxy war". India has been trying the diplomacy route for long but the Pakistani mind is impervious to friendly initiatives. Their response has been that of frequent violations of the ceasefire, and incidence of cross border firings, often to support the infiltrations. Indian forces contain most hostile activity by vigilance and counter action. In sum, the total burden of containment of the insurgency is being borne by Indian Army only, but for whose efforts and dedication, Kashmir may well have been lost. India owes a debt of gratitude to the army and (also the Indian Air Force, especially for their support in 1947-48 war) for their gallant effort for saving Kashmir.

What is the likely future of this insurgency? It is hard to say. Insurgencies with a secure base and support from across a neighboring country are hard to quell. Vigilance and alert counter action can only contain them. There is also need for vigorous and creative propaganda by us. True, the people get economic gain out of the insurgency. A lot of money accrues on account of payments on ponies and porters and from monies spent by the presence of a large military in the state. However, the heaviest burden of the insurgency is being borne by the people of Kashmir, who have not known normal life for decades and their youth who have missed years of proper schooling and upbringing. The politicians are to blame for misleading the common people. The reality is that a small landlocked state like Kashmir cannot function and survive as an independent country. Their inexorable lot is to be a part of India or Pakistan and it should be clear to them by now that if they decide to go with Pakistan, they will be swallowed up by Pakistan and get no democratic rights as witnessed by their brethren in POK.

The Final Solution

India needs to evaluate the situation and respond in a logical manner. We have a number of options vis-à-vis Pakistan. We have to understand that: firstly, the so-called 'proxy war' or operations by 'non-state actors' constitute acts of war by Pakistan and should be treated as such. Secondly, these acts of war should be punished in an effective manner. Thirdly, if Pakistan then chooses to respond by a nuclear strike on India, the onus of starting a nuclear war will thus be on Pakistan and if they do carry out a nuclear strike, we should be prepared to respond with all our might. Fourthly, we must declare in unequivocal terms that India does not accept any difference between tactical nuclear weapons and large yield nuclear weapons and we will respond accordingly. Lastly, India must proclaim that J&K is Indian Land, so any attack on that state will be considered as an act of war on India and we will respond as we did in 1965. In a nutshell, India needs to follow a policy of "enough is enough". Such a policy should be proclaimed to Pakistan and also made clear in unambiguous terms in the capitals of the world, same as was done by Indira Gandhi before the 1971 war. In case we are not prepared to act in this decisive manner, then we should resort to the entire gamut of defensive actions all the way to sealing of the borders and totally severing all connections with Pakistan. It has to be one or the other. We must not persevere in the half way approach that we have been following so far and which has yielded no results. The last option is to continue in the manner of "business as usual" and keep hoping that Pakistan will have change of heart and will mend its ways and be a friendly neighbour. It is also possible that Pakistan might implode under its internal compulsions. USA and China also might find it profitable to withdraw their support to Pakistan. In other words, the solution to the Kashmir imbroglio may lie through Washington, London or Beijing. Till then, India has no choice but to slog on, while our over-worked army bears the burden as an "Unsung Sentinel".

Maoist Insurgency

Apart from the J&K imbroglio, currently a Maoist insurgency is raging in West Bengal, Andhra Pradesh, Bihar, Jharkhand, and Chhattisgarh. The insurgents continue to operate in the vast interior space of the country. This is a leftist, agrarian insurgency with tribal or *adivasi* undertones. It is possibly the greatest potential security threat to the country. As an extension to the recommendations of the Kargil Committee Report, it was decided that in order to free the armed forces to concentrate on professional military tasks, the counter insurgency duties will be the sole responsibility of CRP (Central Reserve Police). It is a forward looking step in theory but in practice, it is beyond the capacity of CRPF. It is not a police job. It has to be handled with military expertise. The fact is that it will take a long time before the CRP is fully kitted, trained and have acquired the military culture. As of now, it is neither good police nor good military. It should be an extension of the army, officered and trained by the army. The leftist cadres are highly trained and equipped with modern weapons so it is really beyond the capability of police. Alongside, the military culture, there is need to improve the intelligence network. The nation needs to take this insurgency very seriously as it has the potential to blow out of control.

At the macro level, India needs to institutionalize a system of in-depth analysis of the causes and nature of insurgencies and modalities of combating them. Such frequency of insurgencies is just not acceptable. We must address the various aspects such as inadequacy of timely warning of untoward situations brewing up, reasons of failure of the initial steps to quell it. We should set up an umbrella organization using the most incisive and coordinated intelligence apparatus employing our best brains. Equally, we must improve the quality of administration and devise measures to discourage errant politicians. Above all, there should be a national debate on the need for a Department of Homeland Security, headed by a minister level political leader. Mr. N.N. Vohra, governor of J&K, speaking on the foundation day of the National Investigation Agency (NIA), suggested an exclusive ministry for 'national security' with a separate cadre of officers.

Duration of Wars and Super Power Intervention

A prominent feature of wars and most other conflicts on the subcontinent is their short duration. Indo-Pak war of 1947 was fought from 26 October 1947 to 31st December 1947. The 1962 operations against China went on for just a month (20 October to 20 November 1962). Indo-Pak war 1965 lasted only 17 days in spite of heaviest engagements of armour. The Indo-Pak war of 1971, most momentous and disastrous for Pakistan, lasted all of 13 days. Again, the operations on Kargil, stretched for little more than a month because of intense fighting on high mountains. It is a telling commentary on limits of war-making capacity of both Pakistan and India. It is also noteworthy that the super powers possess all levers of control over lesser powers, not only with regard to duration of conflicts but also the outcome of conflicts to a large extent. In the 1947 war, India was persuaded upon to halt its advance though the situation appeared favourable for pressing the advantage. Again, in 1965 war, when the balance started tilting in India's favour, the US laid an embargo on supply of ammunition and replacements "on both sides". US also stepped in when Lahore was directly threatened. In 1971, the situation was more critical for Pakistan. After the resounding victory of India and abject surrender of Pakistani forces in Bangladesh, the US was alarmed at the dread prospect of total collapse in both wings of Pakistan. That was the reason for a fervent approach to USSR and the UN for a ceasefire.

The lesson here is that no war may be fought in a vacuum and that the super powers would not permit a significant shift in the global balance of power. Lesser powers are also hostage to dictates of the Cold War and authority of veto-wielding powers. It is reported that at the height of Bangladesh War, the Russians urged India for a quick resolution of the war on account of pressures in the UN. Indeed the stark reality is that lesser powers may not indulge in wars of substance without assured support of a veto-wielding super power. India may not enjoy such support in future scenarios, while Pakistan would appear to have the advantage over us owing to their "all weather friendship" with China. Further, possibility of collusive support between China and Pakistan could conceivably pose a threat of a two-front war to India. On the plus side for India, 1965 was perhaps the last chance for Pakistan to have won Kashmir by force of arms. They may never again have a similar situation of a distinct military edge. This was perhaps their last opportunity. In any case, the advent of nuclear weapons on the sub-continent has radically altered the military situation so that the 1965 type of tank battles will not be possible any more. Anyhow, moral of the story for us is that it is never good to be friendless in the world and that assured support of a super power is essential for achieving anything of substance. Equally, we must acquire the capacity to design and manufacture our own weapons and munitions, and create an indigenous industrial base for manufacture of armaments.

How Do Our Enemies Make War

India has two known adversaries. So, it would be prudent to study the course of past wars and general pattern of the strategy and tactics employed by Pakistan and China. No war is a replica of the previous one; yet an effort to discern the general patterns of behavior and methods adopted by them will be instructive including their national psyche. It is the responsibility of the ministry of external affairs and even more so, the intelligence community to keep abreast of the latest developments in all countries, and in particular that of our adversaries. A case in point is the enormous build-up of military hardware in Pakistan prior to the 1965 War consequent upon their agreement with USA in 1954. The contour of the agreement should have been marked and deduced by our MEA. The agreement was preceded by a state visit of Pakistan's PM Liaquat Ali Khan, for an unprecedented period of 23 days. Similarly, our embassy in Beijing should have been able to spot the tell-tale activity in China prior to the Sino-Indian war of 1962.

Pakistan

Pakistan should be an open book to India. Besides, it has never concealed its visceral hatred of India from the very beginning, indeed this hatred and mistrust of the Hindu majority community gave rise to the two nation theory which formed the basis of a demand for a separate State of Pakistan as a homeland for the Muslims. In fact this sentiment defines the so called "ideology of Pakistan". Hard upon the heels of gaining independence, in a matter of weeks, Pakistan launched an offensive on Kashmir in October 1947 under the garb of a tribal onslaught, to force Maharaja Hari Singh to accede to Pakistan. This was the first Indo-Pak war of 1947-48, the first of four wars between the two countries.

As a matter of fact the first war of 1947-48 set the pattern of the subsequent wars. All were initiated by Pakistan: all were intense short wars with a Pak stamp of daring and an element of originality, and characterized by good tactics at the lower level but a poor grasp of strategy by its generals. Pakistan lost all wars, some disastrously. In all cases, at the end of each conflict and as a result thereof, Pakistani governments in office were booted out. The Pakistani penchant for hasty action and a paranoid preoccupation with internal intrigue and secrecy is so pronounced that very often the right hand did not know what the left was doing. The1947 War (tribal invasion) was a hastily mounted operation and launched in such secrecy as to be as much of a surprise to India as to the major part of the government of Pakistan itself. The entire operation had not been thought through with proper regard to logistics, command and control, or artillery and air support. Yet it was a matter of touch and go for India. The result hung in balance for the first 24 hours when it was not known whether or not the Srinagar airport was already in Pakistan's hands. In the event it was not, because the tribal Lashkars had halted in Baramula for 48 hours of rape and plunder. Unwisely, the Lashkars had been told to live off the country and on the loot from Hindu homes. Even so, the tribals managed to get up to close to Srinagar. There the offensive was routed by resolute resistance by Indian soldiers, ably supported by our air force. The war dragged on for a year thereafter but finally the Indians ejected Pakistani forces from most of Jammu and Kashmir. Worse at the strategic level, the inept and hasty Pakistani offensive forced the Maharaja to accede to India – thus producing a result opposite to what was desired by them.

The Indo-Pak war of 1965 saw large tank battles, and major engagements between massed infantry formations, this war was again initiated by Pakistan. It was triggered by Pakistan's "Operation Gibraltar" on Kashmir; a multi-column infiltration offensive with a view to incite a full scale uprising against India. It was meant as a curtain raiser for a massive military offensive across the LOC with the aim of capturing the entire state of Jammu and Kashmir (operation Grand Slam). In the event their plans failed on all three counts. The half-baked attempt to incite a statewide uprising proved a damp squib. Pakistan's military offensive in J&K stalled against determined Indian forces in Kashmir in spite of massive infusion of armaments by USA. By all accounts it was Pakistan's best shot and they had a chance to get the better of India only if they had got their strategy correct. As it happened, India beat them convincingly and the war ended with Indian forces within tank-gun range of Lahore. To crown all, it provoked India to launch a retaliatory attack on Pakistan across the international boundary which lent a whole new dimension to the Kashmir issue, namely, that India proclaimed Jammu and Kashmir to be an integral part of India and a manifest warning that here to fore, an attack on Kashmir will be considered as an attack on India.

In sum, if the Pakistan misadventure in 1947 propelled the accession of Kashmir to India, its misadventure in 1965, catalyzed an Indian proclamation of a kind of "Monroe doctrine" with regard to the state of Jammu and Kashmir. Next their foolhardy and cruel war on Bangladesh in 1971 cost them half of their country besides debunking their avowed "two nation" theory.

The Kargil fiasco only made sanctity of the LOC into an international commitment. It was also launched with great secrecy and alike other wars it was a disaster for Pakistan. It also ended in strategic loss for them, as having secured a lodgment on the LOC and having got into a favourable position to threaten our road to Ladakh, Pakistan failed to exploit the situation. On the contrary, their action lent weight to our argument that "Kashmir is important to us as our lines of communication to Ladakh run through it". Above all, their cherished myth of superiority of Pakistani arms stood shattered. So was their boast that one Pakistani soldier is the equal of ten Indians soldiers.

In sum, all forays by Pakistan were hastily mounted, in excessive secrecy, with confused aims, and scant regards for dictates of logistics and overall strategy. There has also been an element of treachery as most surprise offensives have followed close on the heels of pronouncements of friendship by them as it happened prior the Kargil attempt. Further their offensives were always preceded by an Israeli- type of preliminary air strike or a ground operation on our air bases. They did it in 1965 and again in 1971. Hence in addition to a detailed analyses of their past operations, India should be on guard for such tactics. India should also beware of Pakistan's irrational behaviour which can pose a serious threat to India. The most serious threat from Pakistan is in the form of Jihadist attacks which have materialized in diverse forms for decades to which India has yet to find an answer.

Pakistani Raid on Pathankot

The latest outrage occurred as the recent attack against our Pathankot airbase on 1-2 January, 2016. The pattern is the same as other such operations: six Jihadis sneaked across the

Indo-Pak border in two groups (2 and 4) and were directed by handlers in Pakistan. The operation was said to have been mounted by Jaish e Muhammad (JeM) Group under Maulana Masood Azar (the same group was involved in the Pakistani attack on the Indian Parliament in 2001). Luckily for India, this operation was badly botched by the attackers. The inter-communication between the two groups broke down (reportedly the group of four mislaid a communication device in the Police SP's car) which delayed the strike by 24 hours. The Indian authorities got the wind of the operation a good 24 hours in advance permitting huge concentration of security personnel including 300 SPG and other specialists and possibly the timely move out of the air assets.

The terrorists could marry up only during night 1/2 January and the group was given their handlers' clearance at 0330 hrs on 2nd January. Since the defenders were alerted, the terrorists could not make headway towards the technical area and the on-site fuel and ammunition depots whose detonation would have caused havoc to the air base, its civil and service population and arguably to the entire town of Pathankot making it into a disaster of unimaginable proportions. Destruction of helicopters and aircraft would have been a greater loss, making it into a major catastrophe.

The terrorists failed despite casualties on Indian side. All six terrorists were killed. The failure on the part of the *jihadis* is amply matched by the failure of the Indians. In spite of prior knowledge and vast resources, Indians failed to seize even a single jihadi alive. One would have expected the security personnel to have cordoned off or ambushed a number of *jihadis*, which would have helped nail Pakistan's lies. As it is, the investigations and blame game will carry on endlessly.

The question is as to how if at all, will India retaliate. A response is clearly mandated because India will have to retaliate against a strike of such daring and a raid of such horrendous potential. It is indeed a 'wake-up call'.

China

India had accepted Tibet as part of China in 1954. As a result, to clear the boundary issue it started sending patrols, upto the areas/points, where bartering of stuff and entering into each other's country used to take place, a practice carrying on for centuries. Line joining these points laterally, used to be a de facto boundary between India and Tibet. Chinese basic problem was Aksai Chin, through which it had constructed a road in 1950 and wanted India to reconcile to which India did not agree, and hence the conflict. Fact of the matter is that India got sucked into an unequal fight against a first rate military in high Himalayas, badly equipped and ill prepared. India had the disadvantage of interference from own civil bureaucracy, faulty intelligence inputs and inept leadership. On the Chinese part, they had made thorough preparation and employed crack mountain troops. We discovered that China has specially trained formations for mountain warfare. India has learnt that it would be inadvisable for us to get involved in a war against any adversary without due preparation. Now, China has built up formidable military capability on the Tibetan Plateau including a vast network of rail and road communications and airfields. So, the situation has become fraught with added difficulty and danger which has perhaps led to our plans for raising a new mountain corps for the eastern sector.

How Does India Make War

India does not have a frame of reference for a purposeful self-analyses of its comparative capacity to wage war nor does it carry out proper professional investigation into different wars that it has fought. This is a major lacuna in our system. At the lower level units do keep up-to-date "war diaries" but no after-action reports or assessments on the entire operations at the higher level, are available or published. The

Henderson Brooks Report on 1962 War has not been officially declassified. There are no official or private authentic accounts or dissertations on other wars with the notable exception of the appointment of a high powered Kargil Committee, which examined the course of the Kargil operations in fair amount of detail. In addition it addressed broader issues of planning, decision making structures and relative roles of different armed services. Consequently, it submitted an exhaustive report and made far reaching recommendations such as merging of the headquarters of the armed services with MoD, and the appointment of a Chief of Defence Staff (CDS) as the overall commander of all forces, constituting a single point advisor to the PM.

Unfortunately, the implementation of the recommendations of the committee has run into a thicket of bureaucratic opposition. The merging of MoD with HQs of services has been only implemented in part and that too in a half-hearted manner. This was followed up by deliberations of a group of ministers (GoM) and subsequently by the Naresh Chandra Committee report, both largely classified but there are reports that the government had approved the concept of a Chief of Defence Staff (CDS), which seems to have been reportedly watered down later by a decision to have, instead, a Permanent Chairman of the present Chiefs of Staff Committee (COSC), which is also said to be meeting with opposition from within the Ministry of Defence (MoD). Other important aspects such as integration of armed services and setting up of integrated commands as against the current single service commands seem to have been shelved.

India may have got the better of Pakistan in all wars fought till date, but it would be imprudent to be overly complacent. Almost seven times larger in size and economy, India was always able to take the field with a distinct military advantage in numbers of men and machines, excepting the 1965 war. We could always muster more divisions, tanks, guns and aircraft and naval vessels. Hence, Pakistan is forever on the lookout to square the edge, which has been the cornerstone of their foreign policy. However they match us in nuclear weapon capability and are closing the gap in military capacity by various means. Pakistan has always been a very bold adversary, bold to the point of rashness. They have also shown an uncanny ability for originality at both strategic and tactical level. Their expertise in Afghanistan and jihadist background will give them a decided edge in warrior ethos. They have often defeated India in diplomacy at international forums. As against that, India has not been proactive and been only reactive to Pakistani initiatives. India is also blamed for being slow to start a war. For example, the one time when we had a legitimate cause to initiate hostilities, ("Op Prakaram" in 2001-02), we massed our army on the Indo-Pak borders and stayed locked in a "stand-off" for a year, but we shied off a war and ultimately acquiesced in a tame withdrawal of our forces "in the face of international pressure"! We made a mess of our affray in Sri Lanka and of course India can never forget the humiliating defeat at the hands of China in 1962.

External Threats and Foreign Policy

In the international circles it is often said that "India punches well below its weight" on the diplomatic front. Our Ministry of External Affairs (MEA) is woefully understaffed and short of talent in certain fields. That may or may not be true but the feeling is inescapable that India does not enjoy the clout that it deserves. To put it simply, India often does not seem to carry sufficient weight on many important issues in the world forums. Sometimes it is also said that India appears to be friendless in the world. The Nehruvian worldview and policy of "friendship to all" may sound good but being friendly to all often implies having no special (committed) friend. Clearly the old concepts of non-involvement and abhorrence of alliances do not work in the imperfect world of today. The truth is that you cannot get something for nothing. Among nations, as among individuals, relationships usually work on the basis of a quid pro quo.

Above all, India needs an assured support of an all-weather and committed friend amongst the permanent members of the Security Council. Russia was a bulwark of strength to us during the Bangladesh war. It is still a permanent member of the Security Council but its position has been weakened by the developments in Crimea and Ukraine. So it may not be so effective in a future crisis involving us. Indeed, Russia may not be willing to go the full length to give India the full throated support that it gave in 1971. Of course the situation will change in a big way, if India itself succeeds in getting inducted into the Security Council as a permanent member but that is still a matter of speculation. During his visit to India, president Obama appeared amenable to this but lately, the US seems to have retracted from this position. China, an all-weather friend of Pakistan has already stated its opposition on this issue and Pakistan is sure to lobby the Islamic bloc against India.

Pakistan has shown formidable prowess in foreign affairs. It will be worth our efforts to study its successes in this respect. Indeed it may be profitable for us to carry out a "case study" of Pakistan's foreign policy and their achievements in this field. Here is a country one-seventh the size and resources of India (India has also a larger Muslim population); with a terrible record of jihadist terrorism, a proven promoter of nuclear proliferation and a willing host to undesirable elements such as Al Qaida, and Taliban on its soil. US openly accuses it of being a treacherous and double-dealing ally. Yet Pakistan has managed to worm its way into the good books of all: USA, China and now, also Russia. It carries a clout which is way beyond its true weight. And it is well worth remembering that they are not trained professional diplomats but only military generals. What is the secret of their success? On the flipside, it would appear that Pakistan's generals have performed far better in foreign affairs than in war. As against that India has very eminent persons as ambassadors, ably supported by PMs who have an international stature. We boast a foreign service which though small in numbers, is packed with brains or at least the top pick of the academic crop. Yet, we are struggling to get the better of Pakistan. We also struggle to forge meaningful alliances with dependable friends.

This is besides the fact that Pakistan's international image has taken a beating since the revelations of David Headley regarding the ISI's role in the attack on Mumbai in 2008 and again due to the May 2011 assassination of Osama Bin Laden by US Navy Seals in an Abbottabad safe house right next door to the Pakistani Military Training establishment. Mrs. Hillary Clinton (the likely US democrat party candidate for presidency) has been particularly scathing in her criticism of the Pakistan's policy of harbouring terrorists (and wild animals) in its backyard.

We also often hear a nebulous comment that India lacks a muscular foreign policy. What does it mean? Does it imply that at the operating level, our officers are lacking in interpersonal skills or that they tend to be timid and not forceful enough in negotiations with representatives of other countries or is it that our negotiators lack the requisite specialized knowledge of say, the weapons and equipment that are being discussed. Or is the problem that of proficiency of language and technical jargon. Very possibly our MEA is engaged in an in-house scrutiny and analysis, which is also backed up by study in concerned departments of the government. The external affairs has also reportedly made a small beginning by deciding to induct non-government domain specialists on a temporary basis. This is a common practice in other countries. In USA for instance, professionals from various fields and universities join the government for short periods often for prestige or patriotic reasons.

The ministry of external affairs of India (MEA) will do well to cast a wide net for specialized talent to enrich their stock. The advantage of posting military officers has been mentioned.

We may also consider employing young men and women from the Indian diaspora abroad to join up as part of a short service cadre. Having been born and brought up in the host country, they will be *au fait* with the language, local idiom and social mores, and will be an asset. The selection and training of new entrants is another area for improvement. Perhaps the combined all-India services examination accords undue weight to academic proficiency and less emphasis on other factors like personality, deportment, and inter personal skills. These aspects need relatively more emphasis, now that boys and girls would increasingly hail from rural areas and poorer sections of the society. We encounter a similar problems in the armed forces and work hard to overcome them. It matters more in the Foreign Service officers because these traits have more salience in developed countries. Selection apart, the in-service training assumes great importance. In sum, there appears to be need for major restructuring in the external affairs cadre. Without doubt, these aspects are known to the ministry and are being addressed.

Apart from the weaknesses at the level of middle rank officers, it is possible that, the criticism regarding a weak foreign policy refers to national policy making echelons high up in the government. If so, it would raise wider issues and factors of national power in diverse fields, such as defence, economy, industrial capacity and political stability. More than that, it may be a reflection on our decision making culture. *Indeed, we also seem to lack the ability to blunt-think and more important, blunt-speak.* Perhaps our PM, council of ministers and bureaucracies lack requisite professional advice or our security structures and advisory processes are unable to provide viable options to the leadership or lack adequate domain expertise. At the operating level there is need for close inter-face between the MEA and the armed forces. While evaluating external threats both must be on the same page. In actual fact, such interaction is minimal. P.R.Chari, a retired bureaucrat and commentator, while writing about the policy process in the MEA, has identified two nodal agencies, The Policy Planning and Review Committee (PPRC) of the MEA, and the Joint Intelligence Committee (JIC) under the cabinet secretary. He goes on to state that "although the PPRC has offered a permanent invitation to the Defence Secretary to participate in its meetings, there was no representation of the armed forces:" "Civil-Military relations and Military Effectiveness" 1980. Anit Mukharjee: Oxford Scholarship Online. DOI: 4.1093/Ac prof: OSO/9780198092384.003.0008. Accessed on 7.5.2015.

Conclusion

In the preceding sections and paragraphs, several suggestions have been made to remedy various weaknesses and problem areas in the existing segments of our society and armed services. To put the record straight, while there are problems and weaknesses, India can legitimately claim an envious record of management and governance during the previous six decades of India as a sovereign nation. First and foremost, we have helped the country steadfastly to integrate, consolidate and progress peacefully despite a bewildering diversity of ethnicity, culture, language and religion, against a backdrop of a very populous country of over a billion plus. This has been a truly remarkable feat if one considers that this "unity in diversity" has been achieved, while adhering to high ideals of democracy: also not under a foreign rule or an authoritative regime but under a democratic model with emphasis on human values and all round development. When India became free country in 1947, many Cassandra's prophesied disaster and break-up of the country but it is to the credit of our leaders that the country was able to recover from the horrendous aftermath of the holocaust of the partition and a Constitution was enacted in record time. This enabled India to emerge as a republic with a judicious distribution of power between the

Centre and the States and a wise distribution of authority at the Center between legislature, Judiciary and the Executive. In short, India has endured as an island of a functional multi ethnic pluralistic democracy amidst a sea of communalistic bigotry in our part of Asia as also Central Asia. The Pak-China nexus is a potential threat but our security system has held off all challenges and dangers. Indeed the challenges serve to keep India alert with security skills honed, warding off complacency and sloth.

The Indian economy has generally progressed and survived the economic upheaval in the world, keeping a steady course. Slowing down in the final stages of UPA rule, it is picking up with the NDA Government aspiring for 8-9%

Growth rate in the near future. Our large Muslim minority has so far seems to have shunned the siren song of radicalization despite the Pakistan example and its efforts. There are huge challenges to overcome yet. Eradication of poverty is still a long way off; 230 million people are still below the extreme poverty line, but the country has staved off a famine since independence. Some 250 to 300 million go without electricity but the country has set ambitious targets of solar and nuclear power generation. Nearly 25 million still defecate in the open but the government is pushing ahead with projects for building millions of lavatories. Everywhere the picture is that of challenges and solutions being tried out on various scales. Education is still a big challenge but the figures for illiteracy are down. Our IITs and IIMs produce world class engineers and management specialists, many of them holding important positions in the United States of America. Indeed there is a new dawn of optimism and hope. To conclude, while still a developing country, India has much to be proud of.

Index

1 Corps, Strike Corps of the Army, 169
1st & 4th Gorkha Rifles, training centre, 166
114 Infantry Brigade, 96, 106
14 Infantry Division, 132
161 Brigade, 51
163 Brigade, 51
2 Corps at Chandimandir, 133, 134
2 Corps under Gen. Tapi Raina, 112
26/11 Pakisan Sponsored Raid on Mumbai, 236
3 Jat Battalion, 84
31 Armoured Division, 171
4 GR Centre, 166
4 Infantry Division, 112
5/8 GR, 64
5th Battalion of the 8th Gurkha Rifles, 38
6/5 GR, 81
8 Gorkha Rifles, 166
9 Infantry Division, 112

Abbasid Caliphs of Baghdad, 217
Accession of Kashmir to India, 50
Acquisition of
  Foreign Technology, 158
  Medium Guns, 155
  Weapons, 151, 152
Aditya, son of author, 174
Administration, 55, 56
  Of Army, Navy and Airforce, 225
Administrative
  Cadre, 238
  Services, 47
  Weapon System, 216
Advanced
  Countries, 224
    USA, UK, Australia, 224
  Technology, 159
  Weapon System, 203
  Weapons, 191
Afghanistan, 114, 161, 253
Aggression in Jammu and Kashmir, 240
Agreement with USA, 246
Agricultural College, Lyallpur, 23
Ahir Company of 13 Kumaon, 105
Air
  Force/Navy-High
    Command Course, 141

Marshal Lal, 86
Support, 200
Aircraft Carriers, 161
Akhnoor, 49, 82
Bridge, 231
Jammu Canal, 49
Aksai Chin, 251
Al Qaeda, 254
Alexander the Great, 93
All
Services Operational Plans, 216
Weather Allies, 109
Weather Road, 75
American Negotiating Team, 155
Ammunition
And Replacement in War
Air Dropping Fruits, 99
Depot, 250
Amnesia, 104
AMUL Milk Cooperatives, 108
AMX-13 Tank, 105
AN 12 Aircraft, 99, 107
Ancient
Mathura, 173
Temples, 174
Andaman and Nicobar Command, (ANC), 206
Anglo-Indian Girls, 143
Anglo-Sikh War, 23
Annexation of -, 190
Dadar and Nagar Haveli, 1954, 190
Goa, 1961, 190
Hyderabad, 1948, 48, 190
Junagarh, 1947, 190
Anti-India Orientation, 77
Anti-
Shia, 109
Tank Missile, 191
Tank Weapons like RCL Guns, 81
Apolitical Nature of Army, 33
Arab Countries, 109
Arctic Cirlce, 62
Area Jhandiala-Guru in Punjab, 76
Arid Zone, 98
Aristocracy, 106
Arjan Singh, Air Marshal, 204
Arjun Tanks, 147
Armed
Forces, 33, 199, 207, 225
Medical College (AFMC), 130, 131
Guards, 47
Police, 180
Revolt of UP Police, 126
Armour
Fights, 70
Piercing (AP), 155
Tactics, 69, 70
Armoured
Division, 73, 78
In Jhansi, Madhya Pradesh, 69
Formations, 87
Personnel Carriers Vehicle (APCs), 70
Arms
And Treasures for Pakistan, 78
Bazar, 153
Army
Central Command, 176
Included States of UP, MP, Bihar and Orissa, 176
College of War, 135
Commander Lucknow, 176
Commanders Meet, 30
Hierarchy, 117, 151
In 1947 War, 204
Of Training Command (ARTRC), 141

Schools, 33
Staff College At Deolali, 91
Training Command, 238
Urgent Needs, 191
Modernization-, 191
Army-Air
Battle Groups, 201
Force Coordination, 86
Art and Science of Leadership, 33
Artillery Capt. Sharma, 68
Arunachal Pradesh, 163
Assassination of Mahatma Gandhi by Nathu Ram Godse, 42
Atik Rahman,
Author's Mentor and Guide, 35
Major, 35
Attack on Parliament, 161
Aul, Madan Gopal, Colonel, 79
Australia, 60, 107
Author,
37 Years of Service in Infantry, 33
Advice to Maj. Gen. P. Chaudhury, 99
Ancestors, 18
Annual Leave to USA, 174
Appointed As Command of 1 Corps, Mathura, 169-188
Appointed As Platoon Commander, 42
Appointed Commanding Officer of 5th Bn, 8 Gorkha Rifles, 79
Appointment As Dy. Chief of the Army Staff at Army HQs, New Delhi, 150-168
Appointment As GOC 1 Corps, 168, 169
As 2nd Lt. on 21-12-1947- 4th Battalion, of 2nd King Edward VII's own Gorkha Rifles, 38
As Commandant of the Army College of War, 135
As Company Commander-Patrol, 67
As Divisional Commander in DB, 131
Assumed the Appointment of GOC-in-C, Central Command Lucknow, 176
At Forman Christian College Lahore, 25
At Ski School for Three Winters, 53
Attended Junior Command Course, 136
Attended National Defence College Course, 132
Avid Reader of George Barnard Shaw, 27
Awarded Param Vishisht Sewa Medal (PVSM), 164
Build House in Defence Colony, 70
Climbed Panchachula Mountain in Kumaon Himalayas with John and His Wife Joan, 54
Commanded A Brigade in Ladakh, 132
Commander, Senior Command Course (SCC), 116, 134
Commissioned Officer, 37
Completion of Tenure in 114 Infantry Brigade, 106
Course at IMA, 30
Daughters, 94
Dy. Chief of Army at Army Headquarters, 30

Early Career, 25
Elder Brother Romesh, 23
Enjoyed Life in California USA after Retirement, 187
Escorted Indira Gandhi PM to Parade in Ceremonial Buggy, 184
Experience at Army HQs, 122
Father Wizard in all Sports, 24
Father-Mehta Dinanath Dutta, 23
First Brush with Smoking, 25
Flee to India After Partition, 18
Friends - Bhupinder, Amrit Verma and Amar Cheema, etc., 37
Got Pakistan's Wireless Network, 87
Grandfather Attended Coronation of Maharaja Ganga Singh of Bikaner, in 1925, 22
Grandfather became Naib Tehsildar in Gurdaspur, 21
Grandfather bought Sandy Lands in Gajsingrur (Rajasthan) Chak of 25 Squares, 22
Grandfather - Mehta Ganda Mall Dutta, 21
Had a Platoon of Ladakhi Scouts, 100
Had Been with His Holiness Dalai Lama in Dharamshala, 54
Had Regard for K Subrahmanyam, 153
Headed A Team to Sweden to Evaluate Bofors, 156
Immediate Ancestors Moved from Zaffarawal to Jhelum District, 20
In 8 GR, 128
In Capacity of Dy. Chief of Army Staff (DCOAS), 125
In Indo-Pak War, 77
Instituted A Set of Studies in Senior Command Course, 139
Joe Rebello from Bangalore, Friend, 33
Joined Alipore Camp Calcutta, 40
Joined Indian Army, 27
Lands in Chak SB in village Phularwan, 20
Left for Leh in Air Force AN 12 Plane, 98
Life After Retirement, 187
Lost All Lands in Sargodha, 48
M Gordon College Campbellpur, 25
Maj. Nandu Jayal of Garhwal Rifles, Friend, 53
Met Army Commander Gen. Navin Rawley, 128
Met Gen. Bhaiya Rajwade, 81
Met Gen. Inder Gill, 167
Middle Level at Missionary School Rawalpindi, 25
Mother Ram Rakhi, 23
Next Assignment as GOC 1 Corps, 157
Officiating As Brigade Major, 64
Older Ancestor—Mehta Balak Ram Dutta, 20

On Return From Canada, Joined 5/8 GR at Yol, 63
On Secret Mission to Sikkim, 127
Organized Adventure Courses for Young Officers, 54
Organized Reconnaissance Tentative Layout (Of the Cantonment), 186
Organized Slalom, downhill and Cross Country Ski Races, 53
Posted As Commander Senior Command Course, 115
Posted to Gorkha Regiment, 39
Posting as Instructor at Staff College Wellington, 89
Posting at 2 Corps under General Raina, 110
Posting at Army HQs as Dy. Director Military Operations, 121
Posting in GSO-2, 69
Posting Order to Ladakh, 97, 135
Promoted As Lt. Col., on 28th Nov., 1963, 79
Promotion as Brigadier to Command 114 Infantry Brigade, 96
Refuge in a Ladakhi Shepherd Hut, 101
Regimental Friend Jarray Nagle, 60
Retired As Army Commander, 187
Room Mate - Jaspal Singh Bedi, 26
Second Regular Course, 29
Served College of Combat for Three Years, 145
Serving in Jammu and Kashmir, 70
Settled in Bhaun, 21
Son Rajiv MBA from Claremont University, USA, 94, 169, 174
Suggestion to Indira Gandhi, 30
Talk with Gen. Manekshaw—about Maths, 26
Training in Deportment, 32
Trauma of Losing Sweetie Daughter and Son Rajiv, 188
Tribe Mohyal Brahmins, 17, 18
Unit 5/8 Gurkha Rifles, (GR), 51
Visit to His Battalion in Palampur (2012), 54
Visit to Leningrad, Kiev, Samarkand, 142
Visit XIV Corps in Jammu Shakargarh Sector, 171
Walked Lakhs of Miles, 33
Was An Army Commander's Suggestion to Selection Board, 117
Was Asked About FEAR FACTOR for a Commander in War, 36
Wife Shobha, 58, 173
With Tikka Khan Capt. At IMA, 113
Younger Son Aditya also settled in California, 188

Author's
Brigade Major (Major Chimni), 101

Community Joined Armed Forces, Police and Administrative Services, 18
First Course at Ski School, 53
First Task – To be Member of Pilot Committee, 57
Jeep Fitted with Oxygen Cylinders, 102
Marriage while at Khadakvasla, 58
Paper on 'What is Wrong with Youth of Our Times', 55
Teaching Career, 120
Train Journey to Wellington from Pune, 90
Unit Placed under 191 Infantry Brigade, 82
Unit Post-War Activity, 88
Awami League Party, 111
Ayub Khan, 82, 85
General, 77, 83
Azad Kashmir, 240
Azhar Sadik, Pakistani Student, 61

Babu-Neta Nexus, 214
Babur, 17, 19
Badhwar, Gen. 69
Badrinath, 179
Baghdad, 217
Bahadur Shah Zafar, Mughal Emperor, 183
Bajpai, Girija Shankar, 128
Bakshi, Harish, Gen., of 5 Gorkhas, 132
Bakshi, Manmohan, Col, 64
Bakshi, MR, 83
Bali, RGR, Maj., Garhwal Rifles, 136
Bali, Sardar Sher Singh, 23
Bamboo Forest, 68
Banerjee, Sushil, Secy. Min. of Defence, 125
Bangaru Laxman, 193
Bangladesh, 114
Government, 112
Operation, 190
War, 112, 245, 254
War or Indo-Pak War of 1971, 110
Basic Military Rules, 110
Battalion of
Grenadiers, 81
Rajputana Rifles, 119
Battalions and Artillery Units, 99
Battle
Groups, 203, 207
Of
Asal Uttar, 1965, 70, 84
Basantar River in 1971, 171
Chushul, 105
Dograi, 84
Gallipoli, 36
Plans, 86
Bauxite or Mineral Deposits, 103
Bay of Bengal, 230
Bed-Rock Training, 136
Bhatnagar, S, Then Defence Secretary, 157
Bhupinder Singh,
Friend of Author from IMA Days, 171
Staff Gen., 171
Bhutan, 108
Army, 166
Distillery, 166
Bhutanese Dragon Dances, 165
Bhutto (ZA), 110, 111, 232, 233

Biannual Army Commandants Conference, 152
Bigoted Sunni Country, Pakistan, 109
Bikram Singh, Brig., 56
Birth of Bangladesh, 110
BJP
  Faction of Jammu, 240
  Government, 158
Blame Game, 127
Blitzkreig Tactics, 113
BMP Vehicles, 191
Bofors
  Gun Controversy, 155
  Howitzer, 191
Bomb Blasts, 161
Brigade Major Wadhwa, 102
British
  And French Forces, 32
  Army, 34, 61
  Gurkhas, 39
  Indian Army, 37, 38, 40, 190
  Leadership, 146
  Resolve to Create Pakistan, 46
  Sergeants, 34
  Soldiers, 222
  Songs, 40
  Union Jack, 37
Brooke, General, 74
BSF (Border Security Forces), 196, 221
Buddhist, 100
Bukharies, 99, 104
Bullet Proof Vest, 191
Bureaucracies, 161
Burma and Cambodia, 214
Bush (Junior), US President, 230
Butcher of East Bengal, 111
Byzantine Politics, 124

Cabinet Committee of Security (CCS), 206
Caliphs, 217, 218
Canada, 60, 107
Canadian
  Army, 61
    Staff College, 60
  Military Establishment, 62
Canal Colonies of Punjab, 22
Captured Haji Pass by India, 84
Carriapa, Field Marshal, 146
CENTO, 78
Central
  Pay Commission
    (Third), 222
    (Fifth), 221
  Reserve Police (CRP), 244
Chakrabarti, Cap. Adjutant, 44
Chakwal in Jhelum District, 23
Chamb-Akhnoor Area, Dogra Country, 89
Chamb-Jaurian Sector in Jammu and Kashmir, 80, 82, 84, 219
Chamkot, Unit's Headquarters, 56
Chandigarh-Leh, 102
Chang La Pass (17590 Ft. High), 98, 102
Chari, PR, Retired Bureaucrat, 255
Chatterjee, Col, NK, 44
  Brigade Commander Program, 68
Chaudhury, General, 86, 101
Choudhury, Mucho, General, 150
Chengis Khan or Nadir Shah, 113
Chibber, Manohar, Col, 90
  Brig., 109
  General, 176
Chief of Defence Staff (CDS), 129, 193, 206, 231, 162, 205-209, 212, 219, 225, 226, 252

System, 215, 216
Chief of General Staff (CGS), 150, 151
Chiefs of Staffs Committee (COSC), 129, 206, 216
China, 113, 163, 219, 246, 251, 253, 254
 And Pakistan, 245
 As a Maritime Power, 189
 Superpower, 85
 Town, 175
China's Plans for Modernization, 163
Chinese
 Claim—Whole of Arunachal Pradesh, 75
 Perceptions, 73
 PLA, 195
 Threat, 209
Chogyal, 127, 128
Chopper Flight, 103
Choppers, 102
Chopra, Gurbaksh, General, 145
 Retired DG of Ordnance Corps, 145
Chowkibal Post, 52
Christian Community of Baltic States, 218
Churchill, Winston, 143
Chushul, 99
 Air Field, 104
 Axis, 101
CISF (Central Industrial Security Force), 196
Civil
 And Military Relations, 215
 Bureaucracies, 207
 Military Corps, 176
 Services, 33, 119
Civilian Leaders, 110
Classified Information, 47
Clinton, Hillary, 255
Collective Training, 104
College
 Of Combat (COC), 135, 142, 151
 Wings, 135
  Higher Command, 135
  Junior Command, 135
  Senior Command, 135
Colonel Reggie Campus, 98
Commandant Army College of Combat Mhow (CAC), 135-149
Commando Attack on Mumbai, 161
Commercial Sea Lanes, 189
Commonwealth Countries, 61
Concept of Security, 233
Concepts of Doctrines, 141
Concessions to Minorities, 48
Continuing In Service Training, 136
Conversion to Islam, 18
Core
 Interest of India, 232
 National Interests, 229
Corps Exercises, 64
Corruption, 147, 154, 193
Cotton Farming, 22
Counter Insurgency
 And Guerrilla Warfare School, 238
 Duties (COIN), 65
 Operations (CIO), 63-95, 189, 225
Court of Rajah of Tehri, 179
Crimea and Ukraine, 254
Cross Country Skiing Training to Baramula, 54
CRPF (Central Reserve Police Force), 196, 221, 244
Cruisers and Destroyers, 113
Cunningham, Sir A, Historian, 19

Curse of Dutts, 20
Customs and Rituals, 66

Dalbir Singh, General, 113
Dalit and Minority, 185
Dance Clubs, 143
Darbuk-Tangtse Route, 101
Darjeeling, 108
Das, DGP, 126
Dealing With
  Intelligence (DMI), 151
  Operations (DWO-DMO), 151
  Weapons (DWE), 151
Defence
  And Forward Outpost, 100
  Armaments, 159
  Committtee, 47
  Manufacturers, 158
  Procurement Procedures (DPP), 158
  Production Policy (DPP), 158, 159
  Public Sector Undertaking (DPSU), 158
  Research and Development Organization (DRDO), 39, 152, 159
  Services Staff College Wellington, (DSSC), 91, 202, 203
  Services Staff College, Oldest Institution, 91
  Support Assistance, 78
Delhi Durbar, 1911, 21
Deportments, 33
Desert Storm (Operation), 93
Destruction of 75 Pakistani Air Force Aircrafts, 86
Dewan Rai Pun Dutt, Descendant of Shiv Datt, 19
Dhar, Moti, Col, Senior Command Wing, 144
Dharmashala, Himachal Pradesh, 54, 63, 199
Dhaula Dhar Mountain Range, 54
Diabolic Malevolence of the Rulers, 48
Dias, John D, died Climbing with US Army team in Alaska, 54
Dikush Sabha Group, 40
Dimapur, 65, 66, 67
Director of Weapons and Equipment (DWE), 152, 156
Directorate of Military Operations at Army HQ, 121
Displacement (People During Partition 7-10 Million), 45
Disputed Territory (Shaksgam Valley), 240
District
  Gurdaspur, 20
  Jhelum, 20
  Nilgiri Tamil Nadu, 91
  Sargodha, 20, 22
  Sialkot, 20
Dogra Regiment, 89
Drafting, Planning Commttee, 171
Drill Square, 30
Drones, 155
Dutt Clan, 18
  Migrated to Arabia, 18
  Participated in Battle of Karbala 687 AD, 18
Dutt Tribe, 19
Dutta,
  Mourn Death of Imam Hussain, 19
  Take Out Tazias, 19
Dutts, Zaffarwal and Kanjrur, Dutts Stonghold, 20
Dwarka Coastal Town, 86

Dy. Chief of the Army Staff (DCOAS), 150-168
Dynasty of Dutts Reached Afghanistan, 19

East
  Bengalis, 111
  India Company, 97
  Pakistan, 108, 162
    Flood of Refugees in India, 108
  Wing of Pakistan, Had More Population, 111
Eastern Naval Command, 205
Ecological Task Forces, 195
Economy of Nations, 153
Electronic Media, 184
Emerson, HW, ICS, 22
Encounter (India), 237
  China, 237
  Pakistan, 237
  The Enemy Within, 237
Energetic Garba Dance, 103
Eskimo Instructions, 62
Ex-Baluch Regiment, 44
Exodus of Refugees to India, 111
Extra Regimental Employment (ERE), 76

F-86, F-104, F-5 Fighter Plains, 113
Fake Currency Racket, 161
Family Lines, 90
Fascism, 21
Fatwal
  Ridge, 81, 88
  Village, 81
Fernandes, George, 193
Fertilizers Units, 196
Firearms, 218
First Summers Swim Club, 104
Fixed Assets, 41
FM Manekshaw Museum at Regimental Centre Shillong, 26
Foreign
  Invasions into India, 189
  Policies, 229
Forward
  Policy, 74
  Positions, 99
Functional Commands, 212
Future War, Preparing for-, 200
Futuristic Warfare, 117

G to G Deal, 155
Gahan, Company Sergeant Major (CSM), 30
Gandhi, Mahatma, 41, 45
  Assassination, 42
Gandhi's
  Quit India Movement, 45
  Philosophy, 153
Gandhi, Mrs Indira PM, 30, 51, 102, 111, 152, 162, 180, 181, 184, 186, 232, 243
  Incarnation of Goddess Durga, 186
Gandhi, Rajiv, PM, 157
Ganganagar Border, Rajasthan, 133
Gangotri-Gaumukh, 134
Garver, John W, Writer, 73
General Henderson Brooke Report, 73, 75
Gentleman Cadets, 34
Georgetown University, 164
German Staff College, 92
Gill, Inder,
  DG Military Operations, 129, 130
  General, 121, 126, 128
  Was Director Military

Operations, 121, 122, 125
Gold Water-Nichols Act, of USA, 204
Golden Gate Bridge, 175
Gorkha
- Regiment Division, 39
- Women, 42

Gould, Col. Head of Academics, 35
Greek Phalanx, 32
Grid of Irrigation Canals, 22
Ground Operations, 203
Guides Cavalry, 23
Gulmarg (at Kashmir), 54, 55, 98
Gupta, MC, Brig., 121
Gurbaksh Singh, General, 152
Gurdyal Singh, Mountaineer, 134
Gurkha
- Battalion (now Rechristened as Gorkhas), 40
- Troops, 39

Gurung Hill, 105

Habibullah, Gen., Commandant, 58
Handling of Weapons, 33
Hando, Ashok, Gen., 171
Handwara to Tithwal, 52
Har Prasad, Gen., 95
Harbakhsh Singh, Brig., 51, 52
Hare Ram Hare Krishna Temple, 173
Hari Singh, Maharaja of Jammu and Kashmir, 50, 247
Harka Bahadur from Lamjhung, Nepal, 42
Harsil and Joshimath, 179
Hasrat Imam Hussain, 18
Hayde, Desmond, Col, 84
Hazari, KK, Maj Gen., 156
Hazrat Mohammed, 18
Headley, David, 255
Hemkunt Saheb (17000 ft above sea level), 179
Henderson Brooks Report, 191, 252
High Technological War, 159
Higher
- Commandant Course (HCC), 139, 141, 203
- Commandant Wing, 139

Highjacking of IC814 to Kandahar, 236
Hilsa Fish, 114
Himalayan Mountain Kingdoms, 230
Hindu
- India, 85
- Majority Community, 247
- Minority, 111
- Muslim Riots, 43
- Nationalist, 42
- Refugees, 114
- Religion, 173
- State of Bikaner, 23

History of Warfare, 32, 56
Homeland for Muslims, 48
Homi Bhabha, 153
Hony. Col. Of 11 GR, 188
Hoon,
- Maj. Prem of Dogra Regiment, 76
- Prem, Brig. 128

Horulam La, 101
Hot Springs, 105
Hoveyda, PM, 109
Humayun, Babur's Son, 20
Hussaini Brahmins, 19
Hyderabad and Junagarh, 48

IAS Lobby, 160
Ice-Hockey Team, 100

Ichogil Canal, 84, 88
ICS (Indian Civil Services), 223
Ideology of Pakistan, 247
Illegally Ceded by Pakistan to China, 230
Impact of Partition on the Army, 39
In Service Training, 33
Inder Gajra, Industrialist of Indore, 187
India
    And Burma, 65
    And Pakistan, 38, 41, 44, 45, 77, 87, 231
    Declared Unilateral Ceasefire, 50
    Defeat by China in 1962, 78
    Gave up Strategic Haji Pass, 88
    Imports about 80% requirement of Weapons, 154
    Inherited First Rate Military, 213
    Nuclear Power, 213
    Proclaim-J&K-Indian Land, 243
    Third Largest Regular Army (Country), 213
India's
    Forward Policy, 73
    Indigenous Manufacture of Arms, 152, 153
    Plans-, 163
    War Efforts, 45
Indian
    19 Division, 51
    Air Force, 59, 74, 86, 163
    Armed Forces, 214
    Arms, 39, 84, 113, 190
    Army, 37, 40, 50, 54, 61, 84, 150, 189, 190, 197
    Centurian Tanks, 84
    Civil Services, 91
    Community of Hindu Merchants, 109
    Debacle of 1962 by China, 85, 219
    Economy, 258
    Forces, 248
        To Tank Gun Range of Lahore, 248
    Independence, 41, 190
    Industry, 158
    Insurgency in Jammu and Kashmir, 161
    Leaders, 45-47
        To Accept Partition, 46
    Military, 214, 217
    Military Academy (IMA), Dehradun, 29, 32, 42, 56, 61, 113, 167, 180
        Golden Jubilee, 181
        Joint Services Wing, 57
    Military Training Team (IMTRAT), 165, 166
    Misadventure in Sri Lanka, 229
    Mujahideen Movement, 161
    Mutiny, 183
    Naval Missile Boats, 86
    Navy, 86, 197
    Ocean, 93
    Rajahs, 32
    Security, 213-227
    Soldiers, 146
    Territory Illegally given to China, 162
    Tricolour, 37
    Troops, 50, 128
India – Rights of Kashmir Including Hunza-Gilgit-Baltistan, 233
Indigenous

Licensed Production in India, 157
Production of Armaments, 152
Indira Gandhi's Assassination, 182
Indo-Gangetic Plains, 189
Indo-Pakistan
Border, 249, 253
Conflict in Kashmir after 1947-48, 239
Relations, 109
War, 51
War 1947-48, 49, 244, 247
War 1965, 77-95, 231, 245, 248
Evaluation, 84
War, 1971, 111
Indo-Soviet Treaty, 108
Of Friendship with Russia, 111
Industrial Units, 179
Industrialization, 195
Infantry, 136
Armour Operation, 203
Battalion, 99
School, 143, 180
Infiltration, 161, 241
Infiltration – Jihadis, 50
Information Technology Revolution, 94
Infusion of Arms by USA, 87
Institutional Reforms, 205
Instrument of Accession, 233
To India, 50
Insurgencies, 189
In India, 237, 238
Motivated by-, 237
Ethno-Linguistics, 237
Leftist Ideologies, 237
Religion, 237
Insurgency, 50, 79
And Counter Insurgency, 237
In Kashmir, 190, 239
Integrated
Command Structure, 210
Commands, 207, 208
Operational Theatre Commands, 210
Operations, 202
Intelligence
Agencies, 68
Bureau Total Failure, 73
Interim Battalion Matches, 100
Internal Security, 230
Duties, 43
International Boundary, 79
Into Pakistan, 162
Interpersonal Skills, 35
IPKF Operations, 205, 229
ISI, 163
Role in Mumbai Attack, 255
Iskandar Mirza, 77
Islamic
Bloc, 254
Countries, 77
Island Territories of Indian Ocean, 230
ITBP, 180

Jaggichand, Director Artillery Maj. General, 156
Jaish-e-Muhammad (JeM), 250
Jammu and Kashmir, 55, 78, 83, 230, 233, 248
Imbroglio, 239, 243
Regiment, 100
Janjua, Brig Amin Gulistan, 35
Ambassador to Nepal, 35
As Governor in Pakistan, 35
Author's Room Mate, 35
Janjuas and Gakkhars, 18
Jenida Town, 112

Jhandiala Guru Area, in Punjab, 76
Jhelum, 48
Jihad, 194
Jihadist, 238, 249, 250, 253
 Attacks, 161
 Infiltration, 238
 Terrorism, 254
Jinnah, 45, 46
 Falling Health of-, 46
 Refused to Support Quit India Movement, 45
Joint
 Ground-Air Operations, 203
 Intelligence Committee, 257
 Planning, 75, 219
Jordan and Iran, 113
Juarian, 82
Juarian-Akhnoor Road, 81
Judicial Commission, 223
Julius Caesar, 218
Junior Command Course, 137
Junior Command Wing (JCW), 136
 Trains Captains and Majors, 136
Jyoti, Author's Daughter Died, 163

K. Natwar Singh, 51
Karachi
 Oil Farm, 209
 Port, 86, 93
Kargil
 Committee, 252
  Report, 243
 Conflict, 1999, 157, 205
 Fiasco, 249
 Offensive, 162
 Operation, 159, 252
 Review Committee, 205
 War, 159, 205
Karu, 104
Kashmir, 48, 79, 80, 85, 160, 190, 231, 238, 242, 246, 249
 Dispute, 232
 In Indian Possession, 50
 Insurgency, 241
 Issue, 248
 Unfinished Business of Partition, 161
Kashmiris, 52
Kaul, BM,
 Later Commander of 4 Corps, 74
 QMG, 74
Kaul, KK, Capt of Deccan Horse, 59, 60
Khalistan, 238
Khandwa or Ratlam, 116
Khulna Town, 112
Kiari and Karu, 99
Kickbacks, 167
King
 George V, 21
 Tribhuvan, 177
Kirkwood Ski Resort, 187
Kissinger, Henry, 235
Kofi Annan, UN Secy. General, 240
Kohima, 67
Kosygin, Soviet Premier, 84
Krishna Rao, 184
 Chief, General, 171, 181
 General, 140, 168
  Retirement, 176
Krishna Sect, 20
Krishannagar West Bengal, 110
Kul Bahadur Havildar, Awarded 'Mentioned in Despatches', 83
Kumaon Regiment, 82
Kurien, Dr. V, 108
Kuwait, 109

Ladakh, 101, 105, 135, 249
  Economy, 105
  In Arid Zone, 98
  Winter, 98
Ladakhi
  Children, 100
  Diet, 100
  Scouts, 100
Lady Shri Ram College for Women, Delhi, 131
Lahore, 84, 85
Lam Dorji, General, 165, 166
Land Route to Afghanistan, 75
Land-Air War, 209
Large Scale Military Operation, No Scope for-, 85
Leadership, 120
Legend *'Hindi Chinni Bhai Bhai'*, 75
Legendary Soldiers, 39
Leh, 99, 112
Lepchas and Sikkimese, 128
Liaquat Ali Khan,
  Former Pakistan PM, 78, 246
Lieutenant Nayar of Indian Navy, 57
Light Machine Guns, 191
Line of Control (LOC), 50, 79, 232, 241, 248, 249
  Against Infiltration, 190
  In Kashmir, 101
  740 Km Long Line, 50
Log Palace in Harsil, 180
Logging Rights, 179
Logistical Planning, 93
Loma Blend, 104
  Notorious for High Winds, 104
Lord
  Krishna, 173
  Mountbatten, Field Marshal, 61
Lukung Hill, 105
Lun Kung, 99

Madras University, 94
Magar Hill, 105
Mahajan, Mehar Chand, Justice and PM of J&K, 50
Maharaja Hari Singh, 50, 247
  Of Jammu and Kashmir, 50
Maj. Koshy of EME, 99
Major
  Changes in British Indian Army After Partition, 38
  Prem Hoon of Dogra Regiment, 76
Make
  In India Initiative, 158
  Shift Bankers, 99
Makran Coast in Afghanistan, 93
Malhotra, OP, General, 151
Malhotra, Smoky, General, 171
Malik, Akhtar Hussain, Maj. Gen., 82
Malik, VP, General, 124, 159
Manali-Leh Road via Tangtse, 104
Mandi State, 22
Manekshaw,
  FM, 125, 187, 205
  General, 86, 112
  General (Col of Regiment), 64
Mansabs To Janjuas-Gakkhars, 17
Maoist Insurgency in-, (MII), 243
  Andhra Pradesh, 243
  Bihar, 243
  Chhatisgarh, 243
  Jharkhand, 243
  West Bengal, 243

Marching Columns, 47
Maritime
  Power, 189
  Trade, 189, 209
  Trade with Middle East and Gulf Countries, 189
Marshall Tito, 109
Marshall Zukhov of Russia, 57
Martial
  Powers, 85
  Races, 121
Mass
  Guerrilla Movement, 111
  Movement, 40
Massive Infiltration into Kashmir, 80
Mata Prasad, 173
Mau Angami, 67, 69
  Angami Leader, 68
  Hunt for-, 67
Maulana Masood Azhar, 250
Maxwell, Neville, Distinguished Journalist, 73, 214
Meadow of Tapovan, 134
Media, 237
Medical
  College Lahore, 23
  Inspection, 53
Mehta Balak Ram Dutta, 20
Mehta Ganda Mal Dutta, 20, 22
Menon, Krishna, Defence Minister, 74, 75
Mentioned in Despatches, 83
Mhow, 42, 116, 117, 142
  Officers Town, 142
  On Malwa Plateau, 142
Migration of Population, 44
Military
  Bases, 66
  Bureaucracies, 207
  Capability, 161
  College of Telecommunication Engineering (MCTE), 142, 167
  Confrontation in Kunjar Kot in Rann, 78
  Crackdown on Eastern Wing, 111
  Crafts, 33
  Culture, 77, 244
  Hardware, 213, 216
  Hospital, 69
  Intelligence (MI), 74
  Operations, 132, 141
  Plane, 49
  Post at Fort Hudson Bay, 62
  Realities, 111
  Secretary, 131
  Special in Dimapur, 79
  Subjects, 33
Mines and Wire Obstacles, 82
Ministry of
  Defence, 75, 97, 107, 123, 125, 129, 135, 158, 160, 187, 206, 208, 215, 219-221, 224-226, 252
  External Affairs, 220, 246, 253, 255, 257
  Home Affairs, 220
Minorities, 238
Misadventure in Sri Lanka, 93
Missile Technology, 75
Missiles, 201
Mobilization Plans, 93, 170
Modern
  Artillery Guns, 191
  Jet Aircrafts, 78
Modernization
  Projects, 216
  Schemes, 147, 194, 215
Modi, Narendra, Indian Prime Minister, 209

Mohyal
  Brahmins, 18, 19
  Celebrated Muharram with Shia Muslims, 19
  Community, 19
Mokama Ghat, Assam, 65
Monroe Doctrine of President Monroe, 230
Mortar Battle, 99
Mountain
  Govardhan, 173
  Kingdom of Bhutan, 165
  Kingdom of Sikkim, 127
  Trishul, 134
  Warfare School, 54
Mountaineering Climbing, 54
Mountbatten, 51
  India's First Governor General, 47
  Lord Louis, 45-47
Movement Tables, 93
Ms Hope, Chogyal's American Wife, 128
Mughal Forces, 19
Mullick, BM, 74
  Intelligence Bureau Chief, 74
  Nehru Confident, 74
Munnawar Tawi, 88
Muslim
  And Non Muslim Soldiers, 41
  Community, 161
  East Bengalis, 114
  League, 49
  League Volunteers, 45
  Majority Kashmir, 241
    Violent Insurgency in-, 241
  Minority, 258
  Minority in India, 48
  Miscreants, 43
  Regiments, 39, 40
  Sepoys from Central India, 40
Mutiny of 1857, 20, 40, 41

Naga
  Hill District, As British Territory, 66
  Insurgency (Erupted in 1958), 66
  Prisoners, 68
Nagaland, 64, 79
Nagas, 65, 66, 67, 69
  Fierce Warrior People, 65
  Untouched by Modern Civilization, 66
Nagas-British Accord, 1880, 66
Nandu, Jayal, Maj. Garhwal Rifles died on Cho Oyu (Tibet), 54
Napoleon, 145
Napoleonic Wars, 32
Naresh Chandra Committee, 206, 225
  Report, 252
Nastachin Pass, 52
National
  Armies, 219
  Defence Academy (NDA), Khadakvasla, 56, 57, 185, 202
  Defence College Courses, 110
  Defence College New Delhi, 106, 107
  Emergencies, 189
  Integration, 36
  Investigation Agency (NIA), 244
  Mega Rally, 223
  Operational Plan, 208
  Security (NS), 107, 139, 141, 159, 189, 190, 225, 229, 233, 234

Advisor, 231
Doctrine (NSD), 229, 231
Guards (NSG), 220
Strategy (NSS), 208, 231
NATO Officers, 61
Natwar Singh, K., 51
Naval
Blockade of Karachi Port and Gwadar Port, 209
Missile Boats in 1971, 209
NDA Government, 193, 258
Nehru, Jawaharlal, PM, 50, 51, 74, 75
And Chou-en Lai, 57
Bias against Armed Forces, 214
Death, 79
Dynasty, 183
Era, 183
Vision, 153
Nepal, 107, 230
Revolution, 177
Nervous System, 92
Neta-Babu Nexus, 193
New
Assault Rifles, 191
Cantonment in Odisha, 186
Tactics and Techniques, 200
Niagara Falls, 62
Nilgiri Hills, 89, 95, 96
Nixon, US President, 113
Despatched Task Force, 113
Non-Aligned India, 78
Non-Military Threats, 234
Climate Change, 234
Famine, 234
Pandemic, 234
Non-Muslim Elements – Transferred from Pakistan to India, 41
North
Korea, 75
West Frontier, 133
Northern Command Located at Rawalpindi, 41
Nuclear
Armed Missiles, 113
Power, 162, 232
Powered Submarines Capability, 161
Proliferation, 254
Weapons, 85, 201, 236, 246

Obama, US President, 254
Oberoi, Tirath Singh, General, 169
Obstacle Course, 33
Officer Exchange Program, 60
Officers of
IAS, IPS, IFS, 107
Majority Community, 40
Minority Community, 40
Officers Training Academy, 167
Oil
Burning Bukharies, 99
Refineries, 196
Old
Cantonments in India, 144
Military Station, Dharmshala, 63
One Rank One Pension (OROP), 72, 221, 223
Operation
1971, 205
Chengiz Khan, 110
Gibralter, 79, 80, 231, 248
Grand Slam (Offensive into Jammu and Kashmir), 79, 80, 83, 231, 248
In Kargil, 245
In Plains, 94
In West Bengal, 112
Of War (OOW), 118, 136, 137

Advance, 136
Attack, 136
Defence, 136
Withdrawal, 136
Prakaram, 253
Operational Command of Army, Shimla, 141
Operations
And Intelligence, 151
Ordnance Factories, 158
Board (OFB), 153
Organizational Skills, 32
Origin of Duttas, 18
Osama Bin Laden Assassination, 255
Ottoman Empire, 218
Overall Force Commander, (OFC), 205
Oxford University, 236

PAC Battalion, 126
Pacific Ocean, 210
Pahlajani, Col., 119
Pakhtun Tribes, 65
Pakistan, 41, 47, 48, 49, 75, 76, 82, 84, 85, 87, 109, 110, 112, 161, 163, 230-233, 240, 242, 247, 252, 254, 255, 258
Access to International Boundary, 231
All Weather Friendship with China, 75, 245
And China, 246
And Indian Armies, 50
Armed Forces, 18
Army, 18, 40, 195, 214, 219
Army Chief, 113
Blunder of Tribal Invasion, 75
Discomfiture on Kashmir, 1948, 77
Four Wars, 190
1947-1948, 1965, 1971 and Kargil Operation, 190
Fuel Installations, 86
Genocide in East Pakistan, 1971, 162
Hatred Against India, 111
Invaded Kashmir, 41
Military, 86, 114
Military Machine, 86
Destroyed, 86
Nuclear Arsenal Larger than India, 233
Occupied Kashmir and Gilgit and Baltistan in Pakistan Possession, 50
Policy of Harbouring Terrorism, 255
Prisoners of War, 114
Transgression, 161
Tribals, 51
Pakistan's
'Operation Gibralter' (infiltration into Kashmir), 79, 80
Foreign Policy, 254
ISI, 241
Misadventure in 1947, 248
Parliament Elections, 111
Pakistan-China Nexus, 258
Pakistani
Air Force, 78, 112
Armed Forces, 195
Army, 241
Bonds with USA, 78
Forces, 248
Forces in East Pakistan, 112
Invaders, 50
Invasion of Kashmir, 93
Jets, 80
Media, 240
Military, 77, 163

Military Capacity, 78, 79
Military Training Establishment, 255
Patton Tanks, 70
Planes, 82
Raid on Pathankot, 249
Taliban, 218
Tanks, 78
Received from US under Military Assistance Program, 78
Tribals, 93
Troops, 88, 114
Panchsheel, 75
Pangong Tso Lake, 102, 103
Largest Salt Water or Blackish Water Lake in Asia, 103
Paniad (Between Gurdaspur and Dinanagar), 19, 20
Pant, KC, Minister of State, 126
Parachute Regiment, 68, 169-170
Paragliding Mountain Hiking, 54
Paramilitary Forces, 93, 197, 213, 220, 238
Parikar, Manmohan, Defence Minister, 223
Parliamentary Standing Committee, 205
Partition, 18, 22, 40, 45, 47, 48, 50, 133
India and Pakistan, 38
Of India, 38, 91
Partition – The Monumental Blunder, 44
Pashmina Wool, 105
Passing Out Parade in Indian Military Academy, 37, 167
Patna High Court, 223
Patnaik, Biju, CM Odisha, 186
Patriotism, 146
Patton, 84
Destruction of-, 97-84
Nagar, 84
Tanks in Chawida-Philora Area, 87
Pay and Pensions, 195
PDP Of Kashmir, 240
Pension Scales, 222
Permit Raj, 154
Persian Gulf, 236
Pilgrimage to Kailash Mansarovar, 179
Pinto, General Wag, 175
Plane Hijacking, 161
Plebiscite, 51
Policy Planning and Review Committee (PPRC), 257
Political
Leaders, 75
Leadership, 162, 213, 214, 219
Masters, 214
Politico-Military
Interface, 162
Leadership, 163
Ponies and Porters, 56
Port of
Gwadar, Pakistani Port, 75
Karachi, 86
Ports of Karachi and Chittagong, 78
Modernization of-,
Potahar Plateau, 17
Area, 18
Praetorian State, 77
Precision Guided Munitions (PGMs), 201
Predatory Neighbours, 235
Primitive Life Style, 66
Princely States (565) To Accede to India, 48

Principal Staff Officers (PSOs), 150, 151, 152
Prisoners of War, 232
Profession of Arms, 132
Professionalism, 136
Of Armed Forces, 229
Proxy War, 190, 242
Prussian
  Army, 92
  General Staff System, 91
  Victories Against Austrian Empire, 92
Pun, Kesh Bahadur Havildar, 83
  Awarded Sena Medal, 83
Punjab Border, 76
Puri, Nimmi, Maj Gen., 175
Pykara Lake, 94

Quattrocchi, 157
  Italian Middle Man, 157
Quebec Heights, 62
Quit India Movement, 45, 47
  Crushed – Repressive Measures, 45

Raheel Sharif, General, 241
Rahib Sidh Dutt, Chieftain, 18, 19
  Left Arabia, 19
  Migrated to Afghanistan, 19
Raina, General, 110, 112, 133, 134, 141, 143
  On Retirement Posted Indian High Commissioner to Canada, 143
Raj Kumar, Lt. General, 174
Raja of Mandi, 21
Rajasthan and Haryana, 53
Rajinder Nath, Brig, 112
Rajiv and Aditya, 166
Rajput Tribes, 17
  Gakkhars, 17
  Janjuas, 17
Ram Rakhi, Daughter of Sardar Sher Singh Bali, 23
Ram Singh, Col. 95
Rama Rao, NT, (Andhra Pradesh), 152
Rana, Vijay Singh, Res. Fellow of IDSA, 209
Ranas, 177
Randhawa,
  Company Coordinator Maj. Jasbir Singh, 81
  Hardyal Singh, Brig., 64
Ranjit Singh of Punjab, 32
Rann of Kutch, 78
Rao, BVR, Lt., Vir Chakra, 83
Rape and Plunder, 247
Redline of Pathankot, 80
Referendum, 39
Refugee
  Camps, 47, 114
  Trains, 47
Regiment 11 GR for Gurkhas, 39
Regimental Durbar, 186
Regional Training Centre, 90
Rehabilitation Ministry, 70
Rehman, Sheikh Mujibur, 111
Repatriation of US Citizens from Lahore Airport, 84
Revolt in East Pakistan, 239
Revolution In
  Communication Technology, 201
  Military Affairs (RMA), 201
River
  Basantar, 171
  Brahmaputra, 65
  Harsil, 179
  Indus, 93
  Indus and Jhelum, 17

Indus near Taxila, 19
Kishan Ganga, 52
Rizang La, 105
Rock Salt Mines, 17
Rocky Hira, Gen., 186
Role of
Army, 67
Unit Commander, 117
Roman
Centurion and Cohort, 34
Legions, 32
Rawley, Navin, General, Army Commander, 128
Rowley, Roger, Brig. DSO, MC, 62
Royal
Bhutan Army, 165, 166
Indian Military College (RIMC), Dehradun, 185
Rundstedt, Gen. of Germany, 200
Russell, Bertrand, 214
Russia, 154, 254
And Pakistan, 234
Russian, 155
Army, 95, 142
Armed Forces, 142
T-90, Tanks, 191

Saharanpur Air Base, 182
Sailing Club on Bercha Lake, 143
Salt
Bearing Hills of Khewra, 17
Marshes, 17
Range, 17
Range and Potahar Plateau, now a part of Pakistan, 17
Samba, Jammu, 20
Sami Khan,
An Army Commander, 137
Brig., 137
San Francisco, 174
Sapra, Maj. Gen., 151
Saraswat Brahmins, 18
Sardar
Bahadur Balesore Rana, 44
Baldev Singh, Defence Minister, 37
Patel, 47, 48, 51
Sartaj Singh Corps Commander Gen., 102
Satbir Singh, Maj Gen., 223
Satellite Surveillance, 87
Satish Isaar, General of Kumaon Regiment, 142
Saudi
Arabia Angle (Truman Factor), 46
Arabian Camp, 109
Savage Rioting, 44
Saxena, Umesh, Brig., 131
Scams, 147
School of Artillery at Deolali, 156
Science of Psychology, 120
Scientists Working in Leh, 100
Screens of Covering Troops, 137
SEATO, 78
Security
Council, 51, 232, 254
Of Arunachal Pradesh, 230
Selection
Board, 28
Process, 61
Selection System, 29
Sen, LP, 51
Sen, Maj. Ajit Ohara, 40
Served in ENSA Group, 40
Senior Commandant Wing (SCW), 138
Separatist Conflicts, 237
Assam, 237
Jammu and Kashmir, 237

Manipur, 237
Nagaland, 237
Punjab, 237
Tripura, 237
Service Chiefs, 203
Settlement at Tashkent, 84
Shah of Iran, 57
Shah Sarup, 20
Shah Sarup and Dholan, Surviving Boys in the Battle of Samba near Jammu, 20
Shahtoosh Wool from Chiru Antilope, 105
Shakti Singh, Brig., 171
Shark Infested Sea, 175
Shastri, Lal Bahadur, 85, 162
Demise, 84
Doctrine, 85
Sheikh Abdullah, 51
Shia Iran, 109
Shimla Conference, 1972, 232
Shivaji's Fort Simhagad, 57
"Shoot and Scoot" Capability, 156
Short Course in Weapons at Saugar, 42
Shortage—Officers Cadre, 194
Shyok, 101, 105
Siachen, 101, 190
Sikhs and Hindus, 25
Sikkim, 128
Acceded to India, 128
Bhutan and Darjeeling, 108
Simla Conference, 1945
Sinclair, Dean of College, 26
Singh, CPN, Governor, 176, 177, 182, 185
Singh, RP, Battalion's Intelligence Officer, 101
Sinha, SK, General, 164
Sino-Indian
Border Issue, 230
Boundary, 75
Boundary Dispute, 219
War, 1962, (SIW), 63-95, 73, 75, 246
Sitadan System, 23
Ski
Poles, 53
Resort, 54
School in Gulmarg, 52
Skiing, Popular Sport in Western Countries, 53
Social
Dislocation, 237
Media, 199
Soft Inner Winter Coat of Tibetan Goat, 105
Solar and Nuclear Power Generation, 258
Sophia College Ajmer, 136
Southern Air Command, 205
Soviet Army Withdrawal, 142
Spangur Gap, 105
Squadron of Armour, 136
Sri Lanka, 107, 219, 230
St. Columbus School, 97
Staff College Wellington, 59, 205
State
Constituent Assembly, 50
Of Jammu and Kashmir, 50, 240
Sting Journalism, 193
Straits of Malacca, 236
Strategic Forces Command (SFC), 206
Strong Indigenous Defence Industrial Base, 158
Submarines with Nuclear Armed Missiles, 113
Sundarji, 176
General, 157
Surrender of Pakistani Forces in Bangladesh, 245

Sushil Kumar, Brig., 104
    Commander of 163 Infantry Brigade, 104
    Course Mate of Author, 104
    General, 164
Swedish Arms Manufacturers (Bofors AB), 156
Swiss Army Officers, 53
    Lt. Zurbrigan, 53
    Maj. Gahluser, 53
System of
    Collecting Blood Money, 67
    Janissaries, 218
    Rotational Presidentship Between Governor and Army Commandant, 177

Tablang of Village Tablang, 106
Tactical
    Exercises without Troops (TEWTs), 92, 137
    Nuclear Weapons, 243
Tactics of Terror, 194
Tagnait, SL, Lt. Col., 89
Taliban, 254
Tangdhar to Tithwal, 56
Tangmarg, 52
Tangtse, 99, 102, 103, 106
    Near Darbuk Units HQs, 98
Tank Battle, 84
Tapi Raina, Brig., 104
Taxation System, 67
Taxila, 19
Teach Grammar of Tactics, 121
Teaching and Consultancy, 59
Techniques of Blitzkrieg, 200
Technologies of Faming, 23
Tehelka Reporters, 192
Ten Conclusions, 73
Territorial
    Gains, 89
    Goals, 230
Terror Stricken against Mosques, 109
Terrorists, 250
    Attack, 190
Thapar, Chief of Army, 75
    General, 75
Thapar, Romela, Dr., 108
    Historian and Author, 108
The Romans, 218
Thimayya, Gen., 51, 52
Think Tank, 107, 140
Thomas, Mathew, General, 184
Threat From Russia, 133
Tibet, 73, 75, 219
    As Part of China, 251
Tikka Khan, 113
    Defence Minister in Bhutto's Government, 113
    General, 111
        Butcher of East Bengal, 111
Timber Business, 179
Tipu Sultan of Hyderabad, 32
Tithwal, 52
    Brigade, 52
    Sector, 51
Toughening Exercises, 33
    And Coordination Training, 53
Traditional Priestly Functions, 18
Training
    Exercises, 119
    Modules, 137
    Of 50 Parachute Brigade, 172
    Schedule, 107
Tri Services, 75, 203
    Institutions, 202
    University, 57
Tribal
    Invasion by Pakistan, 238
    Invasion on Kashmir, 49

Laskars, 204, 247
Tribes of Warrior Brahmins, 17
Tripartite Agreement Between Britain-India-Nepal, 39
Truman, Harry, US Pres., 45, 210
TUFTS College, 188
Turkish Cavalry, 218
TV Serial 'Yes Minister', 124
Two
Front War with India, 245
Nation Theory, 247

UN, 50, 51
Charter, 51
Debate on Jammu and Kashmir, 233
Development Programs, 234
Exclusion of J&K from Annual List of Unresolved Intl. Disputes, (Nov.211), 240
For Ceasefire, 245
Intervention, 85
Security Council, 232, 240
Security Council Resolution 47/21, 1948, 240
Sponsored Ceasefire (23-10-1965), 84, 87
Unarmed Aerial Vehicle (UAV), 155
Unit Commanders with Wars, 117
Unit's
COIN (Counter insurgency) Duties in Nagaland, 65
Peace Tenure, 90
United Kingdom (UK), 46, 60, 107
University of Military Knowledge, 140
UP Armed Constabulary, 126
UP-Tibet Border, 179
UPA Government, 258
Upshi-Manali Road, 104
US, 107, 209, 230, 258
155mm Howitzer, 155
Aid, 79
Aircraft Carrier *USS Enterprise*, 113
And China, 154, 243
And UK, 61
Armaments (to Pakistan), 78
Arms, 154
Build Up Pakistani Strength, 87
Efforts to Save Pakistan, 113
Embargo on Supply of
Ammunition and Replacement, 245
Ammunition Sales to Pakistan, 84
Forces to Iraq for Desert Storm, 93
Influence in UAE, 109
Military, 77
Navy Seals--, 255
Operations in Afghanistan, 93
Pakistan Mutual Defence Assistance Agreement, 77-95
Pressure, 76
USS Enterprise, 113
USSR, 77, 78, 108, 113 142, 245
Uzi, 166
Israeli Submarine Gun, 145

Vaidya, Arun, General, 176
Valley of Flowers, 179
Veto-Wielding Superpowers, 245
Vigilance and Operational Drill, 67

Viking Settlement, 60
Village
  Khurdwar Jhelum, 49
  Of Chamb and Jaurian, 83
Visit to Iran, 108
Vocational and Technical Training Centres, 196
Vohra, AM, General 134
Vohra, NN, Governor of J&K, 244
Von Maltke the Elder, 91, 92

Wahabi Islam, 109
Walker, Gordon, ICS, 22
War
  College, 141, 180, 238
  Military Capacity of Pakistan, 41
  Of 1962 Against China, 229
  Of 1965, 204, 219, 246
  Of 1971, 110
  On Bangladesh 1971, 248
  Veterans Suggestions, 117
  Wastage Rates (WWR), 130
  Zones, 237
Warfare, 35, 121
We (India) a Nuclear Weapon Power, 161
Weapon System, 203
Wedding of Author's Daughter Jyoti at Dehradun, 135
White Revolution in India, 108
Wilson, 179
Wilson Saheb's Palace, 180
  Once Housed Indra Gandhi, PM, 180
Withdrawal of Pakistani Forces, 51
Wolfe, General, 62
Wooden Cottages, 64
World War I, 22
World War II, 27, 29, 42, 45, 132, 201, 210
Wright, Maj., 35

Yahya Khan, Maj. Gen., 82
Yaks, 101
Yol Cantonment, 63, 64
Yugoslavia, 109

Zia-ul-Haq, General, 233
Zia, Gen. of Pakistan, 218
Zoji La, 99
Zoru Bakshi, General (DMO), 130